PATHWAYS TO PEACE

Understanding Death and Embracing Life

MW00651687

CHRISTINE SPENCER

Copyright © 2020 Christine Spencer

All rights reserved. No part of this book may be used or
reproduced by any means, graphic, electronic, or mechanical,
including photocopying, recording, taping or by any
information storage retrieval system without the written
permission of the author except in the case of brief quotations
embodied in critical articles and reviews.

Proisle Publishing
1177 Avenue of the Americas, 5th Floor, New York, NY 10036,
USA
info@proislepublishing.com

ISBN: 978-1-7360197-6-4 (sc)

PROISLE PUBLISHING
SERVICES LLC

CONTENTS

Acknowledgements i

Dedication ii

Preface.. iii

Introduction vi

PART ONE
LIFE AFTER DEATH 1

Chapter One
Heavenly Help.. 3

Chapter Two
What Happens When We Die?... 17

Chapter Three
Similarities in Near-Death Experiences.. 22

Chapter Four
Twenty-Four Inspiring Near-Death Extracts 44

1. Chris' Near-Death Extract – Age 4... 45

2. Randy Geyling's Near-Death Extract – Age 10............................... 50

3. Gracie's Near-Death Extract – Age 11... 54

4. Kesha L. Engel's Near-Death Extract – Age 14............................... 55

5. Dr Eben Alexander's Near-Death Extract.. 57

6. Rev. George Rodonaia's Near-Death Extract.................................. 61

7. Rev. Howard Storm's Near-Death Extract....................................... 64

8. Dr. Dianne Morrissey's Near-Death Extract.................................... 82

9. Mellen-Thomas Benedict's Near-Death Extract.............................. 83

10. Barbara Whitfield's Near-Death Extract.. 97

11. Beverly Brodsky's Near-Death Extract..110

12. Dannion Brinkley's Near-Death Extract..112

13. Rev. Juliet Nightingale's Near-Death Extract..119

14. Elizabeth Kubler Ross' Near-Death Extract..125

15. Mrs Swartz's Near-Death Extract..126

16. Vicky Umipeg's Near-Death Extract..127

17. Jayne Smith's Near-Death Extract..131

18. Rev. Josiane Antonette's Near-Death Extract..136

19. Jake's Group Near-Death Extract..141

20. Rashad's Group Near-Death Extract..143

21. Arthur Yensen's Near-Death Extract..147

22. Frederic Delarue's Near-Death Extract..156

23. Laurelynn Martin's Near-Death Extract..173

24. Doug McMenamin Near-Death Extract..177

Chapter Five
Detailed Experiences from the Spirit World..185

Chapter Six
After Death Communication By Signs..218

Chapter Seven
After Death Communications by Appearances..222

Chapter Eight
After Death Communication by Fragrances..228

Chapter Nine
After Death Communication by Voices..231

Chapter Ten
Was It an Accident?..236

PART TWO
COPING WITH LOSS
Practical Applications, Support and Insights For
The Terminally Ill & Those Dealing With Grief................................... 250

Chapter Eleven
Living with Grief... 255

Chapter Twelve
Terminal Illness 261

Chapter Thirteen
Grief from Divorce... 273

Chapter Fourteen
Conclusions.. 278

ACKNOWLEDGEMENTS

I would like to acknowledge some of the many people who graciously consented to my utilizing their material in this book, subsequently making this book what it is – illuminating, inspiring and full of practical wisdom and knowledge for journeying through life, both on planet earth and transitioning into *life after death*.

My heartfelt thanks goes out to:

Claire Sylvia for her amazing, captivating story.

Dr P.M.H. Atwater for her enlightening contributions and for her generous support.

Bill and Judy Guggenheim for their gracious consent to publish some of their After-Death Communication stories.

Dianne and Mal McKissock for their practical, professional advice on dealing with grief.

Kevin Williams, webmaster of www.near-death.com for his support and enlightening summation of the pertinent messages behind so many Near Death Experiences.Kesha Engel, Rev. Howard Storm, Mellen-Thomas Benedict, Rev. George Rodanaia, Beverley Brodsky, Dannion Brinkley, Barbara Whitfield, Eben Alexander, Rev. Juliet Nightingale's daughter DJamil, Jayne Smith, Josiane Antoinette, Arthur Yensen's son Eric Yensen, Jeanie Dicus, Laurelynn Martin and Doug Mc Menamin's wife Carol for graciously allowing me to reprint some of their inspiring Near Death Experiences.

Julie of www.globalgreyebooks.com for granting me permission to include extracts from *Life In The World Unseen* and *Here and Hereafter.*

Deepest gratitude and love to my Beloved Soul Partner for his Co-Creative efforts in assisting with the polishing and refining of this book.

DEDICATION

TO

Two special souls who had dramatic impacts on my life.

Both are now resting with God and the Angels.

My beautiful friend and mentor, Jenny,

Who believed in me when I did not,

And to my wonderful father, Jack.

Who was one of the gentlest, wisest, and most humble men I have known.

My deepest love and gratitude to you both.

PREFACE

How do you view death? As something to be feared, avoided and not discussed? What happens when we die must be one of the most fiercely contested debates of all time. Human nature being what it is, we often fear what we do not understand and believe we have no control over. There are those who believe we only live once, those who believe in life after death and those who do not know and don't want to know.

So, what would be a reassuring response from our Divine Creator to reduce humanity's fear of death and dying? For some, reassurance can only be found through direct experience. What if a group of people, representing the many colours, cultures and classes of humanity, could be allowed to experience a physical, clinical death; to see for themselves what happens when they die and what it feels like? Then, what if after this direct experience of death, they were assisted in returning to their body? It is easy to imagine how much astonishing clarity those in this group would be able to share. After all, you only need to think back to the major experiences in your life, to know what you learned from having gone through an experience yourself. This group would be able to talk from their own experience of what happens when we die. What they all relate are descriptions of a transforming transition into a realm full of wonder, beauty, peace, and a depth of unconditional love that defies human description.

At the doorway to this higher realm we are even able to discard all pain, all disabilities, all fear, all suffering, all judgments of both ourselves and others, all our negative emotions and human frailties. In exchange, we acquire radiant health, peace and complete inter-dimensional freedom. A powerful and generous exchange wouldn't you agree? An event to be embraced rather than feared by the person passing over. If only they knew that their pain and suffering was about to come to a complete end, and in its place was the caress of the power of our Divine Creator's sublime, all-encompassing unconditional love. It is natural to grieve our loved one's passing, but to know they are at last free from human pain and suffering, in all its forms, is undoubtedly a great comfort and relief.

When we read the illuminating and inspiring accounts from people who have clinically died and returned, we see many parallel interwoven threads of truth. We especially cannot deny the innocent, un-prejudiced children's descriptions of these serene and joyful realms. In fact, it is so glorious that most people who have a near-death experience do not wish to return.

Wonderfully enlightening confirmation of what the Near-Death Experiencers (NDE'ers) have shared is further corroborated in greater detail by Robert Benson's experiences of actually living in these tranquil Realms.

For those of you who have lost a loved one, young or old, I pray these beautiful, uplifting personal experiences will give you comfort and hope in knowing that your beloved is still very much alive and able to be re-united with you at a later date. Some are even fortunate enough to receive some form of communication, as you will read later in the many After Death Communication (ADC) stories in Chapters Six to Eight.

The power and impact of this book is in the collective material and the composite wisdom of all who have graciously contributed their inspiring and illuminating real-life stories. In the case of the near-death extracts, one cannot write about the wonder and majesty of Prime Creator's higher realms unless one has experienced being there. As you will discover throughout this book, the descriptions from those who have *been there* are painted on an astonishing ethereal canvas, that delights the senses and ignites us; that part of us that is our spirit that has been there many times before and, at a deep Soul level, knows the Reality after death only too well.

I have prayed throughout the writing and compiling of this book to our magnificent Creator that I would be guided to words that convey Universal Truth, that this book would carry messages of basic foundational truths about who we are, who God/Source Energy is, and what happens when we die. I will refer to our original Prime Creator primarily as God as for me these words encompass a vastness of Creative Energy that has no beginning or end—an immense radiance of Divine Love and Light that encompasses all creation in all universes. Personally, what label we use to define God matters not as long as it resonates within our own heart and Soul. Equally what term we use to define heaven is insignificant in comparison to discovering what practical steps we can take in the here and now to ultimately experience the wonder and beauty of it.

Throughout this book, when speaking of Prime Creator, The Divine, Father/Mother God, I will sometimes use the singular male version-only for simplicity but God/Source is most definitely not human, thereby is not limited to a single human gender. However, there are many male and female aspects of God. I also like to refer to Source Energy as our Divine Mother – the creative, nurturing, loving, compassionate, feminine side of our Creator. Please feel free to use the name that resonates within your own heart and Soul to address our Divine Creator whilst reading this book.

Within this book are messages of hope, reminders that we are all Divinely Created, eternal, and wonderful Beings. Our very Essence is the life force that enables us to breathe, eat, move, talk, and think. Everything we are, and can do, is made possible because we are all an individualized drop, or facet, of the Cosmic ocean that many call God.

We are all eternal, Divinely Created, wonderful Beings whose Essence is of pure, Divine Love as the individualized facets of the one God that we all are. Whose ultimate destiny is to express that love to ourselves and others and to return to from whence we came. Into the Oneness of All That Is.

We are *all* born as fragile, innocent babies. We must *all* pass-over sometime, for a diversity of reasons. We *then* realize that shedding our human coat allows us to experience life again in a different place and a different time/space reality. How powerful and wonderful for humanity to know this information *before* this happens.

I trust that this book, and many more like it, that have been and will be written, are all playing a part in creating a paradigm shift in the way humanity views death. These powerful experiences are life changing for the individual who experienced them and can also be for those readers who wish to dispel all past misperceptions and misinformation; misunderstandings that have been caused by people's fear of the unknown and *guessing* what happens after death, resulting in a mass consciousness fear of death and dying.

In this book we go beyond the mysterious veil of death's darkness and, through periodic glimpses into what could only be described as a higher dimensional heaven, we discover the All-Pervading Peace, All-Encompassing Love and wonder that awaits us all.

We can rest in the knowing that death ending life is a grand illusion nothing more, nothing less.

> *"The more I observe and study things, the more convinced I become that sorrow over separation and death is perhaps the greatest delusion.*
> *To realize that it is a delusion is to become free.*
> *There is no death, no separation of the substance."*

Mahatma Ghandi

INTRODUCTION

Heaven is attainable for anyone, anywhere, irrespective of what a person has or has not done, or what religion they may or may not believe in. Heaven is not a place as such, but rather an elevated state of consciousness. This book explores pathways to reaching God's higher dimensions, which are so beautifully described in the following Near Death Experiences, and they provide for us an illuminating virtual window to peer through at what happens when we die and where we go after we breathe our last breath.

"Hope Springs Eternal" describes a vital element of the human spirit. Our own Innate Intelligence, or our own Divine Essence within, is naturally full of hope and gives us that inner drive that keeps us striving forward, knowing there is Light at the end of the proverbial tunnel. We can see from the Near-Death Experiences there is much more to that well known saying than meets the eye, as we investigate this literal *Light* that envelopes those who pass into the higher dimensions with an intensity of unconditional love that defies human description.

> *"Hope, like the gleaming taper's light Adorns and cheers our way; and still, as darker grows the night, Emits a brighter ray"*

Oliver Goldsmith

The intent of this book is that many of the experiences, extracts, and insights in this book will shine rays of hope that, in turn, may uplift and illuminate those dark recesses where fear or despair may be lurking. Hope and comfort may come from:

1. The Near-Death Experiences collectively describe a higher-dimensional heaven that is very real; a heaven we can all go to and partake of its beauty and all-encompassing love.

2. Understanding that death is an illusion. The truth is we never die. Instead we shed our earthly garment (our physical body) when we are done with it, and transition into life in another dimension of Peace, Light and Love (heaven).

3. Knowing that our loved ones are still very much alive and are in radiant health. That they are not lost to us forever and that one day we can be re-united.

4. Seeing that we experience a *life review* in which we view the whole of our life; our thoughts, words and deeds and the repercussions thereof after we pass over, in complete honesty, clarity and non-judgment.

5. Realizing that life and death on planet Earth does make sense. That the Individualized part of God that *we are* does have a pre-arranged plan and that *Divine justice is always exacting and fair.*

6. Seeing that we *all* have ONE, non-denominational God/Source of immense love who forgives all and loves all of His/Her creations equally. Realizing that we are *never* judged or condemned by God no matter what we may have done.

In this book all the above issues are addressed and much more. I draw on the insights, experiences and wisdom of those well qualified to share their stories. We look through a virtual window at what happens when we die and look at twenty-four diverse, yet strikingly similar, NDE's. These extracts alone answer so many questions as to the purpose of life, and categorically reveal that we are Eternal Beings that never die. The unequivocal evidence relayed to us by Robert Benson, of how it feels to actually live in these stunningly beautiful realms, qualifies it still further; a world just as real as ours where peace, harmony and love prevails. There is definitely life after death, a wondrous life, just as there are a myriad of beings, as real as we are, in the higher unseen dimensions around us.

Source/God has graciously given us a virtual window so we can view death from a different perspective: from death here on Earth to life continued in other dimensions. It is merely a passing into a different and wondrously beautiful plane of existence, one *even more real* than ours, yet so full of unconditional love and beauty that those who have been pronounced clinically dead, and have had an NDE, are given a fleeting look at what happens when we die. One of the greatest mysteries of life revealed, not once, but millions of times, for hundreds of years, all over the world. In fact, to illustrate just how prevalent NDE's are, in a Gallup Poll conducted within the United States back in 1992 they discovered that 19 million Americans had experienced an NDE and that approximately 774 people a day have some kind of NDE! Not only does it give us real glimpses of life after death but it is the stories behind these NDEs that gives us so much more. They give us an up-close experiential look at God. They can show us, in general, why we are here, what life is for and the repercussions of our words and actions.

These people returned having experienced the inter-connectivity of humanity, and categorically state that we are *all One*. Each person is a special, unique, individualized part of God, interconnected by the fine gossamer web of life pulsating from the *one* original Prime Creator, and that what we do to one, *affects us all.*

These personal testimonies paint an astonishingly detailed, descriptive picture of immense beauty, radiant health; a love that surpasses all earthly understanding and utter joy that awaits us when we do finally pass over. In their extracts they use such descriptive prose to illustrate their NDE that at times it ignites and delights the Soul, as we receive droplets of remembrance of times gone by that our own Souls have known so well. They also provide evidence that we can often be re-united with deceased loved ones. We look at some examples of the twelve striking similarities that weave a common thread through many of the NDE's.

Many of those who have had an NDE wanted to stay in this dimension of immense beauty, and above all, in a love that is so all-encompassing that they want for nothing. A dimension where they are completely free from any form of pain or discomfort. They have retained crystal clear, detailed accounts of what it is like to die. They say these memories of their brief sojourn into heaven are as lucid and detailed today as they were when they took place, which for some was decades ago. This on its own shows that what they experienced was clearly their reality at that time. They were not dreams or hallucinations. Our dream memories are generally short, usually with little detail, and in most instances fade quickly.

The Near-Death Experiences that I have read agree that God is one of unimaginable unconditional love, who loves all creations equally, who is overseeing all of planet Earth, and all the Multiverses and Galaxies in between, (although mankind has free will and thus creates based upon the choices he or she makes and that the subsequent mass consciousness make). God yearns for us to recall who we are, from whence we came, and for us to know that we can never be separated from Source. It is only our belief that creates our illusionary experience of separation and appearing to be apart. We are all primarily spirit— unique, individual creations of the Prime Creator expressing itself through a human body on an experiential lower vibrational planet. We have forgotten who we are and I, for one, believe it is time for us to remember how beautiful and powerful we are when we acknowledge, connect with and embrace our own God Presence.

Not only do these NDE's give us an invaluable glimpse into life after death but they also take away the fear of death and dying. Once we remove the fear of death and replace it with the knowledge that we are Eternal Beings, that are always accountable for our words and deeds, then that naturally frees us up to live life more fully in the here and now.

The real life experiences in this book will give anyone grieving the loss of a loved one comfort in knowing your loved one is still very much alive, in vibrant health and looking forward to being re-united with you when the time is right.

Many people who have experienced NDE's have been told that we, humanity, can collectively change what is happening of this planet. They have been told that our future is not fixed and can be changed. Collectively our planetary awareness is growing at an unprecedented rate as vast amounts of Light are pouring onto Mother Earth. I too believe that we are here to Co-Create with God, to bring peace and unity to this planet and her people. We are ALL extremely powerful, individualized parts of the One God/Goddess and when working in unison with that God-Part of ourselves, our 'I Am' Presence, we can and shall Collectively Co-Create what we DO want to see on this planet.

Pathways to Peace presents twenty-four diverse NDE's from both children and adults. They are from all parts of the globe, representing many races and creeds, even some from people who were originally atheists. Giving even further credence and evidence to support the NDE accounts we have Robert Benson's subsequent chapter as experienced by a man who has lived in these glorious realms for many years now!

Four chapters comprise of short personal accounts from a variety of people who have all had some form of communication from their Loved One after they have transitioned. This is commonly referred to as After-Death Communication or ADC for short.

The following story illustrates the potency of some of these communications and the fact that our loved ones who have passed are still very much alive. Many thanks to Claire Sylvia for kind permission to retell her remarkable story.

Claire Sylvia was a professional dancer with several modern dance companies. As the years passed, her health began to deteriorate. Claire had to undergo a heart and lung transplant. Soon after the transplant, she began having strange and incredibly vivid dreams about a young man she didn't recognize. Eventually, Claire realized that the young man in her dreams was the eighteen-year-old organ donor whose heart and lungs now resided in her chest. Through her continuing 'dream' contacts with her donor, she learned a lot about him including his name. She then decided to do the research to find out if this heavenly higher dimensional information was correct. Her research proved that it was indeed correct. Claire then met the young man's grieving family and shared with them the amazing story of her contact with him from the Other Side through her dreams.

Claire was suffering from primary pulmonary hypertension, a deadly disease. Her only hope for survival was a heart and lung transplant.

Claire's daughter Amara had this to say. *"My mother was basically dying...She prepared herself for death and she was preparing me for her death. She labored to get up in the morning to go to the bathroom. Her breathing was labored and I was afraid every morning whether she would be alive or not."*

The following is a detailed account of Claire's story in her own words.

"I started to have a series of dreams. One dream was that I had the transplant and I had to drink four glasses of milk a day. At the time I questioned this and wondered what this meant? Where did the four glasses of milk come in? I didn't understand what this meant. There was no explanation so I just let it go.

I lived each day with a thought and a prayer that I would live till the next day and that I would live to see my daughter graduate from high school, which was about a year away.

Finally, my prayers were answered; the phone rang and it was the transplant coordinator. She very calmly said, 'We officially got permission to do the heart and lung transplants and we have a donor for you today.'"

I was speechless. All I could say was 'Oh, my God. Oh, my God!' Within hours I was rushed into surgery.

"After a delicate three-hour operation, I awoke. I knew that I would have to take an anti-rejection drug, Cyclosporine. They injected a certain amount of this liquid into two little cups of milk. Then at night, I repeated this same process. I realized that these were the four cups of milk a day in my dream. At first, I didn't accept it, I kept saying to myself that I must have gotten this information from someplace. I kept checking around and nobody had told me. I thought it was bizarre.

When I returned home, another sequence of unexplained occurrences began. My taste in food changed dramatically.

I had a thought one day, 'Why am I cutting up green peppers and putting them into my food?' I used to hate them and I picked them out. Several weeks after the transplant, they told me I could drive by myself. I got in my car and was driving around and I had this yen to find a Kentucky Fried Chicken place to have chicken nuggets. This was something I just don't ordinarily do.

Just when I thought my life couldn't get any stranger, it did, in another mysterious dream.

I'm in an open field and it's very light. It's daytime and I'm in a playful relationship with a young man whom I see clearly. He is tall, has sandy colored hair and his name is 'Tim L'. I come back and say goodbye to him and as we approach each other, we kiss, and as we kiss, I feel as if I inhale him into me. It's like taking this enormous breath. And I know that he will be with me together forever. But it also seemed that this man in my dreams, whom I knew as Tim, must be my donor.

I was very curious to find out who my donor was because of all the things that were happening to me and because of the dreams I was having – and the feeling of living with his presence.

I became convinced that my donor was trying to communicate with me. I contacted the hospital but they informed me that donor records were confidential. When all hope seemed lost, my friend, Fred Stern, called to tell me of a message he received in his own dream.

'I had a clear image of a dream,' says Fred Stern, 'that we had gone to the basement of the public library and had seen in the Portland newspaper a story on either the third or fourth page several days before your operation. A story about the boy who was killed and whom you got your heart from.'

I made arrangements with Fred to meet at the local library.

We met at the public library and we looked at the papers the week preceding my transplant. Sure enough, the day before my transplant, as was in his dream, the obituary of a young man who was killed in a motorcycle accident. He was 18 years old. His name was Tim L. as it was in my dream. It felt like my heart stopped beating for a moment. I was standing up and I remember getting kind of weak all over. My knees went a little weak. It was a shock.

'It was almost like magic,' says Fred Stern, 'like some sense of knowing. It was just wonderful to be a part of it – this unfolding.'

It turned out that Tim L. had died in a motorcycle accident shortly before my life saving surgery.

I was shocked because now it became more real. Now I had all the information. I had the family's name. I had details. This person really existed!

Wanting to know more about my donor, I wrote to Tim's family and made arrangements to meet them.

'I was very excited,' says Tim's sister, Lee Ann, 'and the whole family was very excited to meet Claire. It was like meeting my brother all over again for the very first time – seeing him alive again. Claire was very warm towards us. She was loving. She was loving like Tim was. There was so much feeling that it was absolutely exhausting.'

I then told Tim's family about my dream.

Tim's sister replied, 'My first reaction to Claire's dream was one of disbelief. I really didn't believe it until she just started describing things about my brother – like how he was tall and wiry. She described him almost to a T. She was getting the information from her dream. She described how Tim was loving and that he came to her and wanted to be a friend. I just kind of felt that, Yeah, that's what Tim would do.'

When I met the family, I was trying to corroborate some of the things that had been happening to me. I asked them if he happened to like green peppers and they said:

'Oh, yes, he used to love green peppers. He'd fry them up with cabasa.'

They told me his favorite food was chicken nuggets and that he had apparently just bought them before he died because they had to pull them out of his motorcycle jacket when they found him. When they told me that I said, 'Oh, my God!'

Tim's sister Jackie stated, 'Why would she have a dream about her donor unless God was trying to tell her in a way who we were and trying to make it easier for her to get to us so she could see that there was good out of everything she went through.'

All the images that have come to me since the transplant are, in and of themselves, to do with this new part of me." [1]

How wonderful for Tim's grieving family to know his death literally and figuratively gave new life and that he is still very much alive and able to communicate with the person who was given this 'new life' on planet Earth.

This book is divided into two parts. Part One demonstrates that we are Eternal Beings who, one day, will all return to the One God of love who created us, and that death is nothing to fear. It also shows us that life in other dimensions is very much a reality and that we all have a multitude of unseen *heavenly* higher dimensional helpers who do play an integral part in our daily lives. There is much more to life than that which is seen.

Part Two helps people cope with bereavement, including the little acknowledged grief from the death of a marriage—divorce.

I have also included some support for the carer of the terminally ill as well as for the patient themselves; my dream being to get a copy of this book into as many Hospices around the globe as possible to assist the terminally ill to transition free from fear—in peace, with dignity and serenity. Within these chapters are prayers, practical advice, encouragement, and insights to help people deal with grief.

There is a chapter that asks the question, *Was it an accident?* The stories and insights in this chapter point to the belief that there are no accidents as such, and we will explore this subject in more detail. This may be of some comfort to those who have lived with guilt and blamed themselves or experienced the sudden loss of a loved one, young or old, as a result of an accident.

The many examples in this book, which are taken from a diversity of first-hand experiences, can bring encouragement and give hope to those who have lost a

---

[1] Secret World Of Dreams – Documentary, Questar International.

loved one, whether recently or in the past. Take comfort in knowing that your loved one is still very much alive in another dimension just as real as ours. Death is certainly an illusion. I will be bold and` go one step further and say that death can become a wonderful experience for the person making the transition.

Some of the extracts in this book will undoubtedly expose many readers to new possibilities and expanded parameters of awareness. Be open-minded and then feel for yourself from within your heart what resonates as truth to you.

"The key to growth is the introduction of higher dimensions of consciousness into our awareness."

Lao Tzu

PART ONE:

LIFE AFTER DEATH

CHAPTER ONE

HEAVENLY HELP

There are no religious boundaries when it comes to Near-Death Experiences. Many people, no matter what creed, race or religion, encounter angelic beings when they pass over. Their experiences are so vivid they never forget them. In fact, angel encounters often give survivors a sense of purpose and meaning.

Sarah Powell's story is just one amazing example of the vital role Guardian Angels can play in our lives. Her Guardian Angel, called George, introduced himself to her in her NDE, but also appeared after she had returned to her body while recovering from her terrible ordeal. George gave her hope and encouragement to keep going and told her she would get better. He became her strength to heal herself and when she had, he disappeared.

Deborah Powell's house was broken into by burglars while her youngest daughter Sarah was there alone from school. Deborah came home and found her daughter hog-tied, hands tied to her feet, and having amnesia. Although she couldn't remember what had happened to her, she was deeply depressed, and because of her amnesia, she had to relearn everything all over again.

One month after the crime, Sarah fell down and had what appeared to be a seizure. Sarah was diagnosed with having severe post-traumatic stress disorder, and it was during her seizures that the terrifying details of the crime would enter her memory.

When the burglars entered their home, Sarah became hysterical. One of the burglars attempted to smother her with a pillow. Fighting for her life, she noticed a tattoo on the burglar who was trying to kill her. When he realized she had seen his tattoo, he became enraged and struck her in the head. It was at this point that she died and had a Near-Death Experience.

"After I left my body, I found myself waking up underneath a tree in a place that seemed to be the best place that anyone could possibly be. It's the place I call heaven. It is definitely the place where I want to spend eternity. As I began to look around, I saw a figure approaching me and it turned out to be a good friend of mine. He had passed away four days before. Brian walked up to me and simply explained to me what was happening to me. He said I was going to be okay and that I was going to be spared for a certain reason. I had something to do. He said he had someone to introduce to me. Shortly after, someone else walked up. It was a tall man in a white suit and white top hat who spoke in a British accent.

He said, 'I have been with you for a long time. I've known you all your life, and I've been your Guardian Angel all of your life.' He said he didn't want me to be afraid because of what was happening to me. I wasn't dying. I would have to go back. Then he told me that I was brought there to rest, to gain the courage and energy to go on and finish what I was supposed to finish.

It seemed like everything then started to kind of fade out and then I was back in my room before I knew it. When I woke up again, my dog was licking me in the face and I didn't know where I was or who I was or how I got there or why I was tied up.

Something occurred while in the presence of her psychologist who was making regular visits to Sarah's home to help her regain her memory.

My psychologist was trying to calm me down because no one could. I was at the point where I wasn't even trying to listen to anybody. I was just rocking back and forth and trying to sing to myself. While I was talking to her, a light appeared. It appeared as a circular shape and then came down as a long oval. That was George.

Immediately, I just stopped crying, and Sharon (her psychologist) just seemed to be amazed. She said, 'How come you calmed down so quickly?' And I said, 'He says I am going to be okay, and he is going to take care of me now.' The Guardian Angel Sarah met during her near-death experience, who became affectionately known as George, helped in Sarah's emotional healing and reached out to touch the lives of Sarah's family and friends.

I told my mother to sit down. I said I have a Guardian Angel and he is going to be with me awhile to help us get through this. He says he has been with me a long time since I was a baby. He says that when I was a little kid, I used to laugh at him because he had this big hat that he had to push out of his eyes."

When Sarah's mother heard this, she started to cry. There was a time, when Sarah was two or three years old, when she would laugh a lot in her room. Her mother would peek into the room and ask what Sarah was laughing at.

4

Sarah would say, *"The man with the big hat comes and makes me laugh all the time."* Sarah's mother even keeps drawings that Sarah created of this man who made her laugh as a child.

At this point in her healing, Sarah would frequently receive visitations from George. She would actually be able to see and converse with George even though family members could not see or hear him. Sarah was even able to have George heal her friend who had suffered constantly with various illnesses throughout her life.

When Sarah was fully recovered, George prepared her for his departure. George had a message he wanted to leave with Sarah to share with others, and he wanted her to write it down. The following is the message.

"You must see that everyone within your reach hears about what happened to you. All of it. You must open their eyes and give them hope. Dedicate your soul to healing people simply by talking and letting everyone know how the world is changing. You'll begin to get responses. Ideas will come. Solutions to problems will appear and the people will send you letters supporting you. Some people will be negative, but these are the people who will be harder to reach. Don't let them discourage you. You have proven to be strong and your family as well. I know you can get through this and when you do, you'll come out even stronger than before. Through your mouth, they will hear, because you are a child – a child of God and a child who can bring hope to God's people. Please stay peaceful and one with God."

After receiving this message, George went away and could not be seen by Sarah again. Sarah has this to say about Guardian Angels.

"I think everybody has their own personal Guardian Angel. It's really amazing to think that there's someone just for me – someone that God sent just for me. That's what I always think whenever I feel down."[2]

INTO THE ARMS OF ANGELS

Like Sarah's story, the many first-hand accounts in this book may, at first, stretch your beliefs about the totality of life around us—not just the tangible, seen world, but the wonderful unseen world pulsating with vibrant life, always ready to assist us, both here and when we pass over.

---

[2] Extract taken from www.near-death.com from a documentary entitled, *Angel Stories*.

Here are a few more poignant illustrations, of people who encountered angelic beings when they passed over.

"I was joined by a radiant being bathed in a shimmering white glow." (Beverley Brodsky)

"But then this beautiful Angel appeared beside me. She was really pretty. She looked like a movie star with wings." (Randy Gehling, 10)

"There were always beautiful beings around me as well – helping me . . . guiding me . . . reassuring me . . . and pouring love into me." (Reverend Juliet Nightingale)

"Then in a sacred place somewhere before the light, I found myself being held, gently rocked, nurtured, and embraced in the arms of the one I believed to be the Presence. Whether this was a guide, or even an Angel, it does not matter. For still today this memory is alive . . . My spirit was imbued with a sense of peace, and my soul was engraved with the remembrance of a timeless love." (Lynnclaire Dennis)

"I knew this radiant being was powerful. It was making me feel so good all over. I could feel its light on me – like very gentle hands on me. And I could feel it holding me. But it was loving me with overwhelming power. After what I had been through, to be completely known, accepted, and intensely loved by this Being of Light surpassed anything I had known or could have imagined." (Reverend Howard Storm)

"And now spirits with glowing faces came close to me. They reflect a gentle and powerful light, reminding me of the pictures of beautiful Angels that I love so much. I feel nurtured and loved by them and enveloped by their luminescence." (Josiane Antonette)

Best-selling author Dr. Doreen Virtue, spiritual Doctor of Psychology and a fourth-generation metaphysician, describes angels in this way.

"You have guardian angels with you right now. These beings are pure beings of Divine light who are entirely trustworthy and who want to help you with every area of your life. The word angel means 'messenger of God.' Angels carry messages between the Creator and the created, like heavenly postal carriers."

Angels love everyone unconditionally. They look past the surface and see the Godliness within us all. They focus only on our Divinity and potential, and not on our faults. Angels aren't in anyway judgmental, and they only bring love into our lives. You are safe with the angels, and you can totally trust them.[3]

---

[3] Dr Doreen Virtue, Angels 101. (Hay House Australia, 2006), p. vii, viii.

Not only do people report visits with Guardian Angels, but the Bible refers to angels in many different places, reinforcing what people with Near-Death Experiences say.

There are over 250 references to angels in the Bible. This well-known quote, possibly referring to Guardian Angels, appears in the Bible three times.

> *For he will command his angels concerning you*
> *To guard you in all your ways;*
> *They will lift you up in their hands,*
> *So that you will not strike your foot against a stone.*

Psalm 91:11-12, Luke 4:10-11, Matthew 4:6

Frederic De La Rue's life is a powerful example of divinely directed interaction with Angels. His wonderful NDE is included later within the book. Frederic produces sublime music combining his accomplished skills as a musician and pianist with celestial music he hears and then translates into beautiful music. In Frederic's own words, *"My hands play what the Angels sing in my ears."*

He has many CDs, including one that was channeled specifically for assisting cancer cells, in fact for all cells to heal, entitled *Musical Rapture*. This is available for free from his website www.fredericdelarue.com. Detailed information is available at the end of his NDE.

The following is a channelled extract taken from a source that I consider to be one of the most sacred books of Cosmic Truth I have ever read, entitled *The Elemental Grace Alliance – The God Awakening* by Peter Melchizedek. With over 40 years of spiritual searching through a great number and diversity of spiritual books, that is a lot of books to assist me in making an informed statement.

Angel Yeiazel speaks.

"Yet speaking from Our perspectives, in relationship to Who We Are as the Angelic Host, the third party within the Holy Trinity of Mankind, The Elementals and The Angelic Host, what We provide most of all is the Emotional feelings that support the attainment of Peace, Tranquility, Harmony and Balance and so on. Not only in the Realms of human experience, but also within the vast array of The Elemental, Devic and Nature Kingdoms. We the Angelic Host are the harbingers of Peace and Grace. Not only the Guardian Angels that work with humanity, but All The Angels and Devas of the Natural World. The Ones Who Over Light, Guard and Guide and Bless, the Nature and Elemental Spirits, Plants, animals, rivers, seas, mountains, skies, homes, villages, cities, communities, cultures, countries and Planets. The Whole of Our Beings are imbued with Peace along with many

7

other Virtues that align to the Principles within this Light of Love That We serve God most ardently with.

Peace is the Love Essence and Beauty of Our Beloved Father and the Exquisite Perfection of Our Celestial Mother. How can one describe in words of such Qualities of Peace? The Truth is you cannot, it must be felt, felt within the Heart Mind, Body and Spirit through the Heart of the Emotional Body! And it is through the Angelic Host that these feelings are transmitted and sustained within the Soul Essence of every human being. We are the reservoirs from which humanity and the Elementals draw the Heart Emotion of Peace. Until human beings rediscover this Life Source of Peace within the Core of their being, they will not find their True Identity. Once found, it shall then come forth as the constant flow of Love Substance that will sustain the physical form and give Intelligence to the Mind, continuity to the Divine Consciousness, and activity to the vehicles they presently inhabit.

What a Blessing it will be when men and women, and children of all ages, find the Glory of God within their Hearts and feel this Loving Life Stream of Peace that flows forth with every heartbeat into their world and becomes that for which they Decree and Praise God for. Every human being before they incarnated, applied for the task of Creating the Freedom of Life from within the human experience. It is the Life that you are now living Dear Souls that you have come into so determined to invoke, draw forth, qualify and release into this Universe, bearing your stamp and your name and wearing the colored bands of your Higher Selves. This Life Dear Ones is made up of the Love Substance that We the Angelic Host manifest and give so lovingly and so freely to you to use within your own creative endeavors.

The Earth's Vibrational Frequency is rising rapidly now and so with this increase of speed with which the Electrons rotate around the Atoms, mankind is also feeling a more rapid rate of vibration. That is why so many are finding themselves in states of uncertainty and insecurity, for they are feeling that time is running away with them, that they cannot keep up with the changes that are taking place within and around their lives.

There is also an aspect of the chaos that is being seen around the world for these Higher vibrations cannot sustain lower vibratory states of consciousness or even technology or mechanizations for that matter. So, with the thought forms that one must hold onto the old is naturally giving way to having it taken away by force and which are prompting the defending or fighting for the purpose of keeping. There is no judgment here, just the Peace in these realizations.

Dear Ones, these are all the opposing states of Peace and while these things continue to play out, Peace cannot and will not be found, no matter how much the

8

Angelic Host has to heal and raise humanity above such low Vibrational life experiences.

We The Angelic Host Speaking with One Voice, are here to Love Humanity and the Elementals and support them in every way possible, especially now as the Vibration of Love increases to even Greater rates of Perfection. To 'Protect the Future' We are inviting All of humanity to invoke Our Presence in their lives. Call Us in and feel Our Presence and take advantage of what We have to Gift you with. Ask Us for that which you desire and even if We cannot give that to you, We will soon bring forward Those Who Can. The way forward Dear Souls is the reunification and the reestablishment of the Unity of the Holy Trinity We Hold So preciously within Our Hearts. We the Angelic Host send Peace around the world at this time of New Awareness and shall hold the Visions of Peace so that more human beings can find the Love of God within themselves.

Peace, Peace, Heavenly Peace. For the Greater Glory of God. And So It Is."[4]

Co-Creating with our I Am Presence – God

My next inclusion is not specifically related to Near-Death Experiences however it plays a vital part in the necessary awareness needed to work in harmony with, and in acknowledgment of, our Heavenly Higher Dimensional helpers who are *always* there to assist us to find a level of peace and happiness in our lives regardless of what is going on around us.

Our Father/Mother God wants us to live abundant, happy lives. He/She has designed us to be masterful Co-Creators of our own lives. We are powerful, divinely created masterpieces, and, as such, Source Energy wants us to become the grandest version of ourselves that we can possibly become. Unfortunately, due to lack of understanding, doubt and fear, many people spend the majority of their time de-creating rather than Co-Creating. The God part of us within has the tools to create whatever we desire but many of us have forgotten the blueprints! Regular reminders are good. Then, we can put them into our daily actions, have faith, (and at times lots of patience), knowing that they are on their way, realizing that, invariably it may not happen when or how we think. Divine timing is always precise, according to and in alignment with, our big picture which only our God Presence or I Am Presence knows.

As the energy of our Universe is neutral, what we predominantly think about with feeling is what we attract back to ourselves. Our thoughts are either our greatest asset or our greatest enemy. In Eckhart Tolle's wise words, *"You attract and manifest whatever corresponds to your own inner state."* Unfortunately, most

---

[4] Extract taken from the book, *The Elemental Grace Alliance – The God Awakening* by Peter Melchizedek

9

people's predominant thoughts and feelings are on the very things they **don't want** in their lives. For example, "I can't pay all those bills, I am in so much debt, I don't like my job, I am too fat, I am too thin, I don't want to live in this house, I want more of this or that. The list could go on forever couldn't it? So, if we are concentrating on how sick we feel, guess what? We attract more sickness to us. If we are concentrating on how much debt we have, we attract more debt to ourselves. *This is The Universal Law of Attraction and it is an irrevocable Cosmic Law."*

Some time ago now there was a period in my life that I realized that I had been focusing more on what wasn't working in my life and I was not a 'happy camper' as there was much, to my then perception, majorly out of place. Most major things in my life were associated with hardship and struggle. It was after reading two books by two very different people whom I believe to be modern day Masters that I had my light bulb realizations that did change my whole perspective and subsequently, bit by bit, my ensuing life.

The first book was, *Practising The Power Of Now* by Eckhart Tolle. I had long since read his wonderful book, *The Power Of Now* but at that time I wasn't ready to hear the deeper level messages that spoke to me enough to want to change myself. The second book was the equally wonderful, *Loving What Is* by Byron Katie. Funnily, it was my second read years after the first read that also spoke to my heart understanding rather than to my conditioned, limited, logical 'mind of man' understanding.

Both books say the same things in their own way. They both reiterate many times that ALL negativity and suffering we go through daily comes from mentally opposing *what is* in our lives! I was then constantly and painfully aware that I needed to change so many aspects in my life that weren't okay for me. We can't change what has happened in our life or in the life of those we love so why do we try so hard to do just that. What *is* has already happened. We may not like it, but it can *never* be re-written - it just *is*.

When we mentally stop fighting against what has already happened, surrender to it and live in acceptance of each 'now' moment, a strange and wonderful thing happens. We notice and begin to *live in the now*. Then, we begin to see all the good there is in that now moment and in our life to actually be grateful for. I had blinded myself to all I did have to be grateful for in my life as I was predominantly focused on what I perceived needed to be changed!

One example is that we were living in a run down, large house in a beautiful area close to where our youngest daughter went to High School. There were parts of this house I disliked intensely, (to put it politely), and we'd been there for fourteen years. Due to the fact that the house was so run down we were able to live in a lovely tree lined, park filled, safe area, where my daughter could walk to and from school with ease when I had to work. It had a separate wing that my 'sick' older daughter could call her own, which she needed at that time. If the house hadn't been in such a run down state we wouldn't have been able to afford to live in this district, let alone so close to one of the best High Schools renown for specializing in Musical Theatre, which my daughter loved. The more I surrendered to my situation, (that is to those parts I wasn't able to change at that time), the more peace I felt, and that stillness allowed me to *hear* the guidance my I Am Presence/God Presence, was showing me.

The more I surrendered to every aspect of my then life the more I could see everything I had to be grateful for in my life and there was actually a great deal. So, my focus became those things which I was grateful for, then those positive feelings of gratitude drew more of the same vibrational feelings in and so forth. I had clarity on what direction I should take and I felt a deep peace emanating from my soul/spirit that was completely separate from my still interesting surroundings and situation. I felt a new lightness and happiness bubble up despite those things around me that hadn't actually changed.

"When you completely accept this moment, when you no longer argue with what is, the compulsion to think lessens and is replaced by an alert stillness. You are fully conscious, yet the mind is not labelling this moment in any way. This state of inner non-resistance opens you up to the unconditional consciousness that is infinitely greater than the human mind. This vast intelligence can then express itself through you and assist you, both from within and without."[5]

In Byron Katie's words, *"When we stop opposing reality, action becomes simple, fluid, kind and fearless..... The only time we suffer is when we believe a thought that argues with what 'is.'"*

This is an extract from a book on Cosmic Law.

*"**Law of The Present Moment** - Time does not exist. What we refer to as past and future, have no reality except in our own mental constructs. The idea of time is a convention of thought and language, a social agreement. In truth, we only have this moment. When we hold regret for an occurrence in the past we keep the regret alive with pictures and feelings we conjure up. When we feel anxiety about the future, we keep the anxiety alive with the pictures we imagine. Time is the abstract concept. When we practice remembering that the here and now is all we have, our present moments improve"*

---

[5] Extract taken from, *Practising The Power Of Now* by Eckhart Tolle.

Rev. Howard Storm recalls his experiences with angels.

"During my near-death experience, I was given wonderful insights into the beings we call angels. Angels are messengers of God. There are uncountable kinds of angels. Their numbers exceed the stars." [6]

Both world traditions as well as accounts from Near Death Experiences show us that our Almighty God, Creator of Heaven and Earth and All That Is needs myriads of higher dimensional helpers to run His vast domains. I believe that each one of us has our very own Guardian Angel responsible for watching over us, protecting and guiding us from birth to death. Each angel is available to help us at our every call. However, we must ask them for their help.

When we die, angels are there to help us make the transition into the Divine heavenly realms. I was reminded of a true story that so touched me and has remained etched in my memory.

A little boy drowned in a river close to a large waterfall. All that his distraught parents could think about was this poor little soul falling to his death over this dangerously high waterfall.

A wise friend, who was given this vision, comforted them greatly. She relayed to them how she had seen a glorious golden angel waiting at the top of the waterfall with outstretched arms. She saw the little boy's spirit body leave his physical body at the *top* of the waterfall and fall into the angel's arms. He was safe and alive in spirit.

There is strong evidence to suggest that at the point of death in sudden fatal accidents, the being, human and animal, feels no pain. Our spiritual body merely leaves its physical body. Our Etheric Light body is as real as our physical one; it just exists in a different, higher frequency realm, as do all the higher dimensional Beings. The difference between our dense physical body and our etheric Light body is that our Light body is vibrating at a much higher frequency and, as such, is unable to be seen by most human eyes.

Losing a loved one is hard for adults and children alike. Knowing that loved ones who have passed over are free from pain can alleviate our fears and anxieties.

If you have lost loved ones from a sudden, traumatic accident of one kind or another, it can be comforting to replace any horrific pictures that may haunt you

---

[6] *My Descent Into Death – A Second Chance at Life* (Random House, USA, 2005), p. 135.

of that moment of death, with the image of your loved one and their Guardian Angel waiting with arms outstretched. Imagine they felt no pain, and all they could see at the precise moment of death was this Radiant Being calling to them. Imagine them wrapped in the gentle arms of their own angel filling them with immense love and reassurance whilst assisting them to transition into a higher dimension.

Wouldn't it be wonderful if there exists a place where people who have passed over from sudden accidents are taken to adjust from the instantaneous shock of not having a physical body anymore, and not being with their earthly loved ones— a place where each soul is ministered to by angels, each one radiating a golden glow?

I can't say with absolute certainty that this happens, but I was given a vision that suggests it may. It is a lovely picture to paint for children who have lost someone dear to them through a sudden accident. I imagine the face of each angel exuding pure love, tenderness, and compassion. I wrote this eleven years before I read Robert Benson's first-hand account of buildings that **are** there in the Spirit Realms specifically to look after those who have transitioned suddenly. (Details are in Chapter Five)

If you have children who have also experienced sudden loss, they may have their own concept of Heaven. Be honest with them if you don't know exactly what Heaven looks like. Share with them that you do believe that it is a safe and beautiful place where the departed are still alive in spirit, in radiant heath and where they have gone to be with God and His angels. The young ones of today are so aware that if you ask them what their concept of heaven is they may surprise you with their answer.

Dr Melvin Morse, a Neuroscientist and Pediatrician, recognized as one of the top Pediatricians in the country by Woodward-White's Best Doctor's in America from 1997-2006, is now retired from a busy private practice outside of Seattle, Washington. Dr Morse is now taking his research from his former work in the critical care department of Seattle Children's Hospital, where he investigated children's Near-Death Experiences, and he is teaching how to heal grief and understand death. He continues to research adult and children's Near-Death Experiences, which he has been doing since 1980.

Dr Morse noted eighteen years ago in his book, *Closer To The Light* that hardly a week would go by without a member of his medical staff reporting outer dimensional experiences with their patients, especially close to their passing over.

"These pre-death visions are intensely real experiences that a dying person has while still conscious. Reality is not distorted or altered. The dying patient often

sees God, Angels, dead relatives or visions of Heaven superimposed upon reality or actually present at the deathbed."[7]

Here are a few of Dr Morse's many cases of pre-death visions. *"He was unsedated, fully conscious, and had a low temperature. He was a rather religious person and believed in life after death. We expected him to die, and he probably did too, as he was asking us to pray for him. In the room where he was lying, there was a staircase leading to the second floor. Suddenly he exclaimed: 'See, the angels are coming down the stairs. The glass has fallen and broken.' All of us in the room looked toward the staircase where a drinking glass had been placed on one of the steps. As we looked, we saw the glass break into a thousand pieces without any apparent cause. It did not fall; it simply exploded. The angels, of course, we did not see. A happy and peaceful expression came over the patient's face, and the next moment he expired. Even after his death, the serene, peaceful expression remained on his face.*[8]

The condition of the man suffering from a heart attack had been serious for the last few days. Suddenly he gained consciousness. He looked better and cheerful. He talked nicely to his relatives and requested them to go home. He also said, 'I shall go to my home. Angels have come to take me away.' He looked relieved and cheerful. . . ."[9]

Dr Morse had another eleven-year-old patient John, who was dying. At one point when his relatives were around his bed they were startled when he sat bolt upright and told them Jesus was in the room. And he asked them to pray for him. On another occasion he sat upright again and exclaimed, *"There are beautiful colours in the sky!"*

Near the end John opened his eyes and asked his grieving parents to let him go.

"Don't be afraid," he said. "I've seen God, Angels, and shepherds."

Dr Morse recalls.

---

[7] Morse and Perry, Closer To The Light. (Ivy Books, New York. 1990), p. 57.
[8] Morse and Perry, Closer To The Light. (Ivy Books, New York. 1990), p. 58.

[9] Morse and Perry, Closer To The Light. (Ivy Books, New York. 1990), p. 58.

"As sick as he was, John still begged his family not to feel sorry for him. He had seen where he was going, and it was a joyous and wondrous place. 'It's wonderful. It's beautiful,' he said, his hand held out in front of him.

Soon he laid back and fell asleep. John never regained consciousness and died two days later." [10]

Dr Morse has been a pioneer in endeavoring to help the medical fraternity to understand that these pre-death visions are actually real and can be of great comfort to both the patient and their families. He advocates listening to the patient when they are relaying such information rather than prescribing more drugs, as some do.

Dr Morse studied under another revered Pediatrician Dr Frank Oski, at John Hopkins Medical Centre. Dr Oski was contemplating why some children have to die from congenital defects that he couldn't seem to help. He received a beautiful message from an unexpected source. Dr Morse continues;

"In my own research I have found angels to be an integral part of visions of all kinds. At least 50 percent of the children in my studies see 'guardian angels' as a part of their near-death experience. I have also found that guardian angels lend their help at other times of crisis when a person needs answers to bolster his or her flagging spirit.

Angels are reported under a variety of circumstances. Another account comes from Dr. Frank Oski, a professor of Pediatrics under whom I trained at Johns Hopkins University. Oski is not a new-age guru. Rather he is a demanding Pediatrician with an encyclopedic knowledge of medicine who insisted that his students come to the hospital having read the latest medical-journal articles. Yet to my great surprise Dr Oski has been touched by the same mystical light described by people down through the ages who have had visions, including Near Death Experiences.

As a medical student Oski was enthusiastic about the potential of modern medicine but frustrated by the fact that children die of congenital defects that are beyond anyone's control. One night he went to bed pondering the fate of a dying patient. Although he was doing his best, the child was not improving. He felt powerless to help and went to sleep wondering why this child had to die. About an hour after falling asleep Oski was awakened by a bright light, one that shone in his room like a private sun. Oski could make out the form of a woman in the glow of the intense light. She had wings on her back and was approximately twenty years old.

---

[10] Morse and Perry, Closer To The Light. (Ivy Books, New York. 1990), p. 62.

In a quiet and reassuring voice the woman explained to the speechless Oski why it was that children had to die.

The angel, (I don't know what else to call her), said that life is an endless cycle of improvements and that humans are not perfect yet. She said that most people have this secret revealed to them when they die, but that handicapped children often know this and endure their problems without complaining because they know that their burdens will pass. Some of these children, she said, have even been given the challenge of teaching the rest of us how to love. 'It stretches our own humanity to love a child who is less than perfect,' said the angel. 'And that is an important lesson for us.'

Oski has been courageous enough to talk freely about his experience. He has even written about it in a major Pediatric Journal. In that article he wrote, 'I will make no attempt to convince you as to the reality of my story. But I would merely ask that you keep an open mind on the mysteries of life which occur to you on a daily basis.'"[11]

This is a beautiful message to us all that those who are handicapped in some way have chosen to be born like this, as have all concerned in their family, and they have often chosen to teach those around them by opening them up to a new depth of unconditional love. They are, in fact, very special souls with that intangible special quality of acceptance and unconditional love. As we see from the NDE's their souls know that life is transitory and only for a short period of earthly time, after which they can return and live in radiant health in God's higher spiritual realms.

---

[11] Dr Melvin Morse and Paul Perry, Parting Visions. (Villard Books, N.Y. 1996), pp.16-18.

CHAPTER TWO

WHAT HAPPENS
WHEN WE DIE

For centuries people have pondered over the mysteries of death and dying. The nearest anyone comes to death is when they are *spiritually dead*—when they believe that all there is to life is what can be physically seen by their eyes, touched by their hands, heard with their ears and smelled by their nose. Our world of physicality is but a minute part of the totality of the wonders of life. It is in the higher unseen realms that we truly live in unconditional love, without fear, in absolute freedom.

Dr. P. M. H. Atwater is considered a world authority on near-death experiences and life after death. During Dr. Atwater's lifetime, she was personally involved in witnessing many people dying from varying circumstances. She was pronounced clinically dead three times and subsequently had three personal NDE experiences. Dr. Atwater is one of the original researchers in the field of near-death studies, having begun her work in 1978.

To date, she has nearly 4,500 adult and child NDE experiences in her research database! Dr. Atwater has been invited to address the United Nations twice. She has been given invaluable insights to convey through her books and lectures to help people gain an enlightened and fuller perspective on death and that, although our physical shell dies, our soul lives forever and that we should not fear death. In fact, for the majority it was a blissful, wondrous experience of re-uniting with their Creator and experiencing such a depth of unconditional love that permeated everything and everyone around them to the very core of their being.

WHAT DEATH IS

Dr. Atwater explains.

"There is a step up of energy at the moment of death, an increase in speed as if you are suddenly vibrating faster than before. Using radio as an analogy, this speed-up is comparable to having lived all your life at a certain radio frequency when suddenly someone or something comes along and flips the dial! That 'flip' shifts you to another wavelength. The original frequency where you once existed is still there. It did not change. Everything is still the same as it always was. Only YOU changed, only YOU speeded up or slowed down to allow entry into the next radio frequency up or down the dial.

As is true with all radios and radio stations, there can be bleed overs or distortions of transmission signals due to interference patterns. Normally, most shifts along the dial are fast and efficient, but occasionally one can run into interference perhaps from a strong emotion, a sense of duty, or the need to fulfill a vow, or keep a promise. This interference enables frequencies to co-exist for a few seconds, days or even years. This may well explain the existence of 'hauntings' or 'ghosts'. But, sooner or later, every vibrational frequency will seek out or be nudged to where it belongs.

You fit your particular spot on the dial by your speed of vibration. You cannot co-exist forever where you do not belong. Who can say how many spots there are on the dial or how many frequencies there are to inhabit? No one knows for certain. You shift your frequency in dying. You switch over to LIFE on another wavelength. You are still a spot on the dial, but you move up or down a notch or two.

You don't die when you die. You shift your degree of consciousness and change your speed of vibration. That is all death is—a shift[12]."

This extract is Robert Benson's actual account of what it was like for him when he died and transitioned to **live in** the spirit world, as transcribed by his friend Anthony Borgia.

"I suddenly felt a great urge to rise up. I had no physical feeling whatever, very much in the same way that physical feeling is absent during a dream, but I was mentally alert, however much my body seemed to contradict such a condition. Immediately I had this distinct prompting to rise, I found that I was actually doing so. I then discovered that those around my bed did not seem to perceive what I was doing, since they made no effort to come to my assistance, nor did they try in any way to hinder me. Turning, I then beheld what had taken place. I saw my

---

[12] Dr. P. M. H. Atwater, We Live Forever: The Real Truth About Death, pp. 88-90. Reprinted by kind permission from Dr P.M.H. Atwater.

physical body lying lifeless upon its bed, but here was I, the real I, alive and well. For a minute or two I remained gazing, and the thought of what to do next entered my head, but help was close at hand....

..... I could not resist the impulse to turn and take a last look at the room of my transition. It still presented its misty appearance. Those who were formerly standing round the bed had now withdrawn, and I was able to approach the bed and gaze at 'myself.' I was not the least impressed by what I saw, but the last remnant of my physical self seemed to be placid enough. My friend then suggested that we should now go, and we accordingly moved away. As we departed, the room gradually disappeared."[13]

Life and Death are one thread,

the same line viewed from different sides-

Lao Tzu

WHAT IS A NEAR-DEATH EXPERIENCE OR NDE?

Dr P.M.H. Atwater explains.

"On average, adult and child near-death experiences are without pulse or breathe for about **5 to 20 minutes.** *It is not uncommon for individuals to have been clinically dead for an hour or more and in fact, some have 'woken up' in the morgue! Since* **the brain can be permanently damaged in 3-5 minutes without sufficient oxygen,** *it is important to note that* **one of the striking features of NDE's is that no matter how long the person has been pronounced dead for, there is little or no brain damage. In fact, there is noticeable brain enhancement and a total change in their spiritual belief structure[14]!"**

Dr Atwater has written eight books on her findings.

In Rev. George Rodonaia's case, his corpse was stored in a freezer in the morgue for 3 days, and he revived on the autopsy table as they were cutting open the trunk of his body!

Our Creator – God, has given us wonderful glimpses through people's near-death experiences, a virtual window to peek through at life after death - both of the

---

[13] Taken from, *Life In The World Unseen* by Anthony Borgia

[14] Dr. P. M. H. Atwater, *We Live Forever: The Real Truth About Death.* Dr. Atwater's website address is www.pmhatwater.com, and her blog can be visited at http://pmhatwater.blogspot.com

higher dimensions and of the lower astrals. The Astral plane is a self-created 'hell' of humanity's creation, or rather the absence of love and/or of a belief in Source/God or a higher power.

Naturally, like all information from another source outside of ourselves, this book should always be viewed through glasses of individual discernment. The reality is that NDE's have to be relayed back through human filters of their own concepts and perceptions. I have looked for the common denominators and the parts that ring true for me, the parts that excite and inspire me at a Soul level. One of the reasons God/Source has given us these precious souls and their insights is to help allay our fears of death and dying.

The truth is we never die! However, we do take with us our belief system into our death experience. Neale Donald Walsch outlines how he views this in his book, *Home With God.*

"If you think that you are living or dying without God, you will experience that you are. You may have this experience as long as you wish. You may end this experience whenever you choose.[15]

If you so much as hope that someone will come to help you, you will be surrounded by loved ones and angels. If you so much as hope you will meet Muhammad, Muhammad will guide you. If you so much as hope that Jesus will be there, Jesus will be there. Or Lord Krishna, or the Buddha. Or simply the essence of pure love. Hope plays a wonderful role in death and in life. Never give up hope. Never."[16]

For many NDE's their very real experience of being *"touched by the hand of God"*, radically transforms them. In some cases, like Rev. Howard Storm's, the transformation was from being an Atheist to returning to tell the world about the power of God's unconditional love for all. They come back to Earth with an absolute *knowing* that it was God so imbedded within them.

Researching many NDE's has given me incredible in-depth insights into life in the higher dimensions. Or rather, should I say it has rekindled those deep memories and knowing's that God's higher realms are indeed magnificent and that we are all a part thereof.

I have the deepest respect for these people, for although many have had a wondrously enlightening experience, more often than not they have to come back to lengthy periods of readjustment both physically, mentally and emotionally. Some become depressed as they have just been bathing in a depth of unconditional love that defies human comprehension, back to life in an extremely sick or

---

[15] Walsch, Home With God. (Hodder & Stoughton, London. 2006), p. 1.
[16] Walsch, Home With God. (Hodder & Stoughton, London. 2006), p. 114.

severely damaged human body with all its frailties. They often come thumping back into broken bodies that are in extreme pain. Remembering they have just died - whether from severe accidents, terminal illnesses, electrocution, or medical complications. For many, that pain lasts for months, sometimes years as they fight to regain their health. Often their families, friends or their religious peers do not believe them, and they are frequently ridiculed and occasionally ostracized. In one case I am aware of, the family tried to have the poor person committed after their NDE.

One such inspiring example of returning to a severely damaged body is Dannion Brinkley who felt he was *"doomed to live"* not *"doomed to die"* when he first came back into his seared body. He had come from a place of absolute peace, exquisite love and indescribable beauty during his *"heavenly sojourn"* thumping back into a body that in Dannion's words, *"had been burnt from the inside out,"* by lightning. It was only his sheer determination to survive, to fulfil the missions he had been given, that enabled him to recover. He was in constant agony, his fingernails had been burnt off, and there was nothing left but black stubs. At this point, he was paralyzed, and he looked like something out of a horror movie to the extent that one visitor actually threw up at the sight of him and many more nearly did! He was not expected to live.

So, on behalf of every reader everywhere, of every book written about NDE's, who has received precious insights about life after death I wish to say a heartfelt thank you to all those special souls that have bravely stepped forward to share their inspiring stories so that we, here on planet Earth, can see we need not fear death and can subsequently view 'death' for what it is – a grand illusion.

If you have experienced a Near-Death experience and need support and understanding or wish to share your story, I would suggest going to the International Association for Near-Death Studies at www.IANDS.com. This is a wonderfully supportive international organization with many branches.

21

CHAPTER THREE

SIMILARITIES IN NEAR-DEATH EXPERIENCES

This chapter demonstrates just how many universal factors there are in Near-Death Experiences. With so many common denominators, we can only conclude that they were real. Here are some of the unusual common denominators that so many experienced.

The majority of NDE accounts are astonishingly similar. However, they may have been at other ends of the globe, from other cultures, from other religions, from other times, and from all ages. Some are from innocent children. After being pronounced clinically dead, they discover the following.

1. No emotional attachment to their physical body as they observe it, usually floating above it or on the ceiling. No feelings of pain or discomfort that they were often experiencing before leaving their body behind.

2. Absence of time as we know it.

3. Defies physicality. The blind can see, the deaf can hear, etc. The physical affliction that often led to their death disappears, and they find themselves in radiant health.

4. Complete telepathic communication. No need for words.

5. Often a passageway that leads to unbelievably brilliant light—travelling at immense speed towards the Light.

6. This Light emanates from Source/God, Omnipresent, Omniscient, All-Seeing, All-Knowing and envelopes them in an unconditional Love/Light that is so immense and profound, it defies human description and comprehension.

7. They discover that there is one original Source/God who loves ALL His/Her creations equally, regardless of skin color and ALL religions as they are all stepping-stones to Universal Truth on this free-will planet.

8. They discover that we are ALL interconnected, all a part of the WHOLE. We are all individualized parts of the ONE original Source/Prime Creator, experiencing life then returning to from whence we came – back to 'the Light.'

9. They experience their *Life Review* and are given a screening or interactive/virtual slide show of their whole lifetime and the repercussions of their good and not so good actions, words, and deeds. Feelings of guilt are replaced by feelings of responsibility for them, as they want to rectify them, thus replacing the initial reluctance to return with a genuine desire to do so. Source/God assists us to view our life so we can assess ourselves. Judgment doesn't exist in the higher dimensions. We witness our life in absolute truth without the veil of emotions, deception, misguided perceptions, and indoctrination.

10. They are reunited with beloved family/ friends/ pets that have passed away previously.

11. They experience colors in nature and angelic music of unparalleled splendor. The colors and textures in nature are astonishing. They say there are so many colors they have never seen before and that the beauty is indescribable in human terms. All the flowers and plants are alive with a *"golden inner glow."* The music is celestial with exquisite harmonies and in harmonic perfection that permeates the Soul with serenity and peace.

12. They have total recall of this experience indelibly etched into their memories with lucid clarity as if it were yesterday, sometimes for decades.

Here are some examples.

1. NO EMOTIONAL ATTACHMENT
TO THEIR PHYSICAL BODY

"I feel such a wonderful release! I'm free! I can't resist this new and wonderful tide of energy sweeping my body upward. Now I'm on the hospital room ceiling gazing down! Everything appears so small: I see my bed; my body looks small and colorless; the people around the bed are tiny. Overwhelming grief and sorrow fill the room, and yet I feel completely disconnected from the scene below me. I hover nearer and look at the strange form lying on the bed. I feel compassion beyond words. I understand everything, but I have no feeling of attachment to anyone." (Josiane Antonette)

Barbara was strapped into a circular machine which nurses rotated at intervals, unable to move in any way.

"I lost consciousness. I awoke in the hall in the middle of the night. The lights were dim. It was quiet. I looked up and down the hall and didn't see anyone. I remember thinking that if they caught me out of the circle bed, I'd be in trouble because I wasn't supposed to move. So I turned around to go back into my room and found myself looking into a public address speaker. This isn't possible, I thought. I remembered seeing the speaker when I was admitted. It was mounted on the ceiling at least three or four feet above my head. I moved into my room and looked down into the circle bed and saw....me. I heard myself chuckle because she looked funny with white tape around her nose holding in a tube." (Barbara Whitfield)

"Then I floated above my physical body lifeless and unaware, I wondered, 'Can I save her? Yet, I felt no urge to act. I looked down and knew that the body below me was a previous part of myself. Will it awaken? I wondered . . . . At that moment an awareness overtook me—I am not my physical body! This realization made me feel so free, so wonderful!" (Dr Dianne Morrissey)

"I awakened and found myself floating above my body, off to the right side, looking down, watching the attempts of the medical team trying to revive the lifeless form below. I viewed the scene with detachment." (Laurelynn Martin)

"I watched as Tommy held me and cursed the slowness of the ambulance, which we could hear approaching in the distance. I hovered above the three of them – as the medical technicians loaded me onto the stretcher and wheeled me to the ambulance. . . Without passion or pain, I watched the person on the stretcher." (Dannion Brinkley)

24

"I had no strong feelings about my body lying on the bed. It was almost unfamiliar to me." (Grace Bubulka)

"I jumped out of bed in alarm, looking for my clothes. My uniform wasn't on the chair. I turned around, then froze. Someone was lying in that bed. I took a step closer. He was quite a young man, with short brown hair, lying very still. But the thing was impossible! I myself had just gotten out of that bed . . . . I backed toward the doorway. The man in that bed was dead! I felt the same reluctance I had the previous time at being in a room with a dead person. But . . . if that was my ring, then—then it was me, the separated part of me, lying under that sheet. Did that mean that I was . . . . It was the first time in this entire experience that the word death occurred to me in connection with what was happening. But I wasn't dead! How could I be dead and still be awake? Thinking. Experiencing. Death was different. Death was . . . I didn't know. Blanking out. Nothingness. I was me, wide awake, only without a physical body to function in." (Dr George Ritchie)

2. ABSENCE OF TIME AS WE KNOW IT

"As the brilliance increased and the encompassing rays stretched to meet me, I felt that time, as we know it, was non-existent. Time and existence were a blending and a melding of the past, present and future into this one moment. A sense of all-knowing enveloped me. Every part of my being was satisfied with an unconditional love beyond description. All questions were answered. An inner peace without striving or achieving was created and understood." (Laurelynn Martin)

"I was completely out of time and space as we know it. In this expanded state, I discovered that creation is about absolute pure consciousness, or God, coming into the experience of life as we know it." (Mellen-Thomas Benedict)

"The first awareness was of eternity. . . When we die everything stops. It is like finally getting to the nanosecond, where time stops for us. Like a watch, our body stops at that time. Yet our spirit and consciousness continue to live on in a dimension beyond sequential time." (Dr Gerard Landry)

"Time did not make any sense. Time did not seem to apply. It seemed irrelevant. It was unattached to anything, the way I was. Time is only relevant when it is relative to the normal orderly sequential aspects of life. So I was there for a moment or for eternity. I cannot say, but it felt like a very long time to me." (Grace Bubulka)

"I then remember travelling a long distance upward toward the light. I believe that I was moving very fast, but this entire realm seemed to be outside of time. . . . Space and time are illusions that hold us to the physical realm; in the spirit realm, all is present simultaneously." (Beverly Brodsky)

25

3. DEFIES PHYSICALITY

Rev. Juliet Nightingale was technically blind and bed-ridden, hardly able to sit up, with terminal cancer before her Near-death experience. *"Everything was stunningly beautiful—so vibrant and luminous. . . and so full of life—yes, life! – in ways that one would never see or experience on the physical plane. I was totally and completely enveloped in Divine Love. . . . . There was never any sense of hunger, thirst, weariness or pain. Such things never entered my mind, in fact!"* (Rev. J Nightingale)

"The transition was serene and peaceful. I was walking up a beautiful green hill. It was steep, but my leg motion was effortless, and a deep ecstasy flooded my body. Despite three incisions in my body from the operations, I stood erect without pain, enjoying my tallness, free from inhibitions about it." (Betty Maltz)

"From immense pain, I found myself engulfed by peace and tranquility. It was a feeling I had never known before and have not had since. It was like bathing in a glorious calmness. I had no idea what had happened, but even in this moment of peacefulness, I wanted to know where I was. I began to look around, to roll over in midair. Below me was my own body, thrown across the bed. My shoes were smoking, and the telephone was melted in my hand." (Dannion Brinkley)

"When people die, they don't know that they have died. The world looks the same to them, and they feel completely alive. Whatever trauma a person experienced in dying is only a vivid memory. The suffering is gone, and the person feels physically better than he or she ever did in life." (Rev. Howard Storm)

4. COMPLETE TELEPATHIC COMMUNICATION

"Now – I am filled with the essence of love and compassion. This magnetic power is filling every atom of me. I have never before experienced such depth and power of love. I am the power of love! Merging into an intimate dance wherein all boundaries have disappeared, I feel myself one with these beings of compassion. No words or sounds are being exchanged, and yet communication is happening." (Josiane Antoinette)

"I could hear the Being's message in my head, again as if through telepathy: 'Humans are powerful spiritual beings meant to create good on the Earth. This good isn't usually accomplished in bold actions but in singular acts of kindness between people. It's the little things that count because they are more spontaneous and show who you truly are.'" (Dannion Brinkley)

"Each time I silently posed one of these questions, the answer came instantly in an explosion of light, color, love, and beauty that blew through me like a crashing wave. What was important about these bursts was that they didn't simply silence

my questions by overwhelming them. They answered them, but in a way that bypassed language. Thoughts entered me directly. But it wasn't thought like we experience on Earth. It wasn't vague, immaterial, or abstract. These thoughts were solid and immediate—hotter than fire and wetter than water—and as I received them I was able to instantly and effortlessly understand concepts that would have taken me years to fully grasp in my earthly life." (Dr Eben Alexander)

"*Up there a question would arise in my mind, and the answer would arise at the same time, like a flower coming up right next to it. It was almost as if, (just as no physical particle in the universe is really separate from another), so in the same way there was no such thing as a question without an accompanying answer. These answers were not simple 'yes' or 'no' fare, either. They were vast conceptual edifices, staggering structures of living thought, as intricate as cities. Ideas so vast they would have taken me lifetimes to find my way around if I had been confined to earthly thought. But I wasn't. I had sloughed off that earthly style of thought like a butterfly breaking from a chrysalis.*" (Dr Eben Alexander)

"*The communication was by telepathy and they knew instantly what I was thinking, but their answers were essential, concise and certain.*" (Diego Valencia)

"*There were such feelings of warmth and love coming from the light that it made me feel good. Now it was right before me and instantly began communicating with me. Instantaneously it emanated to me, thought-pattern to thought-pattern. And to describe it I coined the phrase: superluminal telepathic communication: a telepathic thought-pattern to thought-pattern rapport that functioned as fast as or conceivably faster than the speed of light. It was pure communication that was complete in every respect.*" (Tom Sawyer)

5. PASSAGEWAY/TUNNEL TRAVELLING AT IMMENSE SPEED TOWARDS THE LIGHT

"*The tunnel in the NDE is often the pathway to God.*" (Brian Krebs)

"*It was then I saw the tunnel and knew with absolute assurance that I was on my way home, certain that the home that I had long yearned for was in the Light at the other end of this passageway. . . . I was ready, and without hesitation took my first step into the corridor that led toward the Light, crossing an intersection that connected now with forever . . .*" (Lynneclaire Dennis)

"*For a while, I watched on as the nurses and doctors worked quickly to revive me. Then, I lost interest, and my attention turned towards a long dark tunnel. At the end of the tunnel was a very bright light and I floated to the opening. Once inside, I moved with what seemed to be an extraordinary and effortless speed and finally reached the light.*" (Nadia McCaffrey)

"A dot of light appeared far off in front of me. It was just a pinpoint, a tiny speck in the distance, but its brilliance distinguished it from all other lights around me, and I instinctively pressed towards it. Emanating from it was a love and hope and peace that my soul hungered for. I wanted, I needed this brilliant, radiant light. The black tube took the shape of a tunnel now, opening up as I neared its end. The light burst forth before me, filling everything with brightness, and I was coming upon it impossibly fast. Oh, my gosh, I thought, it's brighter than the sun." (Ranelle Wallace)

Dr Melvin Morse, a pediatrician, was called to revive a young girl who nearly died in a community swimming pool. She had had no heartbeat for 19 minutes, yet completely recovered. She was able to recount many details of her own resuscitation, and then said that she was taken down a brick-lined tunnel to a heavenly place. When Dr Morse showed his obvious skepticism, she patted him shyly on the hand and said: *"Don't worry, Dr Morse, heaven is fun!"* (Dr Melvin Morse)

"Then I remember a very powerful force pulling me towards a serene, very beautiful realm, a higher realm. I travelled very slowly along a tunnel toward a bright light, and I could feel an overwhelming sense of warmth and peace and whiteness. I wanted to walk into the whiteness, which was so tranquil and happy." (Helen)

How beautifully this quote from *A Course In Miracles* illustrates the essence of Source Energy and of All That Is.

"Beyond the body, beyond the sun and the stars, past everything you see and yet somehow familiar, is an arc of golden light that stretches as you look into a great and shining circle.

And all the circle fills with light before your eyes.

The edges of the circle disappear, and what is in it is no longer contained at all.

The light expands and covers everything, extending to infinity forever shining and with no break or limit anywhere.

Within it, everything is joined in perfect continuity.

Nor is it possible to imagine that anything could be outside, for there is nowhere that this light is not."[17]

---

[17] Vaughan & Walsh, Gifts From A Course In Miracles. (Penguin Putnam Inc., N.Y. 1995), p. 285.

Dr P.M.H. Atwater, in her book *We Live Forever: The Truth About Death* paints a wondrous picture of her experience of the 'Light' drawn from her three NDE's.

"That light is the very essence, the heart and soul, the all-consuming consummation of ecstatic energy. It is a million suns of compressed love dissolving everything unto itself, annihilating thought and cell, vaporizing humanness and history, into the one great brilliance of All That Is and All that ever was, and All that ever will be. You know it is God. No one has to tell you. You know. You can no longer believe in God, for belief implies doubt. There is no more doubt. None.

You now KNOW God, and you know that you know—and you're never the same again."

". . . . toward the light. Finally, I merged with it, one with the warmth and love. A million everlasting orgasms cannot describe the sensation of the love, warmth, and sense of welcome that I experienced." (Elisabeth Kubler Ross)

"The pinpoint of light became a brilliant white beam a trillion times brighter than the brightest sun imaginable and began to move toward me. At first, it appeared to be bands of multifaceted light being stretched and pulled together. I knew this Light was the Presence of God." (Dr Dianne Morrissey)

"Then I simply remember I became more blissful, more rapturous, more ecstatic. I was just filling and filling with this light and love that was in the light. The dynamics of this light are not static at all. They are so dynamic and so much going on in there of love and joy and knowledge. As you take it into yourself, or as it goes into you and you receive it, your ecstasy level just becomes tremendous." (Jayne Smith)

"There was a light shining. I turned toward the light. The light was very similar to what many other people have described in their near-death experiences. It was so magnificent. It is tangible; you can feel it. It is alluring; you want to go to it like you would want to go to your ideal mother's or father's arms . . . . The light seemed to breathe me in even more deeply. It was as if the light was completely absorbing me. The love light is, to this day, indescribable. I entered into another realm, more profound than the last, and became aware of something more. It was an enormous stream of light, vast and full, deep in the heart of life . . . ." (Mellen-Thomas Benedict)

"When the light came near, its radiance spilled over me, ... The light conveyed to me that it loved me in a way that I can't begin to express. It loved me in a way that I had never known that love could possibly be. IT was a concentrated field of energy, radiant in splendor indescribable, except to say goodness and love. This was more loving than one can imagine . . . ." (Rev. Howard Storm)

29

In Elisabeth Kubler Ross' book, *The Wheel of Life* she explains what she learnt from listening to literally thousands of NDE people describe their experience in the Light.

" . . . . They felt excitement, peace, tranquility and the anticipation of finally going home. The light, they said, was the ultimate source of the universe's energy. Some called it God. Others said it was Christ or Buddha. But everyone agreed on one thing—they were enveloped by overwhelming love. It was the purest of all love, unconditional love."[18]

7. ONE GOD WHO LOVES ALL CREATIONS EQUALLY AND ALL RELIGIONS

"God is not a member of any church or religion. It is the churches and the religions that are members within the vastness and the glory that is God. There is no one religion just as there are no chosen people or person, nor any single way of regarding what cannot be fully comprehended. We are all sons of God in the sense that we are all souls of God's creation, without gender, without form, without nationality, complete and whole and perfect as we explore the never-endingness of God's wonderment." (Dr. PMH Atwater)

"I wanted to know why there were so many churches in the world. Why didn't God give us only one church, one pure religion? The answer came to me with the purest of understanding. Each of us, I was told, is at a different level of spiritual development and understanding. Each person is therefore prepared for a different level of spiritual knowledge. All religions upon the earth are necessary because there are people who need what they teach. People in one religion may not have a complete understanding of the Lord's gospel and never will have while in that religion. But that religion is used as a stepping stone to further knowledge. Each church fulfils spiritual needs that perhaps others cannot fill. No one church can fulfil everybody's needs at every level. As an individual raises his level of understanding about God and his own eternal progress, he might feel discontented with the teachings of his present church and seek a different philosophy or religion to fill that void." (Betty Eadie)

"Doctrine and creed and race mean nothing. No matter what we believe, we were all children joined under one God. The only rule is God's true law: Do unto others as you would have them do unto you." (May Eulitt)

"I asked the light, which I call Christ, how people from other religions get to heaven. I was shown that the group, or organization, we profess alliance to is

---

[18] Elisabeth Kubler Ross, The Wheel of Life (Bantam Books, London, UK, 1998), p. 196.

inconsequential. What is important is how we show our love for God by the way we treat each other. This is because when we pass to the spiritual realm we will all be met by him, which substantiates the passage, 'No one comes to the Father, but by me.' The light showed me that what is important is that we love God and each other, and that it isn't what a person says, but the love in their being that is examined in the afterlife." (Sandra Rogers)

"I asked them, for example, which was the best religion. I was looking for an answer which was like, 'Presbyterians.' I figured these guys were all Christians. The answer I got was, 'The best religion is the religion that brings you closest to God.'" (Rev. Howard Storm)

"The guides taught us that doctrine and creed and race meant nothing. No matter what we believed we were all children joined under one God, and that the only rule was God's true law—do unto others as you would have them do unto you." (May, Rashad and James' group NDE)

"Any complete body of knowledge is like a spoke in a wheel—pointing to the center of ultimate truth. Science, art, music, philosophy and religion run into trouble because they are not yet complete bodies of knowledge even though religion is advertised and sold as such." (Arthur Yensen)

"I asked God, 'What is the best religion on the planet?' The Ultimate Godhead of all the stars tells us, 'It does not matter what religion you are.' . . . More light is coming into all systems now. There is going to be a reformation in spirituality that is going to be just as dramatic as the Protestant Reformation. Everyone thinks they own God, the religions and philosophies, especially the religions because they form big organizations around their philosophy. . . I wish that all religions would realize it and let each other be. It is not the end of each religion, but we are talking about the same God. Live and let live. Each has a different view. And it all adds up to the Big Picture; it is all-important." (Mellen-Thomas Benedict)

8. THEY DISCOVER THAT WE ARE INTERCONNECTED

"I felt so deeply humble and a serious sense of responsibility for every thought and action I made. My only thought was that I wanted to do what was right. How important it was that I be very loving and creative. . . and never damaging in any way. . . and that's the gift. I realized at that point, how totally connected with all life. . . through all the universes. . . I am. I felt one with the All—never separate, never apart. Still, there was no fear. Still, there was only love." (Rev. Juliet Nightingale)

"I perceive how the earth, the sun, the moon, the darkness, the light, the planets, and all forms of life – plants, rocks, animals, people – are interconnected; they come from the same source of light. Everything is united by a transparent net, or

web, and each thread shines with great radiance. Everything pulses with the same luminosity – a magnificent light of unparalleled brilliance." (Josiane Antoinette)

"As soon as the Light touched me, I was transformed. The Light and my spirit merged – I had entered the Light of God, and all sense of my spirit body was gone. My consciousness, fully alive, was now totally connected to God. Within the light, I knew that everyone and everything is connected to it. God is in everyone, always and forever." (Dr Dianne Morrissey)

"We affect each other because we are all a part of each other. We affect all parts of the universe because all parts of creation interweave and interrelate with all other parts." (Dr. PMH Atwater)

"No matter who we are, we are all joined under one God. Our souls are all one. All living things in the universe are connected to one another." (May Eulitt)

9. INTERACTIVE LIFE REVIEW OF EVERY WORD, ACT AND DEED OF THAT LIFETIME

"One of the first things I remember experiencing was the life review—which included everything that I'd experienced in my physical incarnation up to that point. It was like being at the cinema—watching a movie of my life and everything happening simultaneously. I think most NDErs will agree that, the life review is one of the most difficult aspects of the NDE. Viewing your entire life before you— with every thought, word, action, etc.—can be most unsettling, indeed. Yet, what happened was the fact that no one passed judgment on me! I only felt the constant enveloping of divine love from the Being of Light that was always with me. What I came to realize, then, is that we judge ourselves!" (Rev. J Nightingale)

"To my surprise, my life played out before me, maybe six or eight feet in front of me, from beginning to end. The life review was very much in their control, and they showed me my life, but not from my point of view. I saw me in my life – and this whole thing was a lesson, even though I didn't know it at the time. . . . My life was shown in a way that I had never thought of before. All of the things that I had worked to achieve, the recognition that I had worked for, in elementary school, in high school, in college, and in my career, they meant nothing in this setting . . . . What they responded to was how I had interacted with other people." (Rev. Howard Storm)

"This is the way my life was reviewed. I was deeply aware and had profound insight into everything in my life and all of my dealings with others from my birth on to the moment of my near-death experience. All those in the light were witness to this review of my entire life. I was enveloped in a loving feeling and given insight into areas of my weaknesses. I suddenly realized aspects of my life that

were not compatible with eternity in the light. I also knew now how to correct this. I was charged with the accountability of the remainder of my life." (Grace Bulbuka)

"As I turned my eyes left, the entire scene changed into a Life Review, a vivid, three-dimensional colour display of my entire life. Every detail of every second, every feeling, every thought while I had been alive on Earth was displayed before me in perfect chronological order, from my birth to my electrocution. . . . At the same time, to my amazement, I was re-living my entire twenty-eight years simultaneously!" (Dr Dianne Morrissey)

"The voices stopped, and a brief scene flashed before me. A series of pictures, words, ideas, understanding. It was a scene from my life. It flashed before me with incredible rapidity, and I understood it completely and learned from it. . . . . Entirety does not describe the fullness of this review. It included knowledge about myself that all the books in the world couldn't contain. I understood every reason for everything I did in my life. And I also understood the impact I had on others. . . I saw myself repenting of them, sincerely wanting God to remove the weight and guilt of those terrible actions. And He had. I marveled at His sublime love and that my misdeeds could be forgiven and removed so easily. But then I saw other scenes that I hadn't anticipated, things that were just as awful. I saw them in horrible detail and watched the impact they had on others." (Ranelle Wallace)

"By the time my review was finished, I understood. I was aware of an almost cathartic release. I experienced emotion without the physical signs of tears. It brought me to a deep place of understanding and compassion. I never took the time to think how my actions affected others or how I treated myself. I felt a grieving for all my unconscious actions. With awareness of my unaware state, I released all the grief I had ever caused and joyfully moved into forgiveness." (Laurelynn Martin)

"I stared at the beautiful Being of Light who shimmered before me. He was like a bagful of diamonds emitting a soothing light of love. Any fear I might have had at the notion of being dead was quelled by the love that poured from the Being before me. His forgiveness was remarkable. Despite the horrible flawed life we had just witnessed, (Dannion's revealing, not so pleasant life review) deep and meaningful forgiveness came to me from this Being. Rather than issuing a harsh judgment, the being of Light was a friendly counsel, letting me feel for myself the pain and the pleasure I had caused others. Instead of feeling shame and anguish, I was bathed in the love that embraced me through the light and had to give nothing in return." (Dannion Brinkley)

"As this takes place, you have total knowledge. You have the ability to be a psychologist, a psychiatrist, a psychoanalyst, and much more. You are your own

33

spiritual teacher, maybe for the first and only time in your life. You are simultaneously the student and the teacher in a relationship. My life review was part of this experience also. It was absolutely, positively, everything basically from the first breath of life right through to the accident. It was everything. During this life review I experienced what I can only describe as 'in the eyes of Jesus Christ.' Meaning, I watched and observed this entire event as if I were in the eyes of Jesus Christ. Which means unconditionally.” (Thomas Sawyer)

10. REUNION WITH BELOVED FAMILY AND FRIENDS

"Next I was in total blackness. I don't know how I got there. I was floating in darkness with a gentle sense of movement. I was moving away from this life. I had left this life behind. Then I felt hands come around me and pull me into lush warmth. I realized it was my Grandmother. I used to call her Bubbie. She was pulling me close to her in a wonderful embrace. She had been dead for fourteen years, and I never had before thought of her existing beyond her own death. But I knew I was with her." (Barbara Whitfield)

"In the middle of the vapor is a being with the most heavenly smile. Jean Pierre! It is my cousin, Jean Pierre! I am overwhelmed with joy. As I gaze at Jean Pierre, the hospital room disappears. We are suspended in midair. There are no windows or doors, no ceiling or ground. A brilliant radiance fills all space. He slowly approaches my bed and bends to kiss me. I feel the moisture of his lips on my face, the weight of his body against mine, the gentle touch of his hands on me. Jean Pierre is the brother I never had. After a long and painful battle with lung cancer, he died two years ago when he was only twenty-two. I am still grieving his passing." (Josiane Antoinette)

"'RaNelle,' she was more insistent. 'It's Grandma.' And the moment she said this, I recognized her. She was my mother's mother. But she looked different than I had remembered. She was full and rounded and vibrant. She appeared to be about twenty-five years old, but her hair was glorious white, and everything about her was radiantly beautiful. Her body was glorious, and I began to understand why I hadn't recognized her. She had been frail and sick all the years I had known her. Then the realization hit me. Grandma was dead; she had died a couple of years before. And I thought, if she's dead, then what am I doing here?" (Ranelle Wallace)

"I was greeted by acquaintances, friends, my grandparents, my father's best friend, as well as a school chum from seventh grade. One of the most wondrous encounters came when my maternal grandmother approached me carrying a baby. I knew this child was the son I had miscarried in the seventh month of a difficult pregnancy in 1977. Seeing him brought a new peace to my Soul as I

finally realized that this child of my heart had fulfilled his purpose to absolute perfection." (Lynneclaire Dennis)

"Standing in the light was Jake's deceased great-grandfather. His great-grandfather acted as Jake's guide throughout his near-death experience. Jake met with others of his ancestors and had an extensive experience." (Jake)

"They began walking toward the bridge to the city, and Randy saw that the man standing awaiting them was his Grandpa Hansen. Randy ran to his grandfather and felt his strong arms close around him. Grandpa Hansen had been a farmer all of his life in Minnesota. He had died, still, a powerful man, when Randy was six. Randy asked his beloved grandfather if he would now be living with him in heaven. 'One day,' Grandpa Hansen told him. 'But not just yet.'" (Randy Gehling)

"This familiar presence came forward, and my feelings changed to sheer joy when I discovered my thirty-year-old brother-in-law, the one who had died seven months earlier from cancer. My essence moved to meet his essence. I couldn't see with my eyes or hear with my ears, yet I instinctively knew that it was 'Wills.' I heard his smile, saw his laughter and felt his humor. It didn't make sense, but it made complete sense. We were separate but we were also one." (Laurelynn Martin)

11. COLORS AND ANGELIC MUSIC OF UNPARALLELED BEAUTY

"I stood there in this gorgeous meadow, and I remember that the light there was different from the light here on Earth. Though it was not that brilliant white light in which I was involved, it was a more beautiful light. There was a goldenness to this light. I remember the sky was very blue. I don't recall seeing the sun. The colors were extraordinary. The green of the meadow was fantastic. The flowers were blooming all around and they had colors that I had never seen before. I was very aware that I had never seen these colors before and I was very excited about it. I thought I had seen all colors. I was thrilled to death of the beauty that was incredible. In addition to the beautiful colors, I could see a soft light glowing within every living thing. It was not a light that was reflected from the outside from a source, but it was coming from the center of this flower. Just this beautiful, soft light. I think I was seeing the life inside of everything." (Jayne Smith)

"A garden cannot exist on earth like the one I saw. I had been in gardens in California that had taken my breath away, but they were stuck into insignificance by the scene before me now. Here was an endless vista of grass rolling away into shining, radiant hills. We have never seen green in our world like the deep, shimmering green of the grass that grew there. Every blade was crisp, strong, and

charged with light. Every blade was unique and perfect and seemed to welcome me into this miraculous place. And the whole garden was singing. The flowers, grass, trees, and other plants filled this place with glorious tones and rhythms and melodies; yet I didn't hear the music itself. I could feel it somehow on a level beyond my hearing . . . We simply don't have language that adequately communicates the beauty of that world." (Ranelle Wallace)

"I heard what seemed like millions of little golden bells ringing, tinkling; they rang and rang. Many times since, I've heard those bells in the middle of the night. Next, I heard humming and then a choir singing. The singing got louder and louder, and it was in a minor key. It was beautiful and in perfect harmony. I also heard stringed instruments." (Lorraine Tutmarc)

"And so I followed Him into other buildings of this domain of thought. We entered a studio where the music of complexity I couldn't begin to follow was being composed and performed. There were complicated rhythms, tones not on a scale I knew. 'Why,' I found myself thinking. 'Bach is only the beginning!'" (Dr George Ritchie)

"Music surrounded me. It came from all directions. Its harmonic beauty, unlike earthly vocal or instrumental sounds, was totally undistorted. It flowed unobtrusively like a glassy river, quietly worshipful, excitingly edifying, and totally comforting. It provided a reassuring type of comfort, much like a protective blanket that whispered peace and love. I had never sensed anything like it. Perhaps angelic would describe it. This music was sounding within my head, not from an eardrum. Obviously, it was not airborne. Most unusual to me was the absence of any beat. Then I realized that without time this heavenly music could have no beat, which is a measure of time! I was hearing harmonic perfection, undistorted by any interposed medium between me and its source." (Dr Richard Eby)

"And then I heard the MUSIC. It was a tone so sublimely perfect that remembering it still brings me to tears. I knew then, and know now, that I was hearing the symphony of angels, the song of the universe, what some have called the Music of the Spheres. All thoughts melted in its melody, and everything else ceased to be of any importance. I closed my eyes and began to dance, moving to the resonant vibration that coursed through my essence. The melody seemed to issue from a single point and was composed of one verse, a song whose mystical tone my entire being knew and sang. I bathed in its melody as utter joy filled my being, and as the sound washed over my spirit, I felt all confusion purged from my consciousness. . . . The light was getting brighter and warmer as I moved through the tunnel. The MUSIC, the celestial symphony, continued to fill the air with a psalm of Oneness, played on unseen instruments of peace." (Lynneclaire Dennis)

"As we walked toward it, I heard voices. They were melodious, harmonious, blending in the chorus, and I heard the word, 'Jesus.' There were more than four parts to their harmony. I not only heard the singing and felt the singing but I joined the singing. I have always had a girl's body, but a low boy's voice. Suddenly I realized I was singing the way I had always wanted to. . . in high, clear and sweet tones. After a while the music softened, then the unseen voices picked up a new chorus. The voices not only burst forth in more than four parts, but they were in different languages. I was awed by the richness and perfect blending of the words—and I could understand them! I do not know why this was possible except that I was part of a universal experience. The words sung in all the different languages were understandable, but I don't know how or why. We all seemed to be on some universal wavelength. I thought at the time, 'I will never forget the melody and these words. But later, I could only recall two: Jesus and redeemed.'"
(Betty Malz)

"This time we were audience to a choir of angels singing. Angels were totally outside my reality at the time, yet somehow I knew these beautiful beings to be angelic. They sang the most lovely and extraordinary music I had ever heard. They were identical, each equally beautiful." (Dr Allan Kellehear).

12. TOTAL RECALL, INDELIBLY AND CLEARLY ETCHED INTO THEIR MEMORY AS IF IT WERE YESTERDAY

"I can still replay each memory today, and they are as vivid as when they happened twenty-three years ago in my NDE." (Barbara Whitfield)

We have some near-death experiences that have written full-sized books years, sometimes decades later! Arthur Yensen had his experience in 1932 and yet, due to harsh judgment at the time, did not put pen to paper and publish his report until twenty-three years later in 1955!

There is little need to pick out examples to exemplify this fact as you will see when you read the larger accounts that each person has remembered the minutest detail and they have described the experience in the most eloquent, descriptive prose that paints the picture as best they can within our limited human consciousness. Remember, most of the accounts in this book are only a portion of their experience, which is far longer and more detailed in their books.

To round off this chapter, I have included a piece written by Kevin Williams, webmaster of www.near-death.com. Kevin describes what he has discerned from his many, many years of researching NDE's. This piece exemplifies the overall message these people have brought back to pass on to you and me. Some may relate to Kevin's journey of originally being a radical *"I must convert you"* Christian, to wrestling with his doctrinal beliefs, to researching early Christianity, and eventually to finding his answers to the meaning of life in the profound, simplistic wisdom and unconditional love of the NDE's.

Kevin continues.

"Perhaps the main purpose of this website is to help people understand the tremendous importance of unconditional love—the main message of the NDE. Those who experience a NDE learn that loving others is the way to heaven within, heaven on Earth, and heaven after death. NDEs affirm physical existence to be illusionary in that separation exists only in our minds. People who have had a NDE describe an out-of-body existence after death where the oneness of all things cannot be denied. This state of oneness could be described as heavenly if a life of oneness with others had been lived. NDEs reveal love to be the bond which actually connects all things together.

Nevertheless, after death, the only thing we can really take with us is the love we have. Death means stepping into the spiritual condition we have been creating within us all our life.

In the highest afterlife realms, it is said that there is a one-ness that exists which can best be described as a complete realization of a total at-one-ment with God and all things. Love is then the critical factor in determining how close we come to this realization after death.

My mission in life is to promote these NDE truths as a light shining in a world of darkness. As a self-proclaimed NDE evangelist, I seek to end the ignorance of and the fear of death through the promotion of these truths. I am convinced that NDE research is contributing significantly to the spiritual evolution of humanity and that there is no greater endeavour than planting seeds of love and light within other human beings. Love is literally what life, death, and God are all about. It may sound strange but learning about death means learning about love. Love conquers all.

I firmly believe that the insights from near-death accounts are universal and that they speak to the heart of everyone. They are truths already known to all at the deepest core of our beings and transcends death. In this respect, death itself is a Grand illusion.

Reading the beautiful accounts of love and heaven in the by near-death experiences created within me a deep love for near-death experiences. It has also made me a much more spiritual person. Reading enough of these experiences can make a person feel as if they are relearning knowledge that they had forgotten long ago.

My NDE research transformed me away from dogmatic literalism and back into the simple faith. I found myself coming full-circle from the flower child of 'all you need is love' to the unconditional love described in NDEs. Today my desire is to promote NDE research and the spirituality I found in NDEs. As an NDE evangelist, the most important thing in the world for me to emphasize is unconditional love.

In 1977, after reading the Gospel of John, I had a 'born again' experience—a paranormal event of instant spiritual resurrection. Instantly, I transformed into a different person and was never the same person since. I went from being a wild, dope-smoking, hell-raising, alcoholic college student to a transformed fundamentalist Christian. Soon afterwards, I participated in follow-up evangelism with the Billy Graham crusade and the Josh McDowell ministry. I led a significant number of people to Christ and gave speeches at colleges on Christian topics, including Bible prophecy and early Christian history. I was a religious zealot whose Biblical knowledge and 'savior complex' drove me on a crusade to tell those who I perceived were deceived, hell-bound, and lost sinners and who lacked the righteousness I believed I had and who needed the intellectual formula which I possessed that would save their souls. Arrogant, is it not? Later, I learned there is a fine line between ignorance and arrogance. However, at this point in my life, the line was blurred.

When I began to read about near-death experiences, my religious arrogance began to disappear. The spirituality I found in near-death experiences was on a scale far grander than anything I could find in religion. My narrow religious mindset ultimately began to crack as the light of universal love, universal salvation, and a universal God entered in. This ultimately led me to abandon my rigid systematic intellectual, religious theology.

When I began reading about NDEs, I realized how bizarre Christian doctrines were compared to the profound insights found in NDEs. I saw a wonderful simplicity in the concept of universal salvation found in NDEs and the early Christian teachings of Jesus. I eventually had to deal with the contradictions between NDE insights I found and the Christian doctrines that I believed so deeply for so many years. These contradictions ultimately created conflicts in my mind and caused me a lot of mental anguish over the years. Eventually, I discovered that the more NDE concepts I learned and the more I learn about early Christian history, the more I found compatibility with NDE concepts and the teachings of Jesus. If one takes the time to research early Christianity, they will find it compatible with the universal salvation revealed in NDEs.

39

Practicing love for one another is the way to heaven on Earth and heaven within:
Jesus taught people that the way to attain liberation is through the practice of
unconditional love. Love brings about a one-ness between people and is necessary
to attaining the higher dimensions of consciousness. Practicing unconditional
love leads to the manifestation of the spirit within us and in our lives and brings
our spirit into conscious awareness. It is an awakening of unconditional love
within us and is the manifestation of our Holy Spirit within us. However, it is not
enough to merely believe in love. Nor is it enough to merely know about love. To
be spiritual beings living in a physical world, we must live love, manifest love,
and become the embodiment of love. We do not get there by focusing only on the
love and sacrifice of Christ nor through worshipping him.

The Christian life involves taking up our own cross and following in Jesus'
footsteps by practicing unconditional love: We can practice unconditional love by
crucifying our self-centeredness through self-sacrifice and self-denial for the sake
of serving others. 'Crucifying the flesh' also means to put to death the desires of
the lower self—the animalistic desires—to allow our higher self, our spirit, to
come through.

Discovering a higher reality and the supremacy of love: it is the illusion of
separation (i.e., that we are not, in fact, all part of one giant Whole), which is the
source of many of the problems humanity has faced. This constant desire for self
apart from the Whole must be overcome to become the spiritual beings we really
are.

The Life Review after death is for our educational benefit, enlightenment, and
Soul evolution. The Life Review is where we discover what we have been filling
the void within us, our entire life, with. The more we fill our void with love for
others, the more we have evolved as soul. The love we have found within our void
is what draws us into the light.

NDE research dramatically changed my ideas of just about everything on a
massive scale. I learned that God is immensely more loving and infinitely more
forgiving than I ever knew. I knew God would never abandon anyone forever in
hell. The 'God of wrath' I once thought existed I now know to be a man-made
construct for which to project our fear and own personal weaknesses on. Once I
understood that the greatest enemy I will ever have to face and ever have to
conquer is myself, an interesting change occurred within me. The Devil that I used
to blame my sins on and whom I feared all the time evaporated. I began to
appreciate the vastness of God's love for all people, no matter what their religious
or cultural persuasion may be. My narrow religious system cracked and fell away
as it became more and more ridiculous to me. Worse still, I discovered my former
belief system to be highly dishonoring to God in that it portrays him as throwing
the majority of humanity in hellfire to roast and be tortured forever. My former

40

idea of God resembled Charles Manson more than it did of a God of infinite love and I regretted ever having ever believed it. I grew to resent the ignorance within the Church and sympathized with those still trapped by false doctrines.

Nevertheless, once I discovered the kind of love and spirituality found in NDEs, I realized I was no longer concerned about religious dogma anymore. Just follow the simple principle established by Jesus, John, and Paul when they said, 'All you need is love.'

My greatest desire is to promote the supremacy of unconditional love found in NDEs because I believe it is the key to humanity's next stage in human evolution. I believe NDEs will soon prove the survival of consciousness after death without any doubt, and this will bring greater love and unity to the world. Imagine a world where everyone understands that, after death, everyone is accountable for every thought, word, and deed. NDE insights equate death as a process of 'stepping into' the heaven or hell we have created within ourselves during life. The afterlife is a spectrum of existence where the highest heaven is pure unconditional love, and the lowest hell is the absence of love. At death, we awaken to the spiritual environment we have been creating within ourselves and actually inhabiting all our lives. Therefore, death itself is just a body problem. That is all there is to it."
(Kevin Williams)

One of the predominant features of NDE's is the depth of unconditional love felt emanating from Source/God, which envelopes and caresses them. This establishes an inner knowing of the absolute importance of, and a heartfelt desire to, express unconditional love one to another upon their return and that this is indeed a vitally important part of our purpose here on planet Earth.

You will see that the NDE'ers describe Source Energy/God as *"The Light."* They describe *"The Light"* as a brilliance too bright to look upon with the human eye, from which emanates an Omnipresent, All-Encompassing, Unconditional Love. I must admit that before I started reading NDE's I thought of the expression love and light as very airy-fairy. In fact, it is a totally accurate description of Source Energy. It also describes our own Light that can shine forth from our own *Christ Spirit* or Divine Essence from our own portion of that divine radiance that is within us all. Everything in all creation was made from this Light. However, I believe that God is more than The Light but is also darkness, as Source IS in *all* things.

The Light is mentioned many times in the Bible.

There was a man sent from God whose name was John.

The same came to bear witness of the Light that all men
through him might believe. He was not that Light, but was
sent to bear witness of that Light. That was the true Light
which lighteth every man that cometh into the world.

John 1:6-8

When Jesus spoke again to the people he said;
I am the Light of the world. Whoever follows me will never walk in
darkness, but will have the Light of life.

John 8:12

This has been taken literally by most Christian churches to mean that Jesus himself was literally that Light, the only Son of God, and that we needed to follow him and worship him alone. *We are ALL precious Sons/Daughters of God*. The Divine Christ Light within Jesus is the same Divine Christ Light that dwells within us all. He came to show us how to develop our own Light – our own Divine Essence and birthright—to embody and connect with this God-Part of ourselves, the I AM, to overcome *"the things of the Earth"* and thus find peace and happiness from within as opposed to being ruled and dominated unconsciously by life and consequently becoming fearful, victims of life. Our Holy Christ Presence or Higher Self connected to our Mighty I AM Presence is our All-Powerful, individualized facet of God. When Jesus said, *"I AM the Way and the Life"* he meant everyone's I AM is the Way and the Life to inner peace, freedom, and joy.[19]

White Eagle elaborates in the following quote.

"The purpose of life on this Earth planet is that spirit, your spirit, shall shine within the darkness. Your Spirit, which is the Light, was in the beginning: this means that in the beginning of your existence you were Light; and the light shone in the darkness-which is your dense body or the earth-and the earth comprehended it not. You are all familiar with this teaching but you do not think of applying to yourself. You do not understand that in Essence you are Light; and that in the beginning you were Light until you entered the physical body, or that the physical body, and particularly the mortal mind, does not comprehend the Light. You are here to use physical matter and not allow it to dominate you. You are Light; and you have to shine out through the darkness, to transmute the heavy

---

[19] If you are interested in learning how to become the master of your own reality/life and create the life you do desire then "The I AM Discourses" by Ascended Master St Germaine will interest you. They can be found at www.theiamdiscourses.com

atoms of the physical body by the light within you. Miracles happen when the spirit has gained such power of control over the body. " [20]

---

[20] White Eagle, The Living Word Of St John – White Eagle's Interpretation Of The Gospel. (White Eagle Publishing Trust, Cambridge, UK. 2004), pp.18-19

CHAPTER FOUR

TWENTY-FOUR INSPIRING NEAR-DEATH EXTRACTS

This chapter is dedicated to giving the reader a diverse selection of wondrously inspired insights into life after death as seen through the eyes of the people who have clinically died and experienced the higher dimensions and in many cases met with who they perceived to be a part of the Godhead or Christ. Each one paints a unique, personal picture of what can be experienced after we pass over, yet they are strikingly similar in their basic content. You will see just how detailed and real these experiences were and how they witness and describe these sojourns with a Divine poetic eloquence that could only be utilized when you have actually been there.

Children's Near-Death Experiences

Near-death experiences in infants and children fascinate me as the children too have so many similarities and they are usually too young to have their own pre-conceived or pre-conditioned ideas about death and dying. The youngest I am aware of is an 8-month-old who had an NDE after nearly dying from kidney failure.

When she began talking, at two years old, she described to her parents going into a tunnel and a bright light.

Elisabeth Kubler Ross, in her book, *The Wheel of Life* recounts how a twelve-year-old girl had told her that she didn't want to tell her mother about her near-death experience as it had been so wonderful she hadn't wanted to come back. She was reluctant to tell her Mum that there was somewhere even nicer than their home. However, she did tell her father that she had been *"lovingly held"* by her brother. This brother had died a few months before she was born and a brother she had never been told about.

In the same book, Elisabeth Kubler Ross describes how she watched a young five-year-old attempting to convey to his mother through his drawing how lovely his NDE was. Elisabeth continues.

"First he drew a brightly colored castle and said, 'This is where God lives.' Then he added a brilliant star. 'When I saw the star, it said, 'Welcome home.'"[21]

Out of the mouths of babes as they say.

Dr Melvin Morse has been consistently voted as one of America's leading Pediatricians. Dr Melvin Morse has interviewed hundreds of children who have been declared clinically dead. Repeatedly Dr Morse has been told that the end of life is an embracing, joyful experience, not one to be feared. Children too young to have absorbed our adult views and ideas of death recounted first-hand accounts of out of body travel, telepathic communication, and encounters with dead friends and relatives.

The following two NDE's from young children all speak of being *"out of their body"* watching the scene, seeing their body and all were able to describe, in detail, what took place. Both travelled through some form of *"tunnel"* to go to the *"light."*

Dr Morse had this to say;

"My original research and subsequent studies by others have documented that the NDE is real. This understanding that death is in fact, a dynamic spiritual event in which the dying are frequently fully conscious, has profound implications for the living. Nothing less than a new scientific paradigm is at hand. One that will transform human culture as surely as the birth of the written language. I want to be an active part in the birth of this new paradigm." (As do I)

1. CHRIS' NEAR-DEATH EXTRACT—AGE 4

The following NDE is both unusual and wonderful in that Chris, who was four at the time of his NDE, recounts his experience which, in turn, prompted his Mum Patti to speak out about her spiritual experience of seeing her late husband appear before her at the actual accident scene to reassure her he was okay and still alive

---

[21] Elisabeth Kubler Ross, The Wheel of Life (Bantam Books, London, UK, 1998) Pg 194

in Spirit. It sounds like she also had an Angel helping her kick the door open. The whole experience completely changed Patti's foundational beliefs from previous disbelief to belief in God and eternal life.

Dr Morse shares this amazing story.

Mother and Son Experience

"'You have got to tell all the old people so that they won't be afraid to die!'

I nearly choked with emotions as the little boy before me spoke these words. I remembered when I first saw him. His name was Chris. It had been four years earlier when his limp body was brought to the hospital by helicopter. He had nearly drowned after his father lost control of the sedan he was driving and plunged over a bridge and into the freezing waters of a river near Seattle. His brother and mother were in the car too. All were dazed by the impact and stunned by the horror of sinking in the dark waters.

The impact had knocked the father unconscious. The mother was left to find a way out of the rapidly filling automobile. She unfastened her seatbelt and kicked at the passenger window. Nothing happened. Then, as she told me later, 'I felt an indescribable sensation go through my body, and as this happened, I was given the physical strength to kick out the window.' She did this despite three compression fractures sustained during impact.

Chris's mom, Patti, swam out through the passenger window, got to the surface, and grabbed the ski rack that was attached to the top of their car. Somehow, Chris's six-year-old brother, Johnny, had also gotten out of the car and was floating down the river, unconscious. Johnny was almost out of reach before Patti was able to grab him and push him to the top of their car, which was about a foot underwater. The father and little Chris remained trapped inside. For a terrifying moment, Chris struggled as the water enveloped him. Then he lost consciousness and 'went to heaven.' He was submerged in the icy water for almost fifteen minutes. As we spoke in the living room of his house, he told me again in his childlike way what that voyage was like.

'When I died, I went into a huge noodle,' said Chris, who was four years old when the accident happened.

'It wasn't like a spiral noodle, but it was very straight, like a tunnel. When I told my mom about nearly dying, I told her it was a noodle, but now I think that it must have been a tunnel, because it had a rainbow in it, and I don't think a noodle has a rainbow.

I was being pushed along by the wind, and I could kind of float. I saw two small tunnels in front of me. One of them was animal heaven, and the other one was the

46

human heaven. First, I went into animal heaven. There were lots of flowers, and there was a bee. The bee was talking to me, and we were both smelling flowers. The bee was very nice and brought me bread and honey because I was really hungry.

Then, I went to human heaven. I saw my grandmother [who had died years earlier]. Then I saw heaven. Human heaven was beautiful. It was like a castle, but not one of those grungy old places. This was not a golden castle; it was just a regular old castle. As I looked at heaven, I heard music. The music was deafening, and it stuck in my head. I started looking around at it, and then all of a sudden I was in the hospital. Just like that, I woke up, and nurses were standing around me. It was just that easy'

I laughed when he got to the easy part. As I reviewed his case history, I could see that keeping him alive wasn't easy at all. He had been underwater over ten minutes until Dennis Johnson, a carpenter who had witnessed the accident, dove repeatedly to the sunken car and pulled the young boy from the backseat. He then towed Chris to shore and revived him with mouth-to-mouth resuscitation. 'I know he was dead when I reached shore,' said Johnson. 'He wasn't breathing, but I had to try to bring him back to life anyway.' This selfless act of heroism won Johnson a Carnegie Medal for Heroism and a Washington State Patrol Award of Merit, an honor usually reserved for state troopers. Chris was then airlifted to the nearest hospital, where further heroics were required to keep him alive.

Chris's father was the last one to be pulled from the car. He was airlifted to Harbor View Hospital, where extensive efforts were made to resuscitate him. He died despite the efforts.

Now, four years later, Chris was sitting in the living room of his home, casually playing what sounded like avant-garde jazz on a portable keyboard. His mother said he had shown little interest in music before the accident, but afterwards she had to buy him a keyboard so that he could play the hauntingly beautiful tune he had heard while travelling through the 'huge noodle.'

I had been invited to hear Chris's story. An acquaintance of Chris's mom was familiar with my work in near-death studies and thought that I would be interested in talking to her son about his experience at the threshold of death. Even though I have heard hundreds of children describe their near-death experiences, chills ran up my spine as I listened to Chris play the music of his experience. I taped the piece that Chris played and later had a professor of music listen to it. He said it sounded like an advanced piece of jazz being played by a child who had not yet developed the hand-eye coordination necessary to read music and play it. It sounded nothing like the kind of music I would associate with church or death.

I was deeply absorbed in the spiritual concert that was taking place.

47

Suddenly Chris stopped. 'I have to ask you a question,' he said with the sophistication of someone ten years older. 'How do I know that what happened was real? How do I know that I really went to heaven? How do I know that I wasn't just making it all up?'

I had focused on that very question myself for ten years. From the day that I heard my first near-death experience and a little girl patted me on the hand and confidently told me, 'You'll see, Dr Morse, heaven is fun,' I have sought to answer the very question that Chris was asking me. I looked around the living room as everyone waited patiently for my response. Even with the years of research I have done on this topic, this is a difficult question for me to answer. I cleared my throat and smiled nervously at Chris.

'Chris, what happened to you is as real as it gets.'"

Different Experience, Same Question

"'Dr Morse, how do I know that what happened to me was real?'

This time the question didn't come from Chris but his mother, Patti. She had asked me to go into the kitchen so that she could tell me in private what happened to her on that horrible night. She began by saying that neither she nor her husband were religious people. They did not attend church, never prayed, and in fact, did not believe in God. 'My husband was a physicist, and I was just a carefree ski instructor,' she said. 'We had a strong sense of family values, and were deeply in love, but never discussed spiritual matters.'

On the night of the accident, they were returning from the mountains, where Patti had been giving ski lessons to the children of a Seattle Seahawks football player. Her husband was driving too fast for the road conditions. Patti was telling him to slow down when he lost control and skidded off the bridge. 'After we hit the bottom of the river, I knew we had to get out. I unfastened my safety belt and kicked at the passenger window. After I broke the passenger window with my feet, I came to the surface of the water, gasping for air, and grabbed the ski rack. Out of the corner of my eye, I saw my six-year-old son, Johnny, floating down the river. I was barely able to reach him. I realized he wasn't breathing, so I shook him with my free hand. Once I knew he was breathing again, I pushed him to the top of our car and pulled myself up after him. I could feel the strong current of the river so I braced myself against the ski rack to keep us on the roof of the car, while holding Johnny's head out of the water so that he could breathe.

I started screaming for help, louder than I have ever screamed in my life. After several very long minutes, I saw the beam of a tiny flashlight, coming from downstream. Shortly thereafter, a man appeared, jumped in the water and swam out to us. I started screaming about my baby being trapped in the car, and the man dove underwater several times, before coming to the surface with Chris.'

Patti paused for a moment and then told me something she had not mentioned to any of the reporters who had interviewed her: 'When I reached the surface of the water, I sensed that my husband was sitting on the rocks, watching the rescue below. It was eleven at night, pitch-dark and freezing cold, but there he was, sitting on the rocks.' Her husband seemed perfectly content to sit passively while others dove to save his son and himself. Patti became furious with her husband. 'I was as angry as I have ever been with him,' she said. 'I began to scream at him, and when I did that, he disappeared.'

Intellectually Patti felt that her husband was not on that rock. She knew that he was underwater, where rescuers were desperately trying to save him. Still, the sensation was so intense that she will swear to this day that her husband had been sitting right there, watching the proceedings.

Soon after the accident, other visions began taking place. The first of these consisted of several intimate encounters with her deceased husband when Patti was sleeping. However, she distinguished the things she experienced during these vivid encounters as different from her normal dream state. 'It happened as I was waking up, but it was not a dream,' she said. 'It was too real to be a dream! I didn't want it to happen. It just happened.'

In addition to this, Patti also claimed to have actually seen her deceased husband, at least two other times. On one of these occasions, she was wide awake and sitting in her living room. She looked up, and there he was, sitting on the couch. 'He looked very normal. He was not transparent, and he was wearing regular clothing.'

At first, she denied that these visions were anything but 'a crazy widow thing.' Then, about three weeks after the accident, Chris told her and his grandma about his experience of going to see his dead grandmother through the 'huge noodle' and hearing the heavenly music. They listened in mute amazement as he told what had happened when he almost drowned. The effect on Patti was immediate.

'Suddenly it all came together for me,' she said. 'Before hearing his story, I could only sleep for a few minutes without waking up in fear and terror. After hearing Chris's story, I slept six hours and awoke fully rested.'

'Why?' I asked.

'Because of Chris's experience I believe that my husband was letting me know that he was okay,' she said. 'Not that he was going to live, but that it was okay that he had died.'

49

Was Patti's visionary experience 'real?' She didn't wait for me to answer that question. Her son's near-death experience answered that question for her. When Chris told his mother about his experience, she accepted the visions of her husband as real events, not made-up dreams. In short, Chris's experience validated her own. She now believes in God and an afterlife, just as she accepts her husband's message to her that 'everything is going to be all right,' vague and nonspecific though that message might seem to an outside observer.

'My experience was as real as the one Chris had,' said Patti. 'And they have both given us such peace. How could I ever deny that they are real?'

Although she remains both confused and comforted by the various encounters involving her deceased husband, she has now grieved healthily. She feels strongly that her husband was telling her to live and love life rather than to dwell on the reasons for his premature death.

'We lost a lot in that accident,' said Patti. 'But the visions gave us depth, meaning, and the strength to carry on.'

Patti's experience was similar to dozens of cases I have heard over the years. As I searched for near-death experiences to study, I would be approached by people who had had visions like Patti's, experiences that rocked them to their spiritual core and changed the very foundation of their life." [22]

2. RANDY GEHLING'S NEAR-DEATH EXTRACT—AGE 10

Randy was hit by a neighbor's car as he was test driving his brand-new Birthday present – a bicycle. Randy was aware he left his body behind as he continued to fly. He observed his body on the ground below and recognized the car that had just hit him. The moment he started to worry about what was happening his Guardian Angel appeared to reassure him.

"Ten-year-old Randy Gehling of Arlington Heights, Illinois, had been begging for a new bicycle for his birthday all summer long. On September 8, 1988, the tenth anniversary of his arrival on planet Earth, he got his bicycle—but he also came very close to changing his mailing address to Heaven.

Steve and Kathy Gehling, Randy's parents, found the accident bitterly ironic.

'For months he begs for a new bike for his birthday,' Steven said. 'The minute he spotted it on the porch, he tore off the ribbons, ignored the eight little friends

---

[22] Morse and Perry, Parting Visions. (Harper Collins, New York. 1996), pp. 1-8.

gathered for his birthday celebration, and took off for a quick spin around the block. He just didn't seem to see the teenager from across the street using the alley as a shortcut home.'

Kathy remembered the anguish of the long hours that they spent in the waiting room, not knowing for certain whether their son would live or die. 'He had been unconscious ever since the neighbor's boy hit him with his car. His new bicycle was all mangled. Some of the neighbors said that Randy was sent flying fifteen or twenty feet by the impact. All we could do was pray.

After a three-hour surgery, the doctor visited them in the waiting room and told them that the prognosis looked good. Randy was in a recovery room, and as soon as it was advisable, he would be wheeled to a hospital room where they could wait by his bedside. The doctor could not promise whether Randy would be conscious enough to respond to them yet that night.

The next morning at about seven-twenty, about seventeen hours after his accident, Randy opened his eyes, saw his parents at his bedside, and smiled. He accepted their gentle hugs and kisses in silence, then he told them, 'Wow, Mom and Dad, what a trip!'

Steve and Kathy chuckled at their son's first words. Then at a loss for the proper response to such a comment, Steve said, 'Yeah, I guess you really went flying over the handlebars, eh?' Randy nodded, then winced at the pain of the movement. His head was swathed entirely in bandages, leaving him with only a peephole around his eyes and a small open space for his mouth. 'Yeah, I flew up to the stars and went to Heaven. I saw the angels, and I even think I might have seen Jesus. Oh, and I saw Grandpa Hansen, too.'

Steve and Kathy glanced at one another in meaningful silence.

'He's still under the effects of the anaesthetic,' Kathy whispered. 'It's like he's dreaming.'

Randy protested at what he overheard of his mother's whispered analysis. 'It was no dream. I was there!'

Steve and Kathy decided to agree with their son so they would not aggravate his condition so soon after surgery. But over the next days and weeks, they came to have a different opinion of their ten-year-old son's visit to Heaven. They had to admit that Randy may well have experienced much more than a dream.

According to the notes taken by Kathy Gehling here somewhat abbreviated, is Randy's account of his near-death experience:

51

'I didn't really know what had hit me. I just seemed to go flying through the air. And then a really funny thing happened. A part of me—I guess my soul—just kept flying, and I saw my body smash into the ground. I knew it had to hurt to land that hard, so I was happy that I was where I was—wherever that was.

When I got a little higher, I saw that it had been Kurt's car that had hit me. I always told him that he drove too fast in the neighborhood. He would usually just make a face at me or flip me the bird. He should have listened to me. I figured that he must have killed me, and now he would go to jail.'

Randy felt a moment of panic when he realized that he might be dying.

'But then this beautiful angel appeared beside me. She was really pretty. She looked like a movie star with wings. Her voice sounded kind of like Mom's when she is comforting me when I have a stomach ache or something. She told me not to worry. She said that she was with me and that she would stay right by my side. She took my hand, and I felt a lot better.'

Randy said that they soon approached a dark tunnel. When he held back and said that he was afraid to go into the darkness, the angel smiled and told him that this was the only way that they could get to their final destination. I could see a bright light at the far end of the tunnel, so I said 'All right, as long as you don't let go of my hand!'

She laughed and said, 'I told you that I would never leave your side. I have been with you ever since you were born. In fact, I was there at your mother's side when you were born. I am your guardian angel.' Randy asked her what her name was.

'We don't have names in the manner that you mean,' she said, *'but if it makes you feel better to call me something, you may call me, Areo (ah-ree-o).'*

The tunnel did not prove to be such a terrible ordeal after all. Randy and Areo seemed to whoosh through it quickly. 'And then we stood before this totally awesome light,' Randy said. 'It was so bright and powerful that you really couldn't look right at it. I looked at Areo, wondering what we were to do next. She said that we would enter the Light and become One with it. Before I could ask what that meant, she just gave my hand a little tug, and then we were inside the Light.

That was really cool! I kind of felt as though my body exploded—in a nice way—and became a million different atoms—and each single atom could think its own thoughts and have its own feelings. All at once, I seemed to feel like I was a boy, a girl, a dog, a cat, a fish. Then I felt like I was an old man, an old woman—and then a little tiny baby.'*

And then Randy and Areo were standing in what appeared to be a lovely park, bedecked with millions and millions of colorful flowers. Randy could hear beautiful music playing somewhere off in the distance.

'Just a little ways off I could see a bridge with someone standing on it. Beyond the bridge, I saw a golden city with towers like European castles. The whole city seemed to be shining with a light that shot up into the sky like a giant searchlight.

I could see that some of the domes of the city were red, others were gold, and a few were blue. The gates and walls of the city seemed to be made of bright blue, red, and violet lights.'

Randy asked Areo if they were going to visit the city.

The angel nodded. 'That's to be your new home, Randy.' They began walking toward the bridge to the city, and Randy saw that the man standing awaiting them was his Grandpa Hansen.

Randy ran to his grandfather and felt his strong arms close around him. Grandpa Hansen had been a farmer all of his life in Minnesota. He had died, still a powerful man, when Randy was six.

Randy asked his beloved grandfather if he would now be living with him in Heaven. 'One day,' Grandpa Hansen told him. 'But not just yet.'

When Randy questioned his grandfather, he told him that he still had things to learn on Earth. 'You nearly bought the farm this time, Randy-boy,' Grandpa Hansen said with a chuckle. 'But you aren't ready to cash in your chips just yet.'

Areo seemed puzzled. 'But it seemed to me that I was doing the right thing. The word that I received indicated that now was Randy's time to return home.'

Grandpa Hansen shrugged. 'I was told to meet you at the bridge and tell you to take him back home. He's got some lessons that he hasn't learned yet—and lots of work that he hasn't even started to fulfil.'

Before Areo took him by the hand for the return flight home, Randy said that another figure materialized beside Grandpa Hansen on the bridge.

'I knew right away that it was Jesus,' Randy said, convinced of the majestic visitor. 'I knew by his eyes.'

Randy couldn't quite remember all of the things that Jesus said, but he is certain of some of the words.

'Jesus said that I would never quite be the same as I was before I visited Heaven. He said that some of the power of the light would remain within me. And he told me to let the love that I would feel in my heart express itself to all people.

He said that I should never worry if people doubted my story or could not understand what I was telling them.'

'One day,' Jesus said, 'everyone will come to see for themselves what you have seen.'"[23]

Many near-death experiences become catalysts for radical change in that person's life as they view life with expanded awareness, and they become extremely grateful for the precious gift of life. The following is just one of many examples exemplifying this.

3. GRACIE'S NEAR-DEATH EXTRACT—AGE 11

"I was swimming with my sisters when suddenly I found myself unable to reach the top of the water for air. It felt like I had just stepped into nothingness. I went down twice and was coming up for the third time when I managed to yell for help.

Before I was pulled from the water, I saw a filmstrip of my life. It was just like being in a theatre, as I sat crossed-legged and watched the things I'd done wrong to my sisters. I was not judged by the angel, who showed me this. I judged and convicted myself. The Angel hovered in mid-air to the upper left of the screen. I remember thinking that I was leaving my family and sisters, and I started to feel sorrow. The sorrow left immediately, and I felt as if I had been reassured they would be fine.

Then there was such a feeling of bliss that it's indescribable. Since then, I have had a lifetime of unexplained happenings.

My entire outlook is different, and I 'see' with my heart."

---

[23] Brad Steiger, One With The Light.(Penguin Books, N.Y. 1994). Pgs 57-64.

4. Kesha L. Engel's Near-Death Extract—Age 14

Kesha's experience also shows us what can happen when the person who has clinically died was influenced by drugs or the like and in a very depressed, negative state of mind. Although she briefly visited the lower astral as soon as she reached towards the dim light she saw, she was instantly lifted up and surrounded by immense love. Although her own experience was relatively short by our time standards, she returned to her body a totally different girl with a totally new value system that has since been her lifetime foundation.

Kesha explains.

"In February 1974, when I was fourteen years old, I experienced some kind of overdose which nearly killed me. I had willingly and recklessly smoked something called angel dust. Quite a rebel at that time of life, I was expelled from the public-school system—too many truancies and disruptive behavior. I had also been arrested for drug use by undercover cops at the new school.

The night of the overdose, I entered my room and closed the door to the outside world. I drifted into a deep, faraway sleep. The voices from other parts of the house faded into the distance. My body lay listless on the bed, and I was suddenly some place outside of myself—beyond the storm, the suburbs and the city lights.

I was travelling, tumbling through the darkness into a strange void of unfamiliar space. Sharp, stabbing nameless voices, without form, seemed to chase me in the blackness. Loud, buzzing, irritating and incessant taunting seemed to pursue me. It was as if I was spinning, but I had nobody. I felt confused, frightened and utterly alone.

As I reached the peak of my despair, a new thought pierced my awareness. A dim and promising glow appeared in the farthest reaches of space. Intuitively, I knew that the light would save me from this torment. It seemed to magnetize me like a beacon in a sea of darkness, and I knew I had to direct myself to it.

The brilliance grew stronger and more alluring as my desire to be near it surged. In an instant, I was completely and profoundly surrounded by the brightest, most intense and loving light imaginable. It welcomed me with a sense of peace that I had never known before. I was awestruck. I remember thinking, 'How did I get here? Do I really deserve this?'

With that thought, I felt myself slide off the beam as if all my protection vanished. The forces of darkness were just too great. I heard that haunting, malicious laughter again, and it drew me down into an abyss. I wondered how I could retrieve the peace. What had I done wrong? Was it real?

In a flash, I traversed the universe and felt enveloped in serenity once again. This time it was as if I could see without eyes. I perceived an ethereal mist, and a lush, life-filled place awaited me. My energy merged with that of a golden-white glowing Essence—one of complete love and absolute safety. Filled with bliss, I knew I was going home at last.

Yet before I could cross the threshold into my true home, I also knew that I must return. Something unspoken filled my awareness and in seconds, (as if time can be measured at these levels), I was being drawn backwards. I perceived flashes of light swirling quickly by. They were like tiny electrodes of information that contained scenes from my life. A vacuum-like suction swooped me directly from that safe haven, and I awoke to my father's face bent over me.

He was shaking me violently, saying, 'Get up! Get up now!' They had been calling me for half an hour, and I hadn't moved. 'If you don't get up now, we will call the hospital and your parole officer will know that you have been using!'

I felt as if I had been shot back to some kind of hell, disconnected from the light. My dad's nostrils flared with the smoky haze of his cigarette. He paced adamantly, 'Get up,' he commanded when he saw my eyes open. Somehow I was sentenced to live with this family, and it felt so foreign to me. Oh, what a task it was to move. My body felt paralysed initially as if it were filled with lead.

As disconcerting as it was to return to this world, I knew what I had to do. I dragged my sandbagged legs across the floor and reached up to tear a pot leaf poster off the bedroom wall. My dad stood incredulous. His mouth dropped open in disbelief, his eyes widened. 'Do you want me to get rid of this?' he asked. I nodded and proceeded to rip down another blacklight poster of Uncle Sam giving the finger. My dad just shook his head and muttered, Unbelievable.

I could feel his heart lifting as my body grew lighter with every movement. I turned more lights on and proceeded to clear my room of clutter, surrendering all the paraphernalia I had stashed. I stopped using drugs that night.

With the support of some wonderful teachers, I became an honour roll student and learned to meditate while still in high school. I was introduced to the works of Dr Elisabeth Kubler Ross and Dr Raymond Moody, pioneers in the NDE movement. It helped put things in a new context for me. I am grateful for the inner experience and the continuing opportunity to explore this multidimensional world."

Kesha L. Engel, BA, CMT, is now a practitioner in the healing arts field. She is certified in breathe work coaching, SHEN, (an emotional-release bodywork method), cranial-sacral therapy, and hypnosis.

What excites me about so many that experience these spiritual dimensions in their NDEs is that the people, even children such as Gracie and Kesha above, more often than not return *anew,* washed by and so filled with God's unconditional love that they then see life as a precious opportunity to share this wondrous life-changing wisdom. Subsequently they feel drawn to serve humanity by spreading the Universal Truths that are so necessary for all people on Earth to understand and implement to experience lasting happiness and peace within.

The following NDE exemplifies this so completely. Dr Eben Alexander transformed from being an extremely successful, internationally revered Neurosurgeon, who did not believe in, or relate to, the Afterlife, to dedicating the rest of his life to share his wonderful story with the world.

5. DR EBEN ALEXANDER'S NEAR-DEATH EXTRACT

At the time of Dr Eben Alexander's NDE he was a renowned and much revered Neurosurgeon, having practiced Neurosurgery for 25 years and performed over 4,000 operations. His professional career was an extremely successful one, having co-authored over 150 chapters and papers in peer reviewed journals.

Prior to his illuminating Near-Death Experience Eben was a sceptic of anything to do with the afterlife, believing his patients stories to be nothing more than *"fantasies produced by brains under extreme stress."* This makes his extraordinary, radically life-changing NDE all the more powerful and will have caused many scientifically/academically based people to reconsider whether there is indeed more to life than what can be experienced through our physical senses. His vast knowledge of Neuroscience could not be reconciled with beliefs in God, Heaven and the Soul. In Eben's words,

"NDE's such as mine represent the tip of the spear in a rapidly progressing enlightenment of the scientific community around mind-brain relationship, and our understanding of the very nature of reality."

His journey to meet with Source Energy happened while officially comatose for seven days and seemingly brain dead whilst simultaneously discovering in another dimension that nothing is ever what it seems! Eben was forced to re-evaluate the meaning of real and include a vastly more expansive meaning of reality. What became real to him opened up a whole new understanding of *"the meaning of life!"* Eben explains.

"But while I was in a coma my brain hadn't been working improperly. ***It hadn't been working at all.*** *The part of my brain that years of medical school had taught*

me was responsible for creating the world I lived and moved in and for taking the raw data that came in through my senses and fashioning it into a meaningful universe: that part of my brain was down, and out. And yet despite all of this, I had been alive, and aware, truly aware, in a universe characterized above all by love, consciousness, and reality."

On November 10th, 2008 Eben was rushed to hospital and was diagnosed as suffering from a rare illness called bacterial meningo-encephalitis which normally has a 90% mortality rate. The part of the brain that was being attacked controls the emotions and thoughts, essentially medically perceived to be the essence of being human. For the following seven days he lay in a comma in intensive care, each day making the possibility of surviving, let alone without severe brain damage, extremely unlikely. His medical colleagues and family prepared themselves for the worst.

Miraculously, (his recovery is deemed a medical miracle), after seven days his eyes *"popped open"* to the astonishment of all concerned. He awoke with *"memories of a fantastic odyssey deep into another realm- more real than this earthly one!"*

Within a few months Eben had made a remarkable and complete recovery which astonished and perplexed the medical fraternity attending him. As is the case in NDE's Eben not only remembered his voyage into another dimension of life but was able to write down 20,000 words describing his incredible, life-shattering experience in great detail.

Then he started reading other Near-Death Experiences and was astonished by so many similarities between his journey and the journey of so many others reported throughout all cultures, continents and millennia. His journey brought key insights to the mind-body discussion and to our human understanding of the fundamental nature of reality. His experience clearly revealed that we are conscious *in spite of* our brain – that, in fact, *"consciousness is at the root of all existence."*

Once again, we see the same predominant message that Eben came back to espouse was the importance of love of the unconditional kind for ourselves, each other and all of creation. He came to realize that the pure form of love known as Unconditional Love is the basis of everything. In his words, *"How do we get closer to this genuine spiritual self? By manifesting love and compassion."*

Eben returned not believing but *knowing* that the unconditional love that he experienced whilst traversing this new reality of intense love and Light was the single most important scientific and emotional truth in the Universe. In his own words, *"The unconditional love and acceptance that I experienced on my journey is the single most important discovery I have ever made and will ever make."*

Eben experienced undeniably and remarkably the vastness of Creation and now *knows* that life in our physical world, the one we can see with our eyes, is but a miniscule part of the *whole*.

"Only I now have a greatly enlarged conception of what vast and wonderful really mean. The physical side of the universe is as a speck of dust compared to the invisible and spiritual part."

Here are just a few examples of this new *reality* Eben found himself immersed in.

*"Then I heard a new sound: a **living** sound, like the richest most complex, most beautiful piece of music you've ever heard. Growing in volume as a pure white light descended. I was no longer looking at the slowly spinning Light but through it."*

Eben heard a whooshing sound and found himself immersed in the most beautiful world he had ever seen.

Eben recalls, *"Brilliant, vibrant, ecstatic, stunning...I could heap on one adjective after another to describe what this world looked and felt like, but they'd all fall short.*

All those who have experienced NDE's in this book had great difficulty finding adequate words to outline the indescribable beauty and wonder of these realms. On Eben's website he relays the following; *vibrant and dynamic plant life, with flowers and buds blossoming richly and no signs of death and decay, waterfalls into sparkling crystal pools, thousands of beings dancing below with great joy and festivity, all fueled by sweeping golden orbs in the sky above, angelic choirs emanating chants and anthems. The chants and hymns thundering down from those angelic choirs provided yet another portal to higher realms, eventually ushering my awareness into the Core, an unending inky blackness filled to overflowing with the infinite healing power of the all-loving Deity at the source, whom many might label as God, (Allah, Vishnu, Jehovah, Yahweh – the names get in the way, and the conflicting details of orthodox religions obscure the reality of such an infinitely loving and creative source).*

While writing it all up weeks later, God seemed too puny a little human word with much baggage, clearly failing to describe the power, majesty and awe I had witnessed. I originally referred to the Deity as Om, the sound that I recalled from that realm as the resonance within infinity and eternity.

My coma taught me many truths. First and foremost, near-death experiences, and related mystical states of awareness, reveal crucial truths about the nature of existence. Simply dismissing them as hallucinations is convenient for many in the conventional scientific community, but only continues to lead them away from the deeper truth these experiences are revealing to us. The conventional reductive materialist (physicalist) model embraced by many in the scientific community, including its assumption that the physical brain creates consciousness and that our human experience is birth-to-death and nothing more, is fundamentally flawed. At its core, the physicalist model intentionally ignores what I believe is the fundamental of all existence—consciousness itself.[24]

Eben Alexander's Near-Death Experience is a wonderfully inspiring and illuminating story. He is living proof of the power of these transformative NDE's. Now he has dedicated himself to sharing information about NDE's and other spiritually transformative experiences, and what they teach us about consciousness and the nature of reality. **That consciousness is life and life is consciousness.**

Look at the number of lives he has been able to touch since his experience in 2012 and imagine how many more will be. This exemplifies the power of the impact and message these illuminating, revealing and indeed life-changing journeys into life after 'death' can have.

Since *Proof of Heaven* was released in 2012, he has been a guest on The Dr. Oz Show, Super Soul Sunday with Oprah Winfrey, ABC-TV's 20-20 and Good Morning America, FOX-TV's FOX & Friends, and his story has been featured on the Discovery Channel and the Biography Channel. He has been interviewed for over 400 national and international radio and internet programs and podcasts. His books are available in over 40 countries worldwide and have been translated into over 30 languages.

Radical Change

Near-death experiences can bring radical change. Angry atheists have become ordained ministers with a passionate desire to tell as many people as possible that we have a non-denominational, non-judgmental God of immense love available to all of us, regardless of what we may have done in the past. Reverend George Rodonaia's extraordinary case is medically documented and once again demonstrates the miraculous and limitless power of Source Energy both within us and outside of us.

---

[24] Taken from www.ebenalexander.com

6. REV. GEORGE RODONAIA'S NEAR-DEATH EXTRACT

Before he died, Dr PMH Atwater interviewed Rev George Rodonaia and documented his unusual case in her book, *Beyond The Light* Dr Atwater writes.

"George Rodonaia was a vocal communist dissident in Tbilisi, Georgia, in Russia. In 1976 Rodonaia was run over twice by a car driven by a member of the KGB, (the second time was to make sure there was no slip up on the assassination attempt). He was rushed to the hospital, pronounced dead, and his body was taken to the morgue. Morgues in Tbilisi are not like those in the United States. There, bodies are quick-frozen immediately and kept in that state a full three days before any autopsy is performed or the body is dispensed with. After the three days, Rodonaia's body was removed from the freezer vault and wheeled to the autopsy room. A team of doctors began splitting apart his lower torso. As the blade cut through flesh, he managed to force open his eyes. One doctor, thinking this a mere reflex, promptly closed them. He opened his eyes again. Again the doctor closed them. Once more, his eyes popped open, only this time the doctor jumped backwards and screamed! Believe it or not, Rodonaia's own Uncle was one of the attending physicians.

George Rodonaia had earned his master's degree in research psychology and was working towards his doctorate when he was assassinated by the KGB. He felt the pain of being crushed beneath car wheels as he was run over twice by the same vehicle. But what bothered him most was the feeling of unknown darkness that came to envelop him. He thought I am not what I am. I don't exist in my body, yet I am in my thoughts. Being self-aware out of his body was confusing at first until it occurred to him. If I can still think, why don't I think positively? With that, there appeared a pinprick of light, light outside of the darkness. He remembered that physics teaches.

'We see light because it comes to our eye, hits our eye; light outside of darkness is impossible. Every experiment I have is based on my own intelligence, yet my knowledge is not enough to comprehend light or darkness that is in itself intelligent.'

As Rodonaia's sense of logic nullified, he beheld more light, chaos in light, bubbles like balls of molecules and atoms, round, moving, dividing into parts, electrons, protons, dividing into other parts, energy, eternal life-making cells— all moving in spirals. What had seemed chaotic actually had symmetry. He merged with what he saw, living within the living bubbles.

'Never have I seen such beauty or felt so warmly caressed. It is important that I experienced such big happiness because I began to learn that light has a kind of power at this higher level. And there are higher and higher levels, and the highest is God, and everything is under God's direction. Positive thinking links me to this

warmth, this golden spiraling. I obtained my medical doctorate fifteen years before, but I have no words to describe this. All heaviness empties into happiness here. It's better than orgasm, never stops, everlasting unto everlasting.'

Then he thought about his body, and instantly, he was back in the morgue viewing for the first time his green/ blue/ black remains, frozen on a slab. 'I don't want that thing back,' he declared, though an unknown power forced him to linger and look around.

'Two little walls separate you from other bodies. I saw them, all of them. In the darkness I could see. The memory of the car came back. Suddenly I saw the thoughts of everyone concerned with the event, as if they were thinking their thoughts inside of me. I scanned their thoughts and emotions to find truth. I saw my wife go to the grave where I would be buried, and I saw her thinking about herself and what she would do now I was gone'

Rodonaia felt he was able to do as much as he did because time and space, as we know them, do not exist. He returned to the morgue and was drawn to the newborn section of the adjacent hospital where a friend's wife had just given birth to a daughter. The baby cried incessantly. As if possessed of X-Ray vision, Rodonaia scanned her body and noted that her hip had been broken in birth. He verbally addressed her. 'Don't cry. Nobody will understand you. The infant was so surprised at his presence; she momentarily stopped crying.'

'Children can hear and see spirit beings. That child responded to me because, to her, I was a physical reality.

After the attending physicians in the autopsy unit quit screaming at the shock of seeing a dead body come back to life, they rushed Rodonaia to emergency surgery. All his ribs were broken, his muscles destroyed, his feet a horrible mess. It took three days before he could finally move his tongue around enough to speak. His first words warned the doctors about the child with the broken hip. X-Rays of the newborn were taken, and he proved right! Rodonaia remained hospitalized for nine months, during which time he became something of a celebrity.

'Many doctors came to see me. In the Soviet Union psychology is a science concerned with the study of life and death. They were interested in what I could tell them about death. The KGB kept an eye on me all the time I was in hospital, but because I had become so famous, they did not touch me.'

'I later earned my PhD in neuro-pathology, what you call psychiatry, and earned my divinity degree as a direct result of my near-death experience. What I learned in dying, you see, enabled me to make sense of religion and science.'

Years later, the KGB once again became a threat, so Rodonaia and his family secretly slipped away to Moscow and hid from view. They were able to immigrate to the United States in 1989 thanks to political pressure from the American government and through the sponsorship of a friend in Texas.

In October 2004, George passed away due to a massive heart attack. Prior to his near-death experience, George was an avowed atheist; however afterwards he became a Reverend and devoted his time to the study of spirituality. Rev. George Rodonaia held an M.D. and a PhD in neuropathology, and a PhD in the psychology of religion. He delivered a keynote address to the United Nations on the 'Emerging Global Spirituality'."[25]

Dr Atwater continues.

"I knew George well; he was part of my research base and a brief version of his story is in my book, Beyond the Light, I say 'brief' because what happened to George is beyond the scope of books about the near-death phenomenon and could have easily been a book unto itself. George was a vocal Soviet dissident during the time when such a stance could get you killed. And that is exactly what happened—he was assassinated by the KGB. Because his case was highly political, an autopsy had to be performed. His corpse was stored in a freezer vault for three days until then. He revived on the autopsy table as he was being split open by the doctors, one of which was his own uncle. Of all the cases I have investigated in my 26 years of work in the field, his is the most dramatic, the longest, the most evidential, and the most soul-stirring. Now our beloved George Rodonaia has returned 'Home' to stay. During the years afterward, he never failed to share his story and to help others every way he could. My only regret is, he never wrote his own book about his experience. Yet, perhaps he did, on everyone's heart who ever heard him. Blessings, dear George, you will be missed."

This brief extract from Phillip Berman's book, *The Journey Home* poignantly sums up what this remarkable experience gave George Rodonaia and many more like him.

"Many people have asked me what I believe in, how my NDE changed my life. All I can say is that I now believe in the God of the universe. Unlike many other people, however, I have never called God The Light, because God is beyond our comprehension. God, I believe, is even more than The Light, because God is also darkness. God is everything that exists, everything – and that is beyond our ability to comprehend at all. So I don't believe in the God of the Jews, or the Christians, or the Hindus, or in any one religion's idea of what God is or is not. It is all the same God, and that God showed me that the universe in which we live is a

---

[25] Extracts taken from Beyond The Light by Dr P. M. H. Atwater

beautiful and marvelous mystery that is connected together forever and for always.

Anyone who has had such an experience of God, who has felt such a profound sense of connection with reality, knows that there is only one truly significant work to do in life, and that is to love; to love nature, to love people, to love animals, to love creation itself, just because it is. To serve God's creation with a warm and loving hand of generosity and compassion – that is the only meaningful existence."

George's story demonstrates that *anything* is possible – three days dead and frozen – run over twice by the same car to ensure death—and returned a new man. If you're sitting there thinking, *extremely hard to believe,* yes it certainly is, but it is all medically documented and recorded at the hospital. What can we say?

The following near-death extract again re-iterates radical change. It also speaks volumes about our gracious, non-judgmental God of love and answers many questions. In this case, we can see the absolute power of reaching out to God after death. The moment he cried out to God, he was rescued from himself and lifted out of the extremely unpleasant lower astral planes. We see from his NDE that everyone and everything is forgiven by Source/God thus allowing us to begin afresh. This is a lengthy extract, but it encapsulates so much and answers many questions.

7. REV. HOWARD STORM'S NEAR-DEATH EXTRACT

Howard Storm was in intense agony and dying.

"Struggling to say goodbye to my wife, I wrestled with my emotions. Telling her that I loved her very much was as much of a goodbye as I could utter because of my emotional distress.

Sort of relaxing and closing my eyes, I waited for the end. This was it, I felt. This was the big nothing, the big blackout, the one you never wake up from, the end of existence. I had absolute certainty that there was nothing beyond this life – because that was how really smart people understood it.

While I was undergoing this stress, prayer or anything like that never occurred to me. I never once thought about it. If I mentioned God's name at all it was only as a profanity.

For a time, there was a sense of being unconscious or asleep. I'm not sure how long it lasted, but I felt really strange, and I opened my eyes. To my surprise, I was standing up next to the bed, and I was looking at my body lying in the bed. My first reaction was, 'This is crazy! I can't be standing here looking down at myself. That's not possible.' This wasn't what I expected; this wasn't right. Why was I still alive? I wanted oblivion. Yet I was looking at a thing that was my body, and it just didn't have that much meaning to me.

Not knowing what was happening, I became upset. I started yelling and screaming at my wife, and she just sat there like a stone. She didn't look at me, she didn't move – and I kept screaming profanities to get her to pay attention. Being confused, upset, and angry, I tried to get the attention of my room-mate, with the same result. He didn't react. I wanted this to be a dream, and I kept saying to myself, 'This has got to be a dream.'

But I knew that it wasn't a dream. I became aware that strangely I felt more alert, more aware, more alive than I had ever felt in my entire life. All my senses were extremely acute. Everything felt tingly and alive. The floor was cool, and my bare feet felt moist and clammy. This had to be real. I squeezed my fists and was amazed at how much I was feeling in my hands just by making a fist.

Then I heard my name. I heard, 'Howard, Howard – come here.'

Wondering, at first, where it was coming from, I discovered that it was originating in the doorway. There were different voices calling me.

I asked who they were, and they said, 'We are here to take care of you. We will fix you up. Come with us.'

Asking, again, who they were, I asked them if they were doctors and nurses.

They responded, 'Quick, come see. You'll find out.'

As I asked them questions, they gave evasive answers. They kept giving me a sense of urgency, insisting that I should step through the doorway.

With some reluctance, I stepped into the hallway, and in the hallway, I was in a fog, or a haze. It was a light-coloured haze. It wasn't a heavy haze. I could see my hand, for example, but the people who were calling me were 15 or 20 feet ahead, and I couldn't see them clearly. They were more like silhouettes or shapes, and as I moved toward them, they backed off into the haze. As I tried to get close to them to identify them, they quickly withdrew deeper into the fog. So I had to follow into the fog deeper and deeper.

These strange beings kept urging me to come with them.

I repeatedly asked them where we were going, and they responded, 'Hurry up, you'll find out.'

65

They wouldn't answer anything. The only response was insisting that I hurry up and follow them.

They told me repeatedly that my pain was meaningless and unnecessary. 'Pain is bullshit,' they said.

I knew that we had been travelling for miles, but I occasionally had the strange ability to look back and see the hospital room. My body was still there lying motionless on the bed. My perspective at these times was as if I were floating above the room looking down. It seemed millions and millions of miles away. Looking back into the room, I saw my wife and my room-mate, and I decided they had not been able to help me so I would go with these people.

Walking for what seemed to be a considerable distance, these beings were all around me. They were leading me through the haze. I don't know how long. There was a real sense of timelessness about the experience. In a real sense, I am unaware of how long it was, but it felt like a long time – maybe even days or weeks.

As we travelled, the fog got thicker and darker, and the people began to change. At first, they seemed rather playful and happy, but when we had covered some distance, a few of them began to get aggressive. The more questioning and suspicious I was, the more antagonistic and ruder and authoritarian they became. They began to make jokes about my bare rear end, which wasn't covered by my hospital dicky and about how pathetic I was. I knew they were talking about me, but when I tried to find out exactly what they were saying they would say, 'Shhhhh, he can hear you, he can hear you.'

Then, others would seem to caution the aggressive ones. It seemed that I could hear them warn the aggressive ones to be careful, or I would be frightened away.

Wondering what was happening, I continued to ask questions, and they repeatedly urged me to hurry and to stop asking questions. Feeling uneasy, especially since they continued to get aggressive, I considered returning, but I didn't know how to get back. I was lost. There were no features that I could relate to. There were just the fog and wet, clammy ground, and I had no sense of direction.

All my communication with them took place verbally, just as ordinary human communication occurs. They didn't appear to know what I was thinking, and I didn't know what they were thinking. What was increasingly obvious was that they were liars and help was farther away from the more I stayed with them.

Hours ago, I had hoped to die and end the torment of life. Now things were worse as I was forced by a mob of unfriendly and cruel people toward some unknown destination in the darkness. They began shouting and hurling insults at me, demanding that I hurry along. And they refused to answer any question.

Finally, I told them that I wouldn't go any farther. At that time, they changed completely. They became much more aggressive and insisted that I was going with them. A number of them began to push and shove me, and I responded by hitting back at them.

A wild orgy of frenzied taunting, screaming and hitting ensued. I fought like a wild man. All the while, it was obvious that they were having great fun.

It seemed to be, almost, a game for them, with me as the centre-piece of their amusement. My pain became their pleasure. They seemed to want to make me hurt – by clawing at me and biting me. Whenever I would get one off me, there were five more to replace the one.

By this time, it was almost complete darkness, and I had the sense that instead of there being twenty or thirty, there was an innumerable host of them. Each one seemed set on coming in for the sport they got from hurting me. My attempts to fight back only provoked greater merriment. They began to humiliate me in the most degrading ways physically. As I continued to fight on and on, I was aware that they weren't in any hurry to win. They were playing with me just as a cat plays with a mouse. Every new assault brought howls of cacophony. Then at some point, they began to tear off pieces of my flesh. To my horror, I realized I was being taken apart and eaten alive, slowly, so that their entertainment would last as long a possible.

At no time did I ever have any sense that the beings who seduced and attacked me were anything other than human beings. The best way I can describe them is to think of the worst imaginable person stripped of every impulse to do good. Some of them seemed to be able to tell others what to do, but I had no sense of any structure or hierarchy in an organizational sense. They didn't appear to be controlled or directed by anyone. Basically, they were a mob of beings totally driven by unbridled cruelty and passions.

During our struggle, I noticed that they seemed to feel no pain. Other than that they appeared to possess no special non-human or super-human abilities.

Although during my initial experience with them, I assumed that they were clothed, in our intimate physical contact, I never felt any clothing whatsoever.

Fighting well and hard for a long time, ultimately I was spent. Lying there exhausted amongst them, they began to calm down since I was no longer the amusement that I had been. Most of the beings gave up in disappointment because I was no longer amusing, but a few still picked and gnawed at me and ridiculed me for no longer being any fun. By this time, I had been pretty much taken apart. People were still picking at me, occasionally, and I just lay there all torn up, unable to resist.

Exactly what happened was . . . and I'm not going to try and explain this. From inside of me, I felt a voice, my voice, say, 'Pray to God.'

My mind responded to that, 'I don't pray. I don't know how to pray.'

This is a guy lying on the ground in the darkness surrounded by what appeared to be dozens if not hundreds and hundreds of vicious creatures who had just torn him up. The situation seemed utterly hopeless, and I seemed beyond any possible help, whether I believed in God or not.

The voice again told me to pray to God. It was a dilemma since I didn't know-how. The voice told me a third time to pray to God.

I started saying things like, 'The Lord is my shepherd, I shall not want . . . God bless America' and anything else that seemed to have a religious connotation.

And these people went into a frenzy as if I had thrown boiling oil all over them. They began yelling and screaming at me, telling me to quit, that there was no God, and no one could hear me. While they screamed and yelled obscenities, they also began backing away from me – as if I were poison. As they were retreating, they became more rabid, cursing and screaming that what I was saying was worthless and that I was a coward.

I screamed back at them, 'Our Father who art in heaven,' and similar ideas. This continued for some time until, suddenly, I was aware that they had left. It was dark, and I was alone yelling things that sounded churchy. It was pleasing to me that these churchy sayings had such an effect on those awful beings.

Lying there for a long time, I was in such a state of hopelessness, and blackness, and despair, that I had no way of measuring how long it was. I was just lying there in an unknown place – all torn and ripped. And I had no strength; it was all gone. It seemed as if I were sort of fading out, that any effort on my part would expend the last energy I had. My conscious sense was that I was perishing or just sinking into the darkness."

A Rescue from Hell By Jesus Christ

"Now I didn't know if I was even in the world. But I did know that I was here. I was real; all my senses worked too painfully well. I didn't know how I had arrived here. There was no direction to follow, even if I had been physically able to move. The agony that I had suffered during the day was nothing compared to what I was feeling now. I knew then that this was the absolute end of my existence, and it was more horrible than anything I could possibly have imagined.

Then a most unusual thing happened. I heard very clearly, once again in my own voice, something that I had learned in nursery Sunday School. It was the little song, 'Jesus loves me, yes I know. . .' and it kept repeating. I don't know why, but all of a sudden I wanted to believe that. Not having anything left, I wanted to cling to that thought. And I, inside, screamed, 'Jesus, please save me.'

That thought was screamed with every ounce of strength and feeling left in me.

When I did that, I saw, off in the darkness somewhere, the tiniest little star. Not knowing what it was, I presumed it must be a comet or a meteor because it was moving rapidly. Then I realized it was coming toward me. It was getting very bright rapidly.

When the light came near, its radiance spilled over me, and I just rose up – not with my effort – I just lifted up. Then I saw – and I saw this very plainly – I saw all my wounds, all my tears, all my brokenness, melt away. And I became whole in this radiance.

What I did was to cry uncontrollably. I was crying, not out of sadness, but because I was feeling things that I had never felt before in my life.

Another thing happened. Suddenly I knew a whole bunch of things. I knew things. . . I knew that this light, this radiance, knew me. I don't know how to explain to you that I knew it knew me, I just did. As a matter of fact, I understood that it knew me better than my mother or father did. The luminous entity that embraced me knew me intimately and began to communicate a tremendous sense of knowledge. I knew that he knew everything about me and I was unconditionally loved and accepted.

The light conveyed to me that it loved me in a way that I can't begin to express. It loved me in a way that I had never known that love could possibly be. He was a concentrated field of energy, radiant in splendour indescribable, except to say goodness and love. This was more loving than one can imagine.

I knew that this radiant being was powerful. It was making me feel so good all over. I could feel its light on me – like very gentle hands around me. And I could feel it holding me. But it loved me with overwhelming power. After what I had been through, to be completely known, accepted, and intensely loved by this Being of Light surpassed anything I had known or could have imagined. I began to cry, and the tears kept coming and coming. And we, I and this light went up and out of there.

We started going faster and faster, out of the darkness. Embraced by the light, feeling wonderful and crying, I saw off in the distance something that looked like the picture of a galaxy, except that it was larger and there were more stars than I had seen on earth.

There was a great centre of brilliance. In the centre, there was an enormously bright concentration. Outside the centre, countless millions of spheres of light were flying about entering and leaving what was a great being-ness at the centre. It was off in the distance.

Then I . . . I didn't say it, I thought it. I said, 'Put me back.'

What I meant by telling the light to put me back, was to put me back into the pit. I was so ashamed of who I was, and what I had been all of my life, that all I wanted to do was hide in the darkness. I didn't want to go toward the light anymore – I did, yet I didn't. How many times in my life had I denied and scoffed at the reality before me, and how many thousands of times had I used it as a curse. What incredible intellectual arrogance to use the name as an insult. I was afraid to go closer. I was also aware that the incredible intensity of the emanations might disintegrate what I still experienced as my intact physical body.

The being who was supporting me, my friend, was aware of my fear and reluctance and shame. For the first time, he spoke to my mind in a male voice and told me that if I was uncomfortable, we didn't have to go closer. So we stopped where we were, still countless miles away from the Great being.

For the first time, my friend, and I will refer to him in that context hereafter, said to me, 'You belong here.' (Howard believed his friend to be Jesus).

Facing all the splendor made me acutely aware of my lowly condition. My response was: 'No, you've made a mistake, put me back.'

And he said, 'We don't make mistakes. You belong.'

Then he called out in a musical tone to the luminous entities who surrounded the great center. Several came and circled around us. During what follows some came and went but normally there were five or six and sometimes as many as eight with us.

I was still crying. One of the first things these marvellous beings did was to ask, all with thought, 'Are you afraid of us?'

I told them I wasn't.

They said that they could turn their brilliance down and appear as people, and I told them to stay as they were. They were the most beautiful, the most. . .

As an aside, I'm an artist. There are three primary, three secondary, and six tertiary colors in the visible light spectrum. Here, I saw a visible light spectrum with at least 80 new primary colors. I also saw this brilliance. It's disappointing for me to try and describe, because I can't – I saw colors that I had never seen before.

70

What these beings were showing me was their glory. I wasn't really seeing them. And I was perfectly content. Having come from a world of shapes and forms, I was delighted with this new, formless world. These beings were giving me what I needed at that time.

To my surprise, and also my distress, they seemed to be capable of knowing everything I was thinking. I didn't know whether I would be capable of controlling my thoughts and keeping anything secret.

We began to engage in thought exchange, a conversation that was very natural, very easy and casual. I heard their voices clearly and individually. They each had a distinct personality with a voice, but they spoke directly to my mind, not my ears. And they used normal, colloquial English. Everything I thought, they knew.

They all seemed to know and understand me very well and to be completely familiar with my thoughts and my past. I didn't feel any desire to ask for someone I had known because they all knew me. Nobody could know me any better. It also didn't occur to me to try to identify them as uncle or grandfather. It was like going to a large gathering of relatives at Christmas and not being quite able to remember their names or who they are married to or how they are connected to you. But you do know that you are with your family. I don't know if they were related to me or not. It felt like they were closer to me than anyone I had ever known.

Throughout my conversation with the luminous beings, which lasted for what seemed like a very long time, I was physically supported by the being in whom I had been engulfed. We were, in a sense completely stationary yet hanging in space. Everywhere around us were countless radiant beings, like stars in the sky, coming and going. It was like a super magnified view of a galaxy super packed with stars. And in the giant radiance of the centre, they were packed so densely together that individuals could not be identified. Their selves were in such harmony with the Creator that they were really just one.

One of the reasons, I was told that all the countless beings had to go back to their source was to become invigorated with this sense of harmony and oneness. Being apart for too long a time diminished them and made them feel separate. Their greatest pleasure was to go back to the sources of all life.

Our initial conversation involved them simply trying to comfort me.

Something that disturbed me was that I was naked. Somewhere in the darkness, I'd lost my hospital gown. I was a human being. I had a body. They told me this was okay. They were quite familiar with my anatomy. Gradually I relaxed and stopped trying to cover my privates with my hands.

71

Next, they wanted to talk about my life. To my surprise, my life played out before me, maybe six or eight feet in front of me, from beginning to end. The life review was very much in their control, and they showed me my life, but not from my point of view. I saw me in my life – and this whole thing was a lesson, even though I didn't know it at the time. They were trying to teach me something, but I didn't know it was a teaching experience, because I didn't know that I would be coming back.

We just watched my life from the beginning to the end. Some things they slowed down on and zoomed in on and other things they went right through. My life was shown in a way that I had never thought of before. All of the things that I had worked to achieve, the recognition that I had worked for, in elementary school, in high school, in college, and in my career, they meant nothing in this setting.

I could feel their feelings of sorrow and suffering, or joy, as my life's review unfolded. They didn't say that something was bad or good, but I could feel it. And I could sense all those things they were indifferent to. They didn't, for example, look down on my high school shot-put record. They just didn't feel anything towards it, nor towards other things which I had taken so much pride in.

What they responded to was how I had interacted with other people. That was the long and short of it. Unfortunately, most of my interactions with other people didn't measure up with how I should have interacted, which was in a loving way.

Whenever I did react during my life in a loving way, they rejoiced.

Most of the time, I found that my interactions with other people had been manipulative. During my professional career, for example, I saw myself sitting in my office, playing the college professor, while a student came to me with a personal problem. I sat there looking compassionate, and patient, and loving, while inside, I was bored to death. I would check my watch under my desk as I anxiously waited for the student to finish.

I got to go through all those kinds of experiences in the company of these magnificent beings.

When I was a teenager, my father's career put him into a high-stress, twelve-hour-a-day job. Out of my resentment because of his neglect of me, when he came home from work, I would be cold and indifferent toward him. This made him angry, and it gave me further excuse to feel hatred toward him. He and I fought, and my mother would get upset.

Most of my life, I had felt that my father was the villain, and I was the victim. When we reviewed my life, I got to see how I had precipitated so much of that, myself. Instead of greeting him happily at the end of a day, I was continually putting thorns in him – in order to justify my hurt.

72

I got to see when my sister had a bad night one night, how I went into her bedroom and put my arms around her. Not saying anything, I just lay there with my arms around her. As it turned out, that experience was one of the biggest triumphs of my life."

The Therapy of Love and Enlightenment

"The entire life's review would have been emotionally destructive and would have left me a psychotic person if it hadn't been for the fact that my friend, and my friend's friends, were loving me during the unfolding of my life. I could feel that love. Every time I got a little upset, they turned the life's review off for a while, and they just loved me. Their love was tangible. You could feel it on your body; you could feel it inside you; their love went right through you. I wish I could explain it to you, but I can't.

The therapy was their love because my life's review kept tearing me down. It was pitiful to watch, just pitiful. I couldn't believe it. And the thing is, it got worse as it went on. My stupidity and selfishness as a teenager only magnified as I became an adult – all under the veneer of being a good husband, a good father, and a good citizen. The hypocrisy of it all was nauseating. But through it, all was their love.

When the review was finished, they asked, 'Do you want to ask any questions?' and I had a million questions.

I asked, for example, 'What about the Bible?'

They responded, 'What about it?'

I asked if it was true, and they said it was. Asking them why it was that when I tried to read it, all I saw were contradictions, they took me back to my life's review again – something that I had overlooked. They showed me, for the few times I had opened the Bible, that I had read it with the idea of finding contradictions and problems. I was trying to prove to myself that it wasn't worth reading.

I mentioned to them that the Bible wasn't clear to me. It didn't make sense. They told me that it contained spiritual truth and that I had to read it spiritually in order to understand it. It should be read prayerfully. My friends informed me that it was not like other books. They also told me, and I later found out this was true, that when you read it prayerfully, it talks to you. It reveals itself to you. And you don't have to work at it anymore.

My friends answered lots of questions in funny ways. They really knew the whole tone of what I asked them, even before I got the questions out. When I thought of questions in my head, they really understood them.

73

I asked them, for example, which was the best religion. I was looking for an answer which was like, 'Presbyterians.' I figured these guys were all Christians.

The answer I got was, 'The best religion is the religion that brings you closest to God.'

Asking them if there was life on other planets, their surprising answer was that the universe was full of life.

Because of my fear of a nuclear holocaust, I asked if there was going to be a nuclear war in the world, and they said no. That astonished me, and I gave them this extensive explanation of how I had lived under the threat of nuclear war. That was one of the reasons I was who I was. I figured, when I was in this life, that it was all sort of hopeless; the world was going to blow up anyway, and nothing made much sense. In that context, I felt I could do what I wanted, since nothing mattered.

They said, 'No, there isn't going to be any nuclear war.'

I asked if they were absolutely sure there wasn't going to be a nuclear war. They reassured me again, and I asked them how they could be so sure. Their response was: 'God loves the world.'

They told me that at the most, one or two nuclear weapons might go off accidentally if they weren't destroyed, but there wouldn't be a nuclear war. I then asked them how come there had been so many wars. They said that they allowed those few to happen, out of all the wars that humanity tried to start. Out of all the wars that humans tried to create, they allowed a few, to bring people to their senses and to stop them.

Science, technology, and other benefits, they told me, had been gifts bestowed on humanity by them – through inspiration. People had literally been led to those discoveries, many of which had later been perverted by humanity to use for its own destruction. We could do too much damage to the planet. And by the planet, they meant all of God's creation. Not just the people, but the animals, the trees, the birds, the insects, everything.

They explained to me that their concern was for all the people of the world. They weren't interested in one group getting ahead of other groups. They want every person to consider every other person as no lesser or greater than themselves. They want everyone to love everyone else, completely; more even, or at least as much, as they love themselves. If someone, someplace else in the world hurts, then we should hurt – we should feel their pain. And we should help them.

Our planet has evolved to the point, for the first time in our history, that we have the power to do that. We are globally linked. And we could become 'One' People.

The people that they gave the privilege of leading the world into a better age blew it. That was us, in the United States.

When I spoke with them about the future, and this might sound like a cop-out on my part, they made clear to me that we have free will.

If we change the way we are, then we can change the future which they showed me. They showed me a view of the future, at the time of my experience, based upon how we in the United States were behaving at that time. It was a future in which a massive worldwide depression would occur. If we were to change our behaviour, however, then the future would be different.

Asking them how it would be possible to change the course of many people, I observed that it was difficult, if not impossible, to change anything on earth. I expressed the opinion that it was a hopeless task to try.

My friends explained, quite clearly, that all it takes to make a change was one person. One person, trying, and then because of that, another person is changing for the better. They said that the only way to change the world was, to begin with one person. One will become two, which will become three, and so on. That's the only way to affect a major change.

I inquired as to where the world would be going in an optimistic future – one where some of the changes they desired were to take place. The image of the future that they gave me then, and it was their image, not one that I created, surprised me.

My image had previously been sort of like Star Wars, where everything was space-age, plastics, and technology. The future that they showed me was almost no technology at all.

What everybody, absolutely everybody, in this euphoric future spent most of their time doing was raising children. The chief concern of people was children, and everybody considered children to be the most precious commodity in the world. And when a person became an adult, there was no sense of anxiety, nor hatred, nor competition. There was this enormous sense of trust and mutual respect.

If a person, in this view of the future, became disturbed, then the community of people all cared about the disturbed person falling away from the harmony of the group. Spiritually, through prayer and love, the others would elevate the afflicted person.

People, in this best of all worlds, weren't interested in knowledge; they were interested in wisdom. This was because they were in a position where anything they needed to know, in the knowledge category, they could receive simply

75

through prayer. Everything, to them, was solvable. They could do anything they wanted to do.

In this future, people had no wanderlust, because they could, spiritually, communicate with everyone else in the world. There was no need to go elsewhere. They were so engrossed with where they were and the people around them that they didn't have to go on vacation. Vacation from what? They were completely fulfilled and happy.

Death, in this world, was a time when the individual had experienced everything that he or she needed to experience. To die meant to lie down and let go; then the spirit would rise up, and the community would gather around. There would be great rejoicing, because they all had insight into the heavenly realm, and the spirit would join with the angels that came down to meet it. They could see the spirit leave and knew that it was time for the spirit to move on; it had outgrown the need for growth in this world. Individuals who died had achieved all they were capable of in this world in terms of love, appreciation, understanding, and working in harmony with others.

The sense I got of this beautiful view of the world's future was as a garden, God's garden. And in this garden of the world, full of all beauty, were people. The people were born into this world to grow in their understanding of the Creator. Then to shed this skin, this shell, in the physical world, and to graduate and move up into heaven – there, to have a more intimate and growing relationship with God.

Howard's Light Being friends told him more about the new world to come. According to them, God wished to usher in the kingdom within the next two hundred years. This New World Order, according to Howard, will resemble some near-death descriptions of heaven. People will live in such peace and harmony and love that communication will be telepathic, travel instantaneous and the need for clothing and shelter eliminated. The lion will, indeed lie down with the lamb. "

Learning What Happens After Death

"I asked my friend and his friends, about death – what happens when we die?

They said that when a loving person dies, angels come down to meet him, and they take him up – gradually, at first, because it would be unbearable for that person to be instantly exposed to God.

Knowing what's inside of every person, the angels don't have to prove anything by showing off. They know what each of us needs, so they provide that. In some cases, it may be a heavenly meadow, and in another, something else. If a person needs to see a relative, the angels will bring that relative. If the person really likes jewels, they will show the person jewels. We see what is necessary for our introduction into the spirit world, and those things are real, in the heavenly, the divine sense.

They gradually educate us as Spirit Beings and bring us into heaven. We grow and increase, and grow and increase, and shed the concerns, desires, and base animal stuff that we have been fighting much of our life. Earthly appetites melt away. It is no longer a struggle to fight them. We become who we truly are, which is part of the Divine.

This happens to loving people, people who are good and love God. They made it clear to me that we don't have any knowledge or right to judge anybody else – in terms of that person's heart relationship to God. Only God knows what's in a person's heart. Someone whom we think is despicable, God might know as a wonderful person. Similarly, someone we think is good; God may see as a hypocrite, with a black heart. Only God knows the truth about every individual.

I deserved to be where I was – I was in the right place at the right time. That was the place for me, and the people I was around were perfect company for me. God allowed me to experience that and then removed me, because he saw something redeeming in putting me through the experience. It was a way to purge me. People who are not allowed to be pulled into darkness, because of their loving nature, are attracted upwards, toward the light.

I never saw God, and I was not in heaven. It was way out in the suburbs, and these are the things that they showed me. We talked for a long time, about many things, and then I looked at myself. When I saw me, I was glowing; I was radiant. I was becoming beautiful – not nearly as beautiful as them – but I had a certain sparkle that I never had before.

Not being ready to face the earth again, I told them that I wished to be with them forever. I said, 'I'm ready, I'm ready to be like you and be here forever. This is great. I love it. I love you. You're wonderful.'

I knew that they loved me and knew everything about me. I knew that everything was going to be okay from now on. I asked if I could get rid of my body, which was definitely a hindrance and become a being like them with the powers they had shown me.

They said, 'No, you have to go back.'

They explained to me that I was very underdeveloped and that it would be of great benefit to return to my physical existence to learn. In my human life, I would have an opportunity to grow so that the next time I was with them, I would be more compatible. I would need to develop important characteristics to become like them and to be involved with the work that they do.

Responding that I couldn't go back, I tried to argue with them, and I observed that if I bear that thought – the thought that I might wind up in the pit again – I pled with them to stay.

My friends then said, 'Do you think that we expect you to be perfect, after all the love we feel for you, even after you were on earth blaspheming God, and treating everyone around you like dirt? And this, although we were sending people to try and help you, to teach you the truth? Do you really think we would be apart from you now?'

I asked them, 'But what about my own sense of failure? You've shown me how I can be better, and I'm sure I can't live up to that. I'm not that good.'

Some of my self-centeredness welled up, and I said, 'No way. I'm not going back.'

They said, 'There are people who care about you; your wife, your children, your mother and father. You should go back to them. Your children need your help.'

I said, 'You can help them. If you make me go back, there are things that just won't work. If I go back there and make mistakes, I won't be able to stand it because you've shown me I could be more loving and more compassionate and I'll forget. I'll be mean to someone, or I'll do something awful to someone. I just know it's going to happen because I'm a human being. I'm going to blow it, and I won't be able to stand it. I'll feel so bad I'll want to kill myself, and I can't do that because life is precious. I might just go catatonic. So you can't send me back.'

They assured me that mistakes are an acceptable part of being human.

'Go,' they said, 'and make all the mistakes you want. Mistakes are how you learn.'

As long as I tried to do what I knew was right, they said, I would be on the right path. If I made a mistake, I should fully recognize it as a mistake, then put it behind me and simply try not to make the same mistake again. The important things are to try one's best, keep one's standards of goodness and truth, and not compromise those to win people's approval.

'But,' I said, 'mistakes make me feel bad.'

They said, 'We love you the way you are, mistakes and all. And you can feel our forgiveness. You can feel our love any time you want to.'

I said, 'I don't understand. How do I do that?'

'Just turn inward,' they said. 'Just ask for our love, and we'll give it to you if you ask from the heart.'

They advised me to recognize it when I made a mistake and to ask for forgiveness. Before I even got the words out of my mouth, I would be forgiven – but, I would have to accept the forgiveness. My belief in the principle of forgiveness must be real, and I would have to know that the forgiveness was given. Confessing, either in public or in private, that I had made a mistake, I should then ask for forgiveness. After that, it would be an insult to them if I didn't accept the forgiveness. I shouldn't continue to go around with a sense of guilt, and I should not repeat errors – I should learn from my mistakes.

'But,' I said, 'how will I know what the right choice is? How will I know what you want me to do?'

They replied, 'We want you to do what you want to do. That means making choices – and there isn't necessarily any right choice. There is a spectrum of possibilities, and you should make the best choice you can from those possibilities. If you do that, we will be there helping you.'

I didn't give in easily. I argued that back there was full of problems and that here was everything I could possibly want. I questioned my ability to accomplish anything they would consider important in my world. They said the world is a beautiful expression of the Supreme being. One can find beauty or ugliness depending on what one directs one's mind toward.

They explained that the subtle and complex development of our world was beyond my comprehension, but I would be a suitable instrument for the Creator. Every part of the creation, they explained, is infinitely interesting because it is a manifestation of the Creator. A very important opportunity for me would be to explore this world with wonder and enjoyment.

They never gave me a direct mission or purpose. Could I build a shrine or cathedral for God? They said those monuments were for humanity. They wanted me to live my life to love people, not things. I told them I wasn't good enough to represent what I had just experienced with them on a worldly level. They assured me I would be given appropriate help whenever I might need it. All I had to do is ask.

The luminous beings, my teachers, were very convincing. I was also acutely aware that not far away was the Great Being, who I knew to be the Creator. They never said, 'He wants it this way,' but that was implied behind everything they said. I didn't want to argue too much because the Great Entity was so wonderful and so awesome. The love that was emanated was overwhelming.

Presenting my biggest argument against coming back into the world, I told them that it would break my heart, and I would die if I had to leave them and their love. Coming back would be so cruel, I said, that I couldn't stand it. I mentioned that

79

the world was filled with hate and competition, and I didn't want to return to that maelstrom. I couldn't bear to leave them.

My friends observed that they had never been apart from me. I explained that I hadn't been aware of their Presence, and if I went back, I, again, wouldn't know they were there. Explaining how to communicate with them, they told me to get myself quiet, inside, and to ask for their love; then that love would come, and I would know they were there.

They said, 'You won't be away from us. We're with you. We've always been with you. We always will be right with you all the time.'

I said, 'But how do I know that? You tell me that, but when I go back there, it's just going to be a nice theory.'

They said, 'Any time you need us, we'll be there for you.'

I said, 'You mean like you'll just appear?'

They said, 'No, no. We're not going to intervene in your life in any big way unless you need us. We're just going to be there, and you'll feel our Presence, you'll feel our love.'

After that explanation, I ran out of arguments, and I said I thought I could go back. And, just like that, I was back. Returning to my body, the pain was there, only worse than before."[26]

Returning to life wasn't easy for Howard. In addition to his physical problems, he had to face the usual array of uncomprehending and insensitive responses to his new spiritual condition. As he relates it, it began in the hospital.

"I felt this overwhelming sense of love for everyone. I wanted to hug and kiss everyone, but I couldn't even sit up. I would say, 'Oh, you're so beautiful' to anyone and everyone. I was the joke on the floor. People found it very amusing."

Kevin Williams wrote these words about Howard Storm's experience. *"Like other near-death experiences, Howard's sense of empathy expanded, as well as his compassion. He could, he said, feel the emotions of others more powerfully than his own. Howard decided to enter the Christian ministry after his near-death experience."*

Realistically, not every NDE experience is always pleasant. I have purposely omitted all but the above NDE account that had parts that were unpleasant.

---

[26] Judith Cressey, The Near-Death Experience – Mysticism or Madness. Pgs 19-35.

It is empowering to realize that all you can take with you is your consciousness at the time-the love in your heart, or lack of it, and your belief systems or lack of them. For someone who believes there is no life after death and no God, they may well find themselves in a *void of nothingness*, devoid of any form of positive life. For those who believe they will go to a fiery furnace called 'hell' for all they have done if there is a life after death, guess what? They may well find themselves in their conceptual picture of that minus the pain like Howard Storm experienced initially. For those who believe there is no Creator, and that man is the only life form they may find nothing else but a lot more meandering lost souls who believed the same. These are the lower astral realms which are devoid of love. Once again this only validates the importance of having this awareness *before* we 'die'.

There are always exceptions to this as we have seen in some of these NDE's. Even some of those who were atheists and who admitted they were then nasty, selfish people still discovered life after death with a love so all-encompassing that they were changed forever. As you can see Howard Storm was an atheist and returned to become a Reverend because of his profound, life-changing experience. These people had missions to teach what they experienced upon their return and so they did.

It is important to point out here that even those people who have not lived supposedly good lives and who go to a form of 'hell' because they have created it in their mind – none of them will feel any pain, though it will not be a pleasant experience. It will be as if they are observing themselves in a play. This extract is from God's dialogue with Neale Donald Walsch in his book *Home With God*.

"There is no such thing as pain – emotional, physical or spiritual – in the afterlife. I mentioned earlier that even those who imagine they are going to 'hell' and then send themselves there do not suffer. They simply observe themselves having the experience, but without an emotional connection to it."[27]

However, as soon as any of these souls cry out for help. God/Source sends one of his Angels or 'helpers' down to the lower Astrals to assist in the restoration of that soul. What you expect to see after you die is what you will create! So get excited in that, when your time comes, you can create going straight to The Light and merging back into the sublime, ecstatic power of pure unconditional love – of becoming *One*—all you have to do is believe and you too could experience some of the enveloping bliss these NDE'ers have.

Like Revs. George Rodonaia and Howard Storm, Dr. Dianne Morrissey returned a totally changed person from one who disbelieved to one who then embarked on

---

[27] Walsch, Home With God. (Hodder & Stoughton, London. 2006). Pg118.

her own mission; to enable people to have transformational God experiences while here on Earth.

8. DR. DIANNE MORRISSEY'S NEAR-DEATH EXTRACT

When Dianne Morrissey, PhD, was twenty-eight years old, she was electrocuted and had a very profound near-death experience. Her experience transformed her entire life in a big way. Today, she is a certified hypnotherapist and has taught 25,000 people to see and feel God's Presence during their dream state. Her excellent book, *You Can See The Light*, will train you to do this very thing yourself. Her practical techniques teach you how to have a transformational experience and how you can heal your physical body.

Dr. Morrissey was pronounced clinically dead for 45 minutes after being electrocuted by 119 volts.

Dr. Morrissey said, *"I was thrown by such force that my physical body was thrown about 10 feet away from where I was standing, and my head went right through the wall about 1-1/2 feet off the ground. I felt no physical pain. I watched it all happen out-of-my body. When I first came out of my body, I noticed that I was transparent and wondered how I could see so good without my glasses, because I saw them on the floor next to my lifeless body."*

She had found herself floating on the ceiling looking down on her dog who was frantically trying to wake her up. To her sheer amazement, she discovered that she was *"transparent"* and that she could move *"through objects like windows."* She became less and less concerned about her 'dead' physical body as the experience continued.

Dr Morrissey explains, *"I met an angel-like woman on the other side who explained much to me, who helped me with my life review. I went through many tunnels, not just one. I will never forget the love that surrounded me at that moment or the joy that ran through me. Can you imagine being hugged by God and your angel? It's an experience that defies description!*

In this rapturous place, I recognized that there were two aspects of 'me.' My soul was my consciousness, everything that had made me who I had been and what I had become. My spirit, on the other hand, was the part of me that was now transparent and glowing, dressed in white.

Within the light, I knew that everyone and everything is connected to it. God is in everyone, always and forever. Within the light was the cure for all diseases."

9. MELLEN-THOMAS BENEDICT'S NEAR-DEATH EXTRACT

Just like Rev. George Rodonaia's, Rev Howard Storm's, Dr. Dianne Morrissey's and Lynnclaire Dennis' whole worlds and perceptions thereof were annihilated and then divinely remolded by their NDE's, so too was Mellen-Thomas Benedict's.

He confessed that prior to his amazing NDE he was extremely negative and pessimistic about life on planet Earth. He had no interest in any form of spirituality as he saw humanity as some form of blight that was killing our planet.

Deepak Chopra describes Mellen as *"an encyclopedia of the after-life."* Unlike many NDE'ers, Mellen questioned Source along the way and received deeper and deeper understandings from being taken experientially to transcend time and space as we know it to before *"The Big Bang,"* pre-creation as it were, into the all-pervading, never-ending depths of the void before the creation of matter. Mellen could find no words in our vocabulary to adequately describe this experience. Like Lynnclaire Dennis, he also heard The Music of the Spheres. The following extract is taken from Kevin Williams' website www.near-death.com with kind permission.

Mellen-Thomas Benedict was an artist who survived a near-death experience in 1982. He was dead for over an hour and a half after dying of cancer. At the time of his death, he rose up out of his body and went into the light. Curious about the universe, he was taken far into the remote depths of existence, and even beyond, into the energetic void of nothingness behind the Big Bang. During his experience, he was able to learn a great deal of information concerning reincarnation. Because of his near-death experience, he was able to bring back scientific discoveries. Mr Benedict has been closely involved in the mechanics of cellular communication and research dealing with the relationship of light to life called Quantum Biology. This research is providing dramatic new perspectives on how biological systems work. Mr Benedict has found that living cells can respond very quickly to light stimulation resulting in, among other things, high-speed healing. He was a researcher, inventor and lecturer who held six U.S. patents.

Several weeks after Benedict was born, he experienced an NDE when his bowels were ruptured. His body was tossed to one side as a corpse, yet much to everyone's surprise he later revived. As soon as he was big enough to grab hold of crayons, he started what became a compulsive urge to create symbolic renditions of the black/white yin/yang circles of Eastern religious thought. He has no memory of why he drew those particular symbols. He spent his grade school years in a

Catholic boarding school in Vermont and was baptized in the Salvation Army religion as a youngster. He travelled extensively because of a military stepfather until the family finally settled down in Fayetteville, North Carolina. Then, Benedict was diagnosed as having inoperable cancer. He had retired from the frenzy of filmdom by then and was operating his own stained-glass studio. As his condition worsened, he spent more and more time with his art. One morning he awakened knowing he would die the next day, and he did. As the typical heaven-like scenario began to unfold, Benedict recognized what was happening as it was happening. The process was familiar to him because he had read many books about the near-death phenomenon previously.

Mr Benedict's NDE is reprinted here by the permission of his friends Dr Lee Worth Bailey and Jenny Yates. Their excellent book entitled The Near-Death Experience: A Reader, published by Routledge, New York, in 1996 is highly recommended by the webmaster.

A portion of his near-death experience also appears in P.M.H. Atwater's book, Beyond the Light. Concerning Mellen's near-death experience, Dr. Ken Ring remarked, *"His story is one of the most remarkable I have encountered in my extensive research on near-death experiences."*

The Road to Death

"1982 I died from terminal cancer. The condition I had was inoperable, and any kind of chemotherapy they could give me would just have made me more of a vegetable. I was given six to eight months to live. I had been an information freak in the 1970s, and I had become increasingly despondent over the nuclear crisis, the ecology crisis, and so forth. So, since I did not have a spiritual basis, I began to believe that nature had made a mistake and that we were probably a cancerous organism on the planet. I saw no way that we could get out of all the problems we had created for ourselves and the planet. I perceived all humans as cancer, and that is what I got. That is what killed me. Be careful what your world view is. It can feed back on you, especially if it is a negative world view. I had a seriously negative one. That is what led me to my death. I tried all sorts of alternative healing methods, but nothing helped.

So, I determined that this was really just between God and me. I had never really faced God before or even dealt with God. I was not into any kind of spirituality at the time, but I began a journey into learning about spirituality and alternative healing. I set out to do all the reading I could and bone up on the subject because I did not want to be surprised on the other side. So, I started reading about various religions and philosophies. They were all very interesting and gave hope that there was something on the other side.

On the other hand, as a self-employed stained-glass artist at the time, I had no medical insurance whatsoever. So my life savings went overnight in testing. Then I was facing the medical profession without any kind of insurance. I did not want to have my family dragged down financially, so I determined to handle this myself. There was not constant pain, but there were black-outs. I got to the point where I would not dare to drive, and eventually, I ended up in hospice care. I had my own personal hospice caretaker. I was very blessed by this angel who went through the last part of this with me. I lasted about eighteen months. I did not want to take a lot of drugs, since I wanted to be as conscious as possible. Then I experienced such pain that I had nothing but pain in my consciousness, luckily only for a few days at a time."

The Light of God

"I remember waking up one morning at home about 4:30 am, and I just knew that this was it. This was the day I was going to die. So I called a few friends and said goodbye. I woke up my hospice caretaker and told her. I had a private agreement with her that she would leave my dead body alone for six hours since I had read that all kinds of interesting things happen when you die. I went back to sleep. The next thing I remember is the beginning of a typical near-death experience. Suddenly I was fully aware, and I was standing up, but my body was in bed. There was this darkness around me. Being out of my body was even more vivid than ordinary experience. It was so vivid that I could see every room in the house, I could see the top of the house, I could see around the house, I could see under the house.

There was this light shining. I turned toward the light. The light was very similar to what many other people have described in their near-death experiences. It was so magnificent. It is tangible; you can feel it. It is alluring; you want to go to it like you would want to go to your ideal mother's or father's arms.

As I began to move toward the light, I knew intuitively that if I went to the light, I would be dead.

So as I was moving toward the light I said, 'Please wait a minute, just hold on a second here. I want to think about this; I would like to talk to you before I go.'

To my surprise, the entire experience halted at that point. You are indeed in control of your near-death experience. You are not on a roller coaster ride. So my request was honored, and I had some conversations with the light. The light kept changing into different figures, like Jesus, Buddha, Krishna, Mandalas, archetypal images and signs.

I asked the light, 'What is going on here? Please, Light, clarify yourself for me. I really want to know the reality of the situation.'

85

I cannot really say the exact words because it was sort of telepathy. The light responded. The information transferred to me was that your beliefs shape the kind of feedback you are getting before the light. If you were a Buddhist or Catholic or Fundamentalist, you get a feedback loop of your own stuff. You have a chance to look at it and examine it, but most people do not.

As the light revealed itself to me, I became aware that what I was really seeing was our Higher Self matrix. The only thing I can tell you is that it turned into a matrix, a mandala of human souls, and what I saw was that what we call our Higher Self in each of us is a matrix. It's also a conduit to the Source; each one of us comes directly, as a direct experience from the Source. We all have a Higher Self or an Oversoul part of our being. It revealed itself to me in its truest energy form. The only way I can really describe it is that the being of the Higher Self is more like a conduit. It did not look like that, but it is a direct connection to the Source that each and every one of us has. We are directly connected to the Source.

To my surprise, the entire experience halted at that point. You are indeed in control of your near-death experience. You are not on a roller coaster ride. So my request was honored, and I had some conversations with the light. The light kept changing into different figures, like Jesus, Buddha, Krishna, Mandalas, archetypal images and signs.

I asked the light, 'What is going on here? Please, Light, clarify yourself for me. I really want to know the reality of the situation.'

I cannot really say the exact words because it was sort of telepathy. The light responded. The information transferred to me was that your beliefs shape the kind of feedback you are getting before the light. If you were a Buddhist or Catholic or Fundamentalist, you get a feedback loop of your own stuff. You have a chance to look at it and examine it, but most people do not.

As the light revealed itself to me, I became aware that what I was really seeing was our Higher Self matrix. The only thing I can tell you is that it turned into a matrix, a mandala of human souls, and what I saw was that what we call our Higher Self in each of us is a matrix. It's also a conduit to the Source; each one of us comes directly, as a direct experience from the Source. We all have a Higher Self or an Oversoul part of our being. It revealed itself to me in its truest energy form. The only way I can really describe it is that the being of the Higher Self is more like a conduit. It did not look like that, but it is a direct connection to the Source that each and every one of us has. We are directly connected to the Source.

So, the light was showing me the Higher Self matrix. And it became very clear to me that all the Higher Selves are connected as One Being, all humans are connected as one being, we are actually the same being, different aspects of the same being. It was not committed to one particular religion. So that is what was being fed back to me. And I saw this mandala of human souls. It was the most beautiful thing I have ever seen. I just went into it and, it was just overwhelming. It was like all the love you've ever wanted, and it was the kind of love that cures, heals, regenerates.

As I asked the light to keep explaining, I understood what the Higher Self matrix is. We have a grid around the planet where all the Higher Selves are connected. This is like a great company, a next subtle level of energy around us, the spirit level, you might say.

Then, after a couple of minutes, I asked for more clarification. I really wanted to know what the universe is about, and I was ready to go at that time.

I said, 'I am ready. Take me.'

Then the light turned into the most beautiful thing that I have ever seen: a mandala of human souls on this planet.

Now I came to this with my negative view of what has happened on the planet. So, as I asked the light to keep clarifying for me, I saw in this magnificent mandala how beautiful we all are in our Essence, our core. We are the most beautiful creations. The human soul, the human matrix that we all make together is absolutely fantastic, elegant, exotic, everything. I just cannot say enough about how it changed my opinion of human beings in that instant.

I said, 'Oh, God, I did not know how beautiful we are.'

At any level, high or low, in whatever shape you are in, you are the most beautiful creation, you are.

I was astonished to find that there was no evil in any soul.

I said, 'How can this be?'

The answer was that no soul was inherently evil. The terrible things that happened to people might make them do evil things, but their souls were not evil. What all people seek, what sustains them, is love, the light told me. What distorts people is a lack of love.

The revelations coming from the light seemed to go on and on, then I asked the light, 'Does this mean that humankind will be saved?'

Then, like a trumpet blast with a shower of spiraling lights, the Great Light spoke, saying, 'Remember this and never forget; you save, redeem and heal yourself. You always have. You always will. You were created with the power to do so from before the beginning of the world.'

87

*In that instant, I realized even more. I realized that **WE HAVE ALREADY BEEN SAVED**, and we saved ourselves because we were designed to self-correct like the rest of God's universe. This is what the second coming is about.*

I thanked the light of God with all my heart. The best thing I could come up with was these simple words of total appreciation:

'Oh, dear God, dear Universe, dear Great Self, I love my life.'

The light seemed to breathe me in even more deeply. It was as if the light was completely absorbing me. The love light is, to this day, indescribable. I entered into another realm, more profound than the last, and became aware of something more, much more. It was an enormous stream of light, vast and full, deep in the heart of life. I asked what this was.

*The light responded, 'This is the **RIVER OF LIFE**. Drink of this manna water to your heart's content.'*

So I did. I took one big drink and then another. To drink of Life Itself! I was in ecstasy.

Then the light said, 'You have a desire.'

The light knew all about me, everything past, present and future.

'Yes!' I whispered.

I asked to see the rest of the universe; beyond our solar system, beyond all human illusion. The light then told me that I could go with the Stream. I did and was carried through the light at the end of the tunnel. I felt and heard a series of very soft sonic booms. What a rush!

*Suddenly I seemed to be rocketing away from the planet on this stream of life. I saw the Earth fly away. The solar system, in all its splendour, whizzed by and disappeared. At faster than light speed, I flew through the centre of the galaxy, absorbing more knowledge as I went. I learned that this galaxy, and all of the universe, is bursting with many different varieties of **LIFE**. I saw many worlds. The good news is that we are not alone in this universe!*

As I rode this stream of consciousness through the centre of the galaxy, the stream was expanding in awesome fractal waves of energy. The superclusters of galaxies with all their ancient wisdom flew by. At first, I thought I was going somewhere; actually travelling. But then I realized that, as the stream was expanding, my own consciousness was also expanding to take in everything in the universe! All creation passed by me. It was an unimaginable wonder! I truly was a wonder child; a babe in Wonderland!

It seemed as if all the creations in the universe soared by me and vanished in a speck of light. Almost immediately, a second light appeared. It came from all sides, and was so different; a light made up of more than every frequency in the universe.

I felt and heard several velvety sonic booms again. My consciousness, or being, was expanding to interface with the entire holographic universe and more.

As I passed into the second light, the awareness came to me that I had just transcended the truth. Those are the best words I have for it, but I will try to explain. As I passed into the second light, I expanded beyond the first light. I found myself in a profound stillness, beyond all silence. I could see or perceive **FOREVER**, *beyond infinity. I was in the void. I was in pre-creation, before the Big Bang. I had crossed over the beginning of time—the first word—the first vibration. I was in the eye of creation. I felt as if I was touching the Face of God. It was not a religious feeling. Simply I was at one with absolute life and consciousness.*

When I say that I could see or perceive forever, I mean that I could experience all of creation generating itself. It was without beginning and without end. That's a mind-expanding thought, isn't it? Scientists perceive the Big Bang as a single event which created the universe. I saw that the Big Bang is only one of an infinite number of Big Bangs creating universes endlessly and simultaneously. The only images that even come close in human terms would be those created by supercomputers using fractal geometry equations.

The ancients knew of this. They said Godhead periodically created new universes by breathing out, and de-creating other universes by breathing in. These epochs were called yugas. Modern science called this the Big Bang. I was in absolute, pure consciousness. I could see or perceive all the Big Bangs or yugas creating and de-creating themselves. Instantly I entered into them all simultaneously. I saw that each and every little piece of creation has the power to create. It is very difficult to try to explain this. I am still speechless about this.

It took me years after I returned to assimilate any words at all for the void experience. I can tell you this now; the void is less than nothing, yet more than everything that is! The void is absolute zero; chaos forming all possibilities. It is absolute consciousness; much more than even universal intelligence.

Where is the void? I know. The void is inside and outside everything. You, right now even while you live, are always inside and outside the void simultaneously. You don't have to go anywhere or die to get there. The void is the vacuum or nothingness between all physical manifestations—the **SPACE** *between atoms and their components. Modern science has begun to study this space between everything. They call it zero-point. Whenever they try to measure it, their* *instruments go off the scale, or to infinity, so to speak. They have no way, as of yet, to measure infinity accurately. There is more of the zero space in your own body and the universe than anything else!*

What mystics call the void is not a void. It is so full of energy, a different kind of energy that has created everything that we are. Everything since the Big Bang is vibration, from the first word, which is the first vibration.

The Biblical 'I am' really has a question mark after it.

'I am? What am I?'

So creation is God exploring God's Self through every way imaginable, in an ongoing, infinite exploration through every one of us. Through every piece of hair on your head, through every leaf on every tree, through every atom, God is exploring God's Self, the great 'I am.' I began to see that everything that is, is the Self, literally, your Self, my Self. Everything is the Great Self. That is why God knows even when a leaf falls. That is possible because wherever you are is the center of the Universe. Wherever any atom is, that is the center of the universe. There is God in that, and God in the void.

As I was exploring the void and all the yugas or creations, I was completely out of time and space as we know it. In this expanded state, I discovered that creation is about absolute pure consciousness, or God, coming into the experience of life as we know it. The void itself is devoid of experience. It is pre-life, before the first vibration. Godhead is about more than life and death. Therefore there is even more than life and death to experience in the universe!

I was in the void, and I was aware of everything that had ever been created. It was like I was looking out of God's eyes. I had become God. Suddenly I wasn't me anymore. The only thing I can say, I was looking out of God's eyes. And suddenly I knew why every atom was, and I could see everything.

The interesting point was that I went into the void. I came back with this understanding that God is not there. God is here. That's what it is all about. So this constant search of the human race to go out and find God . . . God gave everything to us, everything is here—this is where it's at. And what we are into now is God's exploration of God through us. People are so busy trying to become God that they ought to realize that we are already God, and God is becoming us. That's what it is really about.

When I realized this, I was finished with the void and wanted to return to this creation or yuga. It just seemed like the natural thing to do.

Then I suddenly came back through the second light, or the Big Bang, hearing several more velvet booms. I rode the stream of consciousness back through all

90

of creation, and what a ride it was! The superclusters of galaxies came through me with even more insights. I passed through the centre of our galaxy, which is a black hole. Black holes are the great processors or recyclers of the universe. Do you know what is on the other side of a black hole? We are our galaxy; which has been reprocessed from another universe.

In its total energy configuration, the galaxy looked like a fantastic city of lights. All energy this side of the Big Bang is light. Every sub atom, atom, star, planet, even consciousness itself is made of light and has a frequency and/or particle. Light is living stuff. Everything is made of light, even stones. So everything is alive. Everything is made from the light of God; everything is very intelligent. "

The Light of Love

"I began my return to the life cycle, it never crossed my mind, nor was I told, that I would return to the same body. It just did not matter. I had complete trust in the light and the life process. As the stream merged with the great light, I asked never to forget the revelations and the feelings of what I had learned on the other side.

There was a 'Yes.' It felt like a kiss to my soul.

Then I was taken back through the light into the vibratory realm again. The whole process reversed, with even more information being given to me. I came back home, and I was given lessons on the mechanics of reincarnation. I was given answers to all those little questions I had.

'How does this work? How does that work?' I knew that I would be reincarnated.

The Earth is a great processor of energy, and individual consciousness evolves out of that into each one of us. I thought of myself as a human for the first time, and I was happy to be that. From what I have seen, I would be happy to be an atom in this universe. An atom. To be the human part of God. . . this is the most fantastic blessing. It is a blessing beyond our wildest estimation of what blessing can be. For each and every one of us to be the human part of this experience is awesome, and magnificent. Each and every one of us, no matter where we are, screwed up or not, is a blessing to the planet, right where we are.

So I went through the reincarnation process, expecting to be a baby somewhere. But I was given a lesson on how individual identity and consciousness evolve. So I reincarnated back into this body.

I was so surprised when I opened my eyes. I do not know why, because I understood it, but it was still such a surprise to be back in this body, back in my room with someone looking over me crying her eyes out. It was my hospice caretaker. She had given up an hour and a half after finding me dead. She was sure I was dead; all the signs of death were there—I was getting stiff. We do not know how long I was dead, but we do know that it was an hour and a half since I was found. She honoured my wish to have my newly dead body left alone for a few hours as much as she could. She had an amplified stethoscope and many ways of checking out the vital functions of the body to see what was happening. She can verify that I really was dead.

It was not a near-death experience. I experienced death itself for at least an hour and a half. She found me dead and checked the stethoscope, blood pressure and heart rate monitor for an hour and a half. Then I awakened and saw the light outside. I tried to get up to go to it, but I fell out of bed. She heard a loud clunk, ran in and found me on the floor.

When I recovered, I was very surprised and yet very awed about what had happened to me. At first, all the memory of the trip that I have now was not there. I kept slipping out of this world and kept asking, 'Am I alive?' This world seemed more like a dream than that one.

Within three days, I was feeling normal again, clearer, yet different than I had ever felt in my life. My memory of the journey came back later. I could see nothing wrong with any human being I had ever seen. Before that, I was really judgmental. I thought a lot of people were really screwed up, in fact I thought that everybody was screwed up but me. But I got clear on all that.

About three months later a friend said I should get tested, so I went and got the scans and so forth. I really felt good, so I was afraid of getting bad news.

I remember the doctor at the clinic looking at the before and after scans, saying, 'Well, there is nothing here now.'

I said, 'Really, it must be a miracle?'

He said, 'No, these things happen; they are called spontaneous remission.'

He acted very unimpressed. But here was a miracle, and I was impressed, even if no one else was.

The Lessons He Learned

"The mystery of life has very little to do with intelligence. The universe is not an intellectual process at all. The intellect is helpful; it is brilliant, but right now, that is all we process with, instead of our hearts and the wiser part of ourselves.

The center of the Earth is this great transmuter of energy, just as you see in pictures of our Earth's magnetic field. That's our cycle, pulling reincarnated souls back in and through it again. A sign that you are reaching human level is that you are beginning to evolve an individual consciousness. The animals have a group soul, and they reincarnate in group souls. A deer is pretty much going to

92

be a deer forever, but just being born a human, whether deformed or genius, shows that you are on the path to developing an individual consciousness. That is in itself part of the group consciousness called humanity.

I saw that races are personality clusters. Nations like France, Germany and China each have their own personality. Cities have personalities, their local group souls that attract certain people. Families have group souls. Individual identity is evolving like branches of a fractal; the group soul explores within our individuality. The different questions that each of us has, have been very, very important. This is how Godhead is exploring God's Self—through you. So ask your questions, do your searching. You will find your Self, and you will find God in that Self, because it is only the Self.

More than that, I began to see that each one of us humans are soul mates. We are part of the same soul 'fractaling' out in many creative directions, but still the same. Now I look at every human being that I ever see, and I see a soul mate, my soul mate, the one I have always been looking for. Beyond that, the greatest soul mate that you will ever have is yourself. We are each both male and female. We experience this in the womb, and we experience this in reincarnation states. If you are looking for that ultimate soul mate outside of yourself, you may never find it; it is not there. Just as God is not there. God is here. Don't look 'out there' for God. Look here for God. Look through your Self. Start having the greatest love affair you ever had . . . with your Self. You will love everything out of that.

I had a descent into what you might call hell, and it was very surprising. I did not see Satan or evil. My descent into hell was a descent into each person's customized human misery, ignorance, and darkness of not-knowing. It seemed like a miserable eternity. But each of the millions of souls around me had a little star of light always available. But no one seemed to pay attention to it. They were so consumed with their own grief, trauma and misery. But, after what seemed an eternity, I started calling out to that light, like a child calling to a parent for help. Then the light opened up and formed a tunnel that came right to me an insulated me from all that fear and pain. That is what hell really is.

So what we are doing is learning to hold hands, to come together. The doors of hell are open now. We are going to link up, hold hands, and walk out of hell together.

The light came to me and turned into a huge golden angel. I said, 'Are you the angel of death'

It expressed to me that it was my Oversoul, my Higher Self matrix, a super-ancient part of ourselves. Then I was taken to the light.

93

Soon our science will quantify spirit. Isn't that going to be wonderful? We are coming up with devices now that are sensitive to subtle energy or spirit energy. Physicists use these atomic colliders to smash atoms to see what they are made of. They have got it down to quarks and charm, and all that. Well, one day they are going to come down to the little thing that holds it all together, and they are going to have to call that . . . God. With atomic colliders, they do not only see what is in here, but they are creating particles. Thank God most of them are short-lived milliseconds and nanoseconds. We are just beginning to understand that we are creating too, as we go along.

As I saw forever, I came to a realm in which there is a point where we pass all knowledge and begin creating the next fractal, the next level. We have that power to create as we explore. And that is God expanding itself through us.

Since my return I have experienced the light spontaneously, and I have learned how to get to that space almost any time in my meditation. Each one of you can do this. You do not have to die to do this. It is within your equipment; you are wired for it already.

The body is the most magnificent light being there is. The body is a universe of incredible light. Spirit is not pushing us to dissolve this body. That is not what is happening. Stop trying to become God; God is becoming you. Here.

The mind is like a child running around the universe, demanding this and thinking it created the world. But I ask the mind:

'What did your mother have to do with this?'

That is the next level of spiritual awareness. Oh! My mother! All of a sudden you give up the ego, because you are not the only soul in the universe.

One of my questions to the light was, 'What is heaven?'

I was given a tour of all the heavens that have been created: the Nirvanas, the Happy Hunting Grounds, all of them. I went through them. These are thought form creations that we have created. We don't really go to heaven; we are reprocessed. But whatever we created, we leave a part of ourselves there. It is real, but it is not all of the soul.

I saw the Christian heaven. We expect it to be a beautiful place, and you stand in front of the throne, worshipping forever. I tried it. It is boring! This is all we are going to do? It is childlike. I do not mean to offend anyone. Some heavens are very interesting, and some are very boring. I found the ancient ones to be more interesting, like the Native American ones, the Happy Hunting Grounds. Egyptians have fantastic ones. It goes on and on. There are so many of them. In each of them, there is a fractal that is your particular interpretation unless you are part of the group soul that believes in only the God of a particular religion. Then you are very close, in the same ballpark together. But even then, each is a little bit different. That is a part of yourself that you leave there. Death is about life, not about heaven.

I asked God, 'What is the best religion on the planet? Which one is right?'

And Godhead said, with great love, 'I don't care.'

That was incredible grace. What that meant was that we are the caring beings here.

The Ultimate Godhead of all the stars tells us, 'It does not matter what religion you are.'

They come and they go, they change. Buddhism has not been here forever, Catholicism has not been here forever, and they are all about to become more enlightened. More light is coming into all systems now. There is going to be a reformation in spirituality that is going to be just as dramatic as the Protestant Reformation. There will be lots of people fighting about it, one religion against the next, believing that only they are right.

Everyone thinks they own God, the religions and philosophies, especially the religions because they form big organizations around their philosophy. When Godhead said, 'I don't care,' I immediately understood that it is for us to care about. It is important because we are caring beings. It matters to us, and that is where it is important. What you have is the energy equation in spirituality. Ultimate Godhead does not care if you are Protestant, Buddhist, or whatever. It is all a blooming facet of the whole. I wish that all religions would realize it and let each other be. It is not the end of each religion, but we are talking about the same God. Live and let live. Each has a different view. And it all adds up to the Big Picture; it is all-important.

I went over to the other side with a lot of fears about toxic waste, nuclear missiles, the population explosion, the rainforest. I came back loving every single problem. I love nuclear waste. I love the mushroom cloud; this is the holiest mandala that we have manifested to date, as an archetype. It, more than any religion or philosophy on Earth, brought us together all of a sudden, to a new level of consciousness. Knowing that maybe we can blow up the planet fifty times, or 500 times, we finally realize that maybe we are all here together now. For a period, they had to keep setting off more bombs to get it into us. Then we started saying, 'We do not need this anymore.'

Now we are actually in a safer world than we have ever been in, and it is going to get safer. So I came back loving toxic waste because it brought us together.

These things are so big. As <u>Peter Russell</u> might say, these problems are now 'soul size.' Do we have soul size answers? **YES!**

The clearing of the rain forest will slow down, and in fifty years there will be more trees on the planet than in a long time. If you are into ecology, go for it; you are that part of the system that is becoming aware. Go for it with all your might, but do not be depressed. It is part of a larger thing.

Earth is in the process of domesticating itself. It is never again going to be as wild a place as it once was. There will be great wild places, reserves where nature thrives. Gardening and reserves will be the thing in the future. Population increase is getting very close to the optimal range of energy to cause a shift in consciousness. That shift in consciousness will change politics, money, energy.

What happens when we dream? We are multi-dimensional beings. We can access that through lucid dreaming. In fact, this universe is God's dream. One of the things that I saw is that we humans are a speck on a planet that is a speck in a galaxy that is a speck. Those are giant systems out there, and we are in sort of an average system. But human beings are already legendary throughout the cosmos of consciousness. The little bitty human being of Earth/Gaia is legendary. One of the things that we are legendary for is dreaming. We are legendary dreamers. The whole cosmos has been looking for the meaning of life, the meaning of it all. And it was the little dreamer who came up with the best answer ever. We dreamed it up. So dreams are important.

After dying and coming back, I really respect life and death. In our DNA experiments, we may have opened the door to a great secret. Soon we will be able to live as long as we want to live in this body. After living for 150 years or so, there will be an intuitive soul sense that you will want to change channels. Living forever in one body is not as creative as reincarnation, as transferring energy in this fantastic vortex of energy that we are in. We are actually going to see the wisdom of life and death and enjoy it.

As it is now, we have already been alive forever. This body that you are in, has been alive forever. It comes from an unending stream of life, going back to the Big Bang and beyond. This body gives life to the next life, in dense and subtle energy. This body has been alive forever already."

Mellen passed over himself on March 31[st,] 2017. Thank you Mellen, you left us all a great legacy with all you experienced and shared with the world.

96

Back to Broken Bodies

People who have a NDE invariably come crashing back into *broken* bodies and have much to overcome, both physically and mentally. Barbara was certainly no exception. She came home weighing in at only 83 pounds and having to wear a full body cast that weighed 30 pounds. She had little help, had just undergone a wonderful life-changing event; however, no-one understood or wanted to. In her words, *"I spent the six months in the body cast thinking about my NDE but trying not to tell anyone."* Her revealing experience re-shaped her life, one in which she has gone on to assist a multitude of people who needed her newly acquired wisdom and knowledge in many diverse arenas.

She is a Thanatologist (thanatology is the study of death and dying), popular speaker, workshop presenter, a NDEer, and therapist in private practice in Atlanta, Georgia. She has been on the board of Directors for the Kundalini Research Network and was on the faculty of Rutgers University's Institute on Alcohol and Drug Studies for 12 years.

Barbara spent six years researching the after-effects of her NDE at the University of Connecticut Medical School. She was a member of the executive board of the Kundalini Research Network and has sat on the executive board of the International Association for Near-Death Studies. She is a consulting editor and contributor for the Journal of Near-Death Studies.

Barbara has been a guest on several major television talk shows including Larry King Live, The Today Show, Unsolved Mysteries, Good Morning America, Oprah, and CNN.

Barbara's life review enabled her to not only view her own life revealing the reasons behind her actions and the repercussions thereof but also those of her mother's, Grandmother's and father's and explained why they were like they were. This has enabled her to offer healing counsel and therapies for abuse and addiction cases, especially those who were children when it occurred. Her contact details are at the end of this NDE.

10. BARBARA HARRIS WHITFIELD'S NEAR-DEATH EXTRACT

Healing: Barbara's Story

"My work with dying people probably would have never come about if I hadn't died myself. I know that sounds strange. How many of us die and get to come back

and talk about it? Not many -- we may think -- but that's not true. In 1984, a Gallup poll reported that one in every nineteen Americans has had an NDE. And these first numbers include only adults. Since that time, we have acquired data on childhood NDEs, and they are almost as prevalent as adult experiences.

I want to share my own NDE with you, most importantly, to tell you about what we call the life review. Our research shows that only in about 20 per cent of NDEs is there a life review. Since my NDE over twenty years ago, I have focused my heart and my life on the knowledge I received from the life review.

Some NDErs report seeing their life review as if they are watching the pages in a book. Others describe it as a film. My life review appeared as a cloud filled with thousands of bubbles. In each bubble, there was a scene from my life. I had the feeling I could bob from bubble to bubble, but overall it had the feeling of a linear sequence in which I relived all thirty-two years of my life.

During a life review, many of us experience not only our own feelings but the feelings of everyone else -- as though all other people participating in our lifetimes are joined. We can feel, then, how everything we've ever done or said affected others. The sense is that we don't end at our skin. It is an illusion that we are separate. This deep review of our life shows us that at a higher level of consciousness, we are all connected.

This new perspective totally changes our values and attitudes about the way we want to live. Materialism decreases and altruistic values become greater in most NDErs' lives. Almost all of us talk about a sense of mission. If we were spiritual before, the shift in values and attitude is not as apparent as it is in someone like me. I had become an atheist when I numbed out at an early age. Subsequently, my changes have been obvious and profound."

A Need for Surgery

"I was born with a deformity -- a curvature in my lumbar spine called scoliosis. It never bothered me until 1973 when it suddenly became the focus of my life. The pain emanating from my lower back became overwhelming, and the drugs I was given to control it numbed everything out. I was hospitalized four times in the next two years, each time for two weeks and with traction and injections of Demerol to help alleviate the pain. Looking back on it now, like many other NDErs I believe that my life had gotten off track and my back pain was a metaphor for my life.

In 1975, at the age of thirty-two, I was admitted for the fifth time to the hospital. I underwent surgery -- a spinal fusion. I awoke after the five-and-a-half-hour operation in a Stryker-frame circle bed. This strange bed looks like a Ferris wheel for one person. There are two big chrome hoops with a stretcher suspended in the middle. Three times a day, the nurses would place three or four pillows over me and then another stretcher on top of them. They would strap these two stretchers together with me in the middle, like a human sandwich, and turn the bed on. It would rotate me up, and then it would slowly move me around onto my belly. The pillows made it more tolerable because I was very thin. I had lost more than thirty pounds over the two years of pain and using Valium as a muscle relaxant. The surgery on my spine prevented me from any movement at all. I couldn't move. The bed moved me. The reason for using this bed, and for rotating me forward and face down, was to drain my lungs and allow the skin on my back to breathe so I wouldn't develop bedsores. I remained in this bed for almost a month, and then I was placed in a full-body cast from my armpits to my knees.

About two days after surgery, complications set in and I started to die. I remember waking up in the circle bed and seeing this huge belly. I had swelled up. The swelling was pulling my incisions open and it hurt. I called for my nurse, and then I started screaming.

People in white came rushing in. It was a dramatic scene like you see on television. I had no idea what was going on because I hadn't become a respiratory therapist yet. It seemed like everybody was pushing carts and machinery, throwing things back and forth over me. They hooked me up to all kinds of machinery, tubes, monitors and bags."

Barbara Whitfield's First NDE

"Everything that was going on was loud and overwhelming. I lost consciousness.

I awoke in the hall in the middle of the night. The lights were dim. It was quiet. I looked up and down the hall and didn't see anyone. I remember thinking that if they caught me out of the circle bed, I'd be in trouble, because I wasn't supposed to move. So I turned around to go back into my room and found myself looking directly into a public-address speaker. This isn't possible, I thought. I remembered seeing the speaker when I was admitted. It was mounted on the ceiling at least three or four feet above my head. I moved into my room and looked down into the circle bed and saw -- me. I heard myself chuckle because she looked funny with white tape around her nose holding in a tube.

I was out of pain. I felt calm -- incredibly peaceful -- in a way I had never felt before. So I hung out with her for a while, but I knew that wasn't me.

Next, I was in total blackness. I don't know how I got there. I was floating in darkness with a gentle sense of movement. I knew I was moving away from this life. I had left this life behind.

Then I felt hands come around me and pull me into lush warmth. I realized it was my grandmother. I used to call her Bubbie. She was pulling me close to her in a wonderful embrace. She had been dead for fourteen years, and I never had before thought of her existing beyond her death. But I knew I was with her.

I suddenly realized that what I had believed in the past might not be real. Maybe my belief systems were really messed up. Maybe this was real and everything else had been an illusion. As I was thinking about how off base my beliefs had been, and as I realized that my grandmother holding me was real, I felt like I released a load of toxic pain [1]. And as I experienced that release, there was a sudden replay of every scene my grandmother and I had shared during our nineteen years together in this life. It wasn't just my memories of her -- it was also her memories of me. And our memories became one. I could feel and see and sense exactly what she was feeling, seeing and sensing. And I knew she was getting the same thing from my memories. It was both of us together, replaying everything that we meant to each other. It was wonderful.

I can still replay each memory today, and they are as vivid as when they happened twenty-three years ago in my NDE. One of my favorite scenes is when we were cooking together. I was three or four years old. We were alone in her kitchen, but the whole family was going to come for dinner, so there was expectancy in the air. My Bubbie pulled over a heavy wooden chair from her kitchen table to the stove and picked me up and put me on it. She stood behind and very close to me to help and protect me. One at a time, she would put a little bit of mixture in my hand, and I would form it into a ball and drop it into this huge pot of boiling water. The pot was almost as tall as I was on the chair. The pungent smell of fish saturated the already humid air. I would put my hands to my nose and yell Yuk! And she would laugh. After we finished, she pulled the chair with me on it into the middle of the kitchen. I screamed and laughed because it felt like she was taking me on a ride. She wiped my hands with a wet cloth, but I smelled them and yelled Yuk! Again. I watched her take a lemon and cut it in half. She rubbed a lemon half on my hands and then wiped them with her already stained and wet apron. Then she looked at me with such love in her eyes and said, don't move. Bubbie will be right back. She came back with her hairbrush and brushed my hair for what seemed like a very long time. It felt so good. Then she made me long curls, twisting each lock of my hair around her fingers. When she was finished, and she lifted me down to the floor, I ran into her bedroom and looked in the mirror. I looked just like Shirley Temple.

When the whole family sat down for dinner that evening, she told everyone I had made the fish. My aunts looked at me, very impressed. And as they tasted it, they nodded their heads in approval and told my mother what a good cook I was.

After our memories ended, I stayed with my grandmother for a while. I loved her so much. Then I started moving away. I had no control over what was happening, but it felt all right that I was moving away from her. I understood that she would

100

be waiting for me to return and that this place she was in was eternal. So was I. My life had been a brief moment in eternity, and I had no concerns or doubts that as this bigger eternal reality unfolded, it was perfect. Besides, the one I had just endured for thirty-two years was so painful and constrictive. This new reality felt like it would continually expand and flow.

At that time, I wouldn't have called where I was a tunnel, but later, as a researcher, I realized that tunnel is the closest word we have on this plane. Whatever it was that I was moving through started off totally black. Then I became aware that there was energy churning through the blackness. As I watched the energy move, shades of grey to almost white separated from the churning. Out of the darkness, Light was coming, and the Light was moving way ahead of me. The Light and I were moving in the same direction, but it was far, far ahead.

My hands were expanding. They felt like they were becoming infinitely large. A gentle breeze was wrapping around my body, and I could hear a low droning noise that beckoned me. This unusual sound was taking me to the Light.

Suddenly I was back in my body, back in the circle bed, and it was morning. Two nurses were opening my drapes. The sunlight was startling. It hurt my eyes. I asked them to close the drapes. I tried to tell my nurses and then several doctors that I had left the bed. They told me that it was impossible and that I had been hallucinating."

Barbara Whitfield's Life Review

"About a week later, I again left my body in the circle bed. I had been taken off the critical list, but I was still debilitated and sick. I had been rotated forward onto my face. I was uncomfortable. I seemed to have been left in that position for too long. I reached for the call button, but it had slipped away from where it was clipped on the bedsheet. I started to call, then yell, then scream frantically, but my door was closed. No one came. I wet the bed. I became hysterical. I separated from my body.

As I left my body, I again went out into the darkness. Only this time I was awake and could see it happening. Looking down and off to the right, I saw myself in a bubble -- in the circle bed -- crying. Then I looked up and to the left, and I saw my one-year-old self in another bubble -- face down in my crib -- crying just as hard. I looked to the right and saw myself again in the circle bed, then to the left and saw myself as a baby -- back and forth about three more times; then I let go. I decided I didn't want to be the thirty-two-year-old Barbara anymore; I'd go to the baby. As I moved away from my thirty-two-year-old body in the circle bed, I felt as though I released myself from this lifetime. As I did, I became aware of an energy that was wrapping itself around me and going through me, permeating me, holding up every molecule of my being.

101

It was not an old man with a long white beard. It took me a long time to use the word, God. In fact, I never used any word until I saw the movie Star Wars and heard about The Force. By then, I was already reading quantum physics, trying to figure out how I could explain what had permeated me and was me . . . and you . . . and all of us. Now it was here, and it was holding me. It felt incredible. There are no words in English, or maybe in this reality, to explain the kind of love God emanates. God was totally accepting of everything we reviewed in my life. In every scene of my life review, I could feel again what I had felt at various times in my life. And I could feel everything everyone else felt as a consequence of my actions. Some of it felt good, and some of it felt awful. All of this translated into knowledge, and I learned -- oh, how I learned! The information was flowing at an incredible breakneck speed that probably would have burned me up if it weren't for the extraordinary energy holding me. The information came in, and then love neutralized my judgments against myself. In other words, as we relived my life, God never judged me. God held me and kept me together. I received all information about every scene -- my perceptions and feelings -- and anyone else's perceptions and feelings which were in the scene. No matter how I judged myself in each interaction, being held by God was the bigger interaction. God interjected love into everything, every feeling, every bit of information about absolutely everything that went on so that everything was all right. There was no good and no bad. There was only my loved ones from this life trying to be, or just trying to survive and me.

I realize now that without this God force holding me, I wouldn't have had the strength to experience what I am explaining to you.

I -- we at this point, for we are one, a very sacred one -- God and I were merging into one sacred person. We went to the baby I was seeing to my upper left in the darkness. Picture the baby being in a bubble and that bubble in the centre of a cloud of thousands and thousands of bubbles. In each bubble was another scene in my life. As we moved toward the baby, it was as though we were bobbing through the bubbles. At the same time, there was a linear sequence in which we relived thirty-two years of my life. I could hear myself saying, No wonder, no wonder. I now believe my no wonders meant. No wonder you are the way you are now. Look what was done to you when you were a little girl.

My mother had been dependent on drugs, angry, and abusive, and my father wasn't there much of the time and did little to intervene. I saw all this childhood trauma again, in my life review, but I didn't see it in little bits and pieces, the way I had remembered it as an adult. I saw and experienced it just as I had lived it at the time it first happened. Not only was I me, but I was also my mother. And my dad. And my brother. We were all one. Just as I had felt everything my grandmother had felt, I now felt my mother's pain and neglect from her childhood. She wasn't trying to be mean. She didn't know how to be loving or kind. She didn't

102

know how to love. She didn't understand what life is really all about. And she was still angry from her own childhood, angry because they were poor and because her father had grand mal seizures almost every day until he died when she was eleven. And then she was angry because he left her.

Everything came flooding back, including my father's helplessness at stopping the insanity. If my father was home when my mother exploded into one of her rages, he would close all the windows so the neighbors wouldn't hear, and then he would go outside and visit with them. Again I witnessed my brother's rage at my mother's abuse, and then his turning around and giving it to me. I saw how we were all connected in this dance that started with my mother. I saw how her physical body expressed her emotional pain. I watched as I grew up and left my parents' house when I was eighteen. By that point, I had watched my mother undergo twenty-six operations, twenty-five of which were elective. I saw myself as a child praying for a doctor who could help my mother. One part of her body or another was always in pain. She had two spinal fusions on her neck, two or three on her lumbar spine. Both knees, both elbows and one wrist were operated on.

As my life review continued, I again experienced my mother starving herself because she was told she had gotten chubby. Then she had to have several surgeries for intestinal problems and constipation, and during those stays in the hospital, they would tube feed her because she was so thin. She even had her toes shortened. They called it hammertoe surgery. The real reason was that she had a huge collection of high-heeled shoes that were size four and one-half. (She always insisted on wearing spike heels even with her bad back.) Her feet were growing (as all of ours do as we get older), but she wanted them to remain a size four and one-half. I watched myself with her in a bubble as her orthopedic surgeon said, Florence, you have two choices. Get shoes a half size bigger or shorten your toes! He was laughing, but she chose the surgery. She was in plaster casts for six weeks, taking even more painkillers and sleeping pills.

I also saw her go through psychiatric hospitalizations. During one of these, around 1955, I couldn't visit her for three weeks. I was about eleven and was sure I had done something wrong. In one bubble, I could see myself finally being allowed to visit her. I looked big for my age and my five-foot-two-inch frame towered over her four-foot-eleven one. She weighed about eighty-eight pounds. I was chunky. She lived on black coffee, sedatives, painkillers and tranquillizers. I loved to eat.

In the bubble, I was pleading with her to cooperate with the doctors so she could come home. She said, Oh, honey. This is like a job. I don't need to be in here, but Daddy has three (health insurance) policies, so I make us money when I'm here. Blue Cross pays all the medical expenses, and we get to keep the rest from the other two policies. I could now feel her saying that and she meant it. She believed

103

it. I continued watching and realized that nothing could have helped my mother because she had no real understanding of why she was there. I could hear myself saying, No wonder, no wonder. And then the benevolent energy that was holding me would hold me tighter and with even more love.

We continued watching my mother in pain, always seeing doctors and always receiving prescription pain killers, sleeping pills and tranquillizers. My only feelings during this time were ones of loneliness. I felt so alone when she was in the hospital. Then I watched her abuse me when she was home. I could now feel that she abused me because she hated herself. I saw myself down on my knees by the side of my bed, praying for a doctor to help my mother. What I didn't realize as a child, but was understanding in the life review, was that she didn't want anyone to help her. She thought her job in life was to have doctors and be a patient. And she enjoyed being taken care of in the hospital.

I saw how I had given up myself in order to survive. I forgot that I was a child. I became my mother's mother. I suddenly knew that my mother had had the same thing happen to her in her childhood. She took care of her father during his seizures, and as a child, she gave herself up to take care of him. As children, she and I both became anything and everything others needed. As my life review continued, I also saw my mother's soul, how painful her life was, how lost she was. And I saw my father, and how he put blinders on himself to avoid his grief over my mother's pain and to survive. In my life review, I saw they were good people caught in helplessness. I saw their beauty, their humanity and their needs that had gone unattended to in their own childhoods. I loved them and understood them. We may have been trapped, but we were still souls connected in our dance of life by an energy source that had created us.

This is when I first realized that we don't end at our skin. We are all in this big churning mass of consciousness. We are each a part of this consciousness we call God. And we're not just human. We are Spirit. We were Spirit before we came into this lifetime. We are all struggling Spirits now, trying to get being a human right. And when we leave here, we will be pure Spirit again.

As my life review continued, I got married and had my own children and saw that I was on the edge of repeating the cycle of abuse and trauma that I had experienced as a child. I was on prescription drugs. I was in the hospital. I was becoming like my mother. And at the same time, this energy holding me let me into its experience of all this. I felt God's memories of these scenes through God's eyes just as I had through my grandmother's eyes. I could sense God's divine intelligence, and it was astonishing. God loves us and wants us to learn and wake up to our real selves -- to what is important. I realized that God wants us to know that we only experience real pain if we die without living first. And the way to live is to give love to ourselves and to others. We are here to learn never to withhold our love. But only when we heal enough to be real can we understand and give love the way love was meant to be.

As my life unfolded before my eyes, I witnessed how severely I had treated myself because that was the behaviour shown and taught to me as a child. I realized that the only big mistake I had made in my life of thirty-two years was that I had never learned to love myself.

And then I was back, but not in my body. I was behind the nurse's station. I saw a metal circle with pillows tossing behind glass. They were the pillows I had urinated on when I separated from my body. I was watching them in a dryer.

I heard two nurses talking about my case and about how my day nurse was so upset after she found me that they had sent her home early. Then they were saying that I was going to be in a body cast for six months, even though they had told me six weeks because my doctors thought that I couldn't handle knowing. So they were not going to tell me the truth.

Then I was back in my body, back in the circle bed. The same two nurses came in to check on me, and I said to them, I left the bed again.

'No, honey. You're hallucinating,' they said.

I was not on painkillers at this point, so I insisted, No, I'm not hallucinating. I left the bed.

No, you're hallucinating. You can't leave the bed, they said.

Please call my day nurse and tell her I'm okay, I responded. Tell her I'm not angry with her. I know she was sent home early. And don't lie to me by telling me I'm going to be in a body cast for six weeks. Tell me the truth. I know I'm going to be in a body cast for six months. And you should have washed those pillows before you put them in the dryer. I don't care for myself, but I care for the next patient."

Following My Heart

"A month after I came home from the hospital, my parents came over to visit me. They had taken care of my children for the month I was in the circle bed, so I understood why they couldn't visit me in the hospital. However, I couldn't understand why they weren't coming to my house. I spent every day in bed. I weighed eighty-three pounds, and the body cast weighed thirty pounds. I wondered when they were coming so I could tell them about my experience. Finally, they came, and I blurted out how much I loved them and that everything that had happened to us was all right. I think I even told them that I forgave them.

They looked at me like I was really strange and quickly left. After that, I insisted on seeing a psychiatrist, hoping he would understand what I had experienced. The doctor I saw didn't understand. No one understood NDEs back then, so I realized that I couldn't talk about it. I spent the six months in the body cast, thinking about my NDE but not trying to tell anyone. Once I was out of the cast and went through some physical therapy to regain my strength, I decided to put the NDE away and follow my heart.

First, I volunteered to work in the emergency room of the hospital, where I had been a patient. I had many opportunities there to be with and touch dying people. I felt real when I worked there. And everyone else was real, too. In a setting where life and death are on the edge every moment, only truth is spoken. My personal life, however, was at the opposite end of the spectrum. My husband, my friends and most family members were caught up in their own games. No one seemed to be communicating honestly. There was so much denial of feelings. I can't deny that I too had been a part of it - part of the materialism and part of the numbness. But now, I was different. It wasn't their fault. I had changed. The only place I felt real besides the hospital was on a college campus.

I became a respiratory therapist working in the emergency room and the ICU, and my patients were telling me about their experiences as they were dying. And the ones who returned to their bodies told me about their NDEs. I started writing about all this, in those days calling my topic the emotional needs of critical-care patients. Surprisingly, I was being invited to speak at professional conferences and being published in respiratory therapy journals. The emotional needs of patients was a new and hot topic in healthcare in the late 1970s and early 1980s.

Finally, I became a researcher and could look for the answers I so longed to find. Because my research was conducted at a university medical school, all kinds of new knowledge were available to me. I could frame and reframe not only the hundreds of experiences I was studying but also my own personal one. The story of my NDE is in this book, so we can have a foundation for the way I participated in and describe the other stories you are about to read."

Processing My Life Review

"The NDE is never over if we invite it to continue to affect us. It can continue to grow in our lives if we nurture it. It continues to interpret for us what we are doing here, what life may be all about.

Before my NDE and life review, I knew I had been abused physically and emotionally by my mother and neglected by both parents. I remembered most everything. The problem was that those memories of abuse did not arouse any emotional reactions in me. In order to deal with the emotional and physical pain, I had numbed myself not only as a child going through pain but also as an adult remembering it. I protected myself with my own emotional Novocain, so I couldn't feel anything that had happened in my childhood. Unfortunately, the numbness

106

continued in my adult life. Once I experienced my life review, I could remove the Novocain from my past and re-glue the pieces of my life together. I could begin to learn about all the new feelings that were coming up.

Psychiatry calls emotional Novocain psychic numbing. It is a common approach used by children to get through painful times. Once we grow up, we have the choice of staying numb or remembering and working through all those buried but painful numbed-out memories. In my life review, I also saw the beginnings of abuse in the way I was reacting to my children. For me, it wasn't just a choice of numbness or healing. I needed to break the chain of abuse. I needed to save my children from what I had been through."

Starting to Wake Up

"I learned in my life review that the only thing that is real is love, and the only way to share love is by being real. Being real happens when we acknowledge our feelings and continually share our truth. When we feel our feelings and are real, we share our truth out of love. Then our relationship with God and our self is healthy.

My parents and the rest of my family and friends certainly weren't the exception to the rule when it came to not understanding my new attitude. I facilitated support groups for the International Association of Near-Death Studies (IANDS) for twelve years, and the biggest problem NDErs talk about is that no one understands us. We experience a profound change in our values and attitudes and need to talk about it in a support group. It is as though we had lived our lives in black and white and were suddenly shown colors. We no longer fear death. And this is just the first of many paradoxes: Because we don't fear death, we don't fear living. We love life in a whole new way. We are more willing to take risks to help others. We work with the dying because we get as much as we give by helping.

Our research also shows that a history of childhood trauma, abuse and neglect is more frequent among NDErs than among the control group. Many people I have interviewed who have had an NDE came from an abusive childhood steeped in addiction. We all have the same story. We talk about how every time our parents started drinking or taking pills . . . they were gone. Even if their bodies were still there, they were gone. And so we grew up numb. Because our parents had numbed out, so did we. But our NDEs brought us back. They reminded us of who we are. And to maintain our real selves, we have to learn to feel our feelings, share our truth and give our love. I wrote in detail about the childhood abuse factor in my last book, Spiritual Awakenings. Childhood abuse or trauma has always been of interest to me because of my own history, and because I hear about it so often in support groups or when I give talks. Now it has been demonstrated statistically in the research.

I also wrote in Spiritual Awakenings that we should not blame anyone, but instead, we should break the chains of abuse. When we die -- if we re-experience our lives from everyone else's perspective as well as our own -- there is only information and feelings, perceptions and knowledge. We really can't judge or blame others because we suddenly understand from where we and everyone else is coming. We only judge here in this earthly reality. Over there, with God, I was just learning about this. The knowledge of what had happened was pouring into me, and I was saying my no wonders! Over and over again. I came to believe that God doesn't judge but wants us to learn, so we won't make the same mistakes again. My experiences showed me that God wants us to extend love, not fear. If I can understand my childhood, and I can name, express and let go of the emotions I have held in since I was a little girl, I won't repeat my past. My parents repeated their pasts because they didn't know any better. Before my NDE and my life review, the old way of conflict and numbness controlled me. Suddenly, I was catapulted out of time and embraced by a whole different way. Just as fast, I was back here wanting to forge new ground. I have had a great opportunity, and now I want to share it. But I don't blame, and I certainly don't want to judge anyone, including my parents.

And now, almost twenty-three years later, my parents have died -- my dad in late 1992 and my mom in early 1994. My life review had set the scene for the way I helped my father die and the way I observed my mother die. In fact, my life review, what I learned in it and, even more importantly, what I experienced in it -- that a divine energy connects all of us -- have since orchestrated all my relationships. With each person I have attended in the dying process, I have also witnessed this spiritual energy. I have given talks for hundreds of hospice workers, and almost everyone agrees that this energy is present. Hospice workers often tell me their stories of God's loving energy being present during a client's death.

In all of the stories in this book, I feel connected to this energy through my heart. The prayer within my heart is constant and is the background music orchestrating my experiences. When we are connected to God's loving energy, it is the most powerful force in the universe."

Excerpt taken from the book title, *Final Passage* Chapter One. All content copyright 2003, 2004 Barbara Harris Whitfield. All rights reserved. Used by permission.[28]

---

[28] Barbara Harris Whitfield is the author of many published articles and five books, The Power of Humility (HCI), Full Circle: The Near Death Experience and Beyond (Pocket Books), Spiritual Awakenings: Insights of the NDE and Other Doorways to Our Soul (Health Communications, Inc.), and Final Passage: Sharing the Journey as This Life Ends (Health Communications, Inc.).

The following table is taken from her book, Victim to Survivor and Thriver.[29]

Victim	Survivor	Thriver
Depression	Movement of feelings	Aliveness
Doesn't deserve to enjoy life	Struggling to heal	Gratitude for everything in life
Low self-esteem/shame/unworthy	Sees self as wounded and healing	Sees self as overflowing miracle
Hyper-vigilant	Learning to relax	Experiences peace
Confusion and numbness	Learning to grieve, grieving past, ungrieved traumas	Grieving current hurts, losses and traumas
Hopeless	Hopeful	Trust real self and life
Hides personal story	Tells their story to safe people	Transforms story to Hero's Journey
Feels Defective	Compassion for others and eventually self	Open heart for self and others
Own needs come last	Learning healthy needs	Placed self-first
Allows repeated dramas	Sees drama patterns	Creates peace
Believes suffering is the human condition	Feels some relief	Finds peace and joy
Always serious, can't laugh	Beginning to laugh	Experiences healthy humor
Inappropriate humor, teasing	Feels appropriate painful feelings	Uses healthy humor
Numb or angry around toxic people	Increased awareness of pain and dynamics	Healthy boundaries with all people
Lives in the past	Aware of patterns	Lives in Now
Angry at religion	Understanding the difference between religion & spirituality	Enjoys personal relationship with Higher Power

Barbara's site, www.barbara-whitfield.com, which she shares with her husband, best-selling author Dr Charles L. Whitfield, provides timely and helpful information on recovery from abuse, trauma, and addiction. Her site is a member of the communities of several web-rings dealing with recovery issues, abuse, trauma, PTSD, depressive illness and moving forward into a whole life.

You can contact Barbara directly via email at bw11@me.com. Extract taken from www.near-death.com by Kevin Williams with kind permission by Barbara.

[29] From Whitfield B 2011 Victim to Survivor and Thriver Muse House Press, Atlanta GA and Whitfield C, Whitfield B 2019 Dragon Energy: Myth and Reality Muse House Press Atlanta GA. Both available at Amazon.Com

Barbara's thought-provoking realizations after her insightful NDE have and shall continue to help so many people.

11. BEVERLEY BRODSKY'S NEAR-DEATH EXTRACT

In the following NDE Beverley Brodsky was struck by a drunken driver and fell off the back of a motorcycle, suffering a fractured skull and numerous broken bones in her head. She was taken to UCLA hospital where she was in and out of a coma for two weeks. Miraculously she was able to hold the feeling of sublime delight she experienced and was oblivious to any pain for two months after she returned home. She was even sent home from the hospital without any pain medication.

Beverly Brodsky was raised in a conservative Jewish family in a mostly Jewish neighborhood in Philadelphia. She went through her teens as an atheist. Since learning of the Holocaust at age eight, she had turned angrily against any early belief in God. How could God exist and permit such a thing to occur? In July 1970, her questions were answered when a motorcycle accident led to her near-death experience. Kenneth Ring describes Beverly Brodsky's NDE as *"possibly the most moving in my entire collection."* Evelyn Valarino and Kenneth Ring kindly share Beverley's testimony from their book, *Lessons From The Light*.

"Somehow, an unexpected peace descended upon me.

I found myself floating on the ceiling over the bed, looking down at my unconscious body.

I barely had time to realize the glorious strangeness of the situation—that I was me but not in my body—when I was joined by a radiant being bathed in a shimmering white glow. Like myself, this being flew but had no wings. I felt a reverent awe when I turned to him; this was no ordinary angel or spirit, but he had been sent to deliver me.

Such love and gentleness emanated from his being that I felt that I was in the presence of the Messiah. Whoever he was, his presence deepened my serenity and awakened a feeling of joy as I recognized my companion. Gently, he took my hand, and we flew right through the window. I felt no surprise at my ability to do this. In this wondrous presence, everything was as it should be.

Beneath us lay the beautiful Pacific Ocean . . . But my attention was now directed upward, where there was a large opening leading to a circular path. Although it seemed to be deep and far to the end, a white light shone through and poured out into the gloom to the other side where the opening beckoned. It was the most brilliant light I had ever seen, although I didn't realize how much of its glory was veiled from the outside. The path was angled upward, obliquely, to the right. Now still hand in hand with the angel, I was led into the opening of the small, dark passageway.

I then remember travelling a long distance upward toward the light. I believe that I was moving very fast, but this entire realm seemed to be outside of time. Finally, I reached my destination. It was only when I emerged from the other end that I realized that I was no longer accompanied by the being who had brought me there. But I wasn't alone. There, before me, was the living presence of the light. Within it, I sensed an all-pervading intelligence, wisdom, compassion, love, and truth.

There was neither form nor sex to this perfect being. It, which I shall in the future call he, in keeping without our commonly accepted syntax, contained everything, as white light contains all the colors of a rainbow when penetrating a prism. And deep within me came an instant and wondrous recognition: I, even I, was facing God.

I immediately lashed out at him with all the questions I had ever wondered about; all the injustices I had seen in the physical world. I don't know if I did this deliberately, but I discovered that God knows all your thoughts immediately and responds telepathically. My mind was naked; in fact, I became pure mind. The ethereal body which I had travelled in through the tunnel seemed to be no more; it was just my personal intelligence confronting that universal mind, which clothed itself in a glorious, living light that was more felt than seen since no eye could absorb its splendor.

I don't recall the exact content of our discussion; in the process of return, the insights that came so clearly and fully in heaven were not brought back with me to earth. I'm sure that I asked the question that had been plaguing me since childhood about the sufferings of my people. I do remember this: there was a reason for everything that happened, no matter how awful it appeared in the physical realm. And within myself, as I was given the answer, my own awakening mind now responded in the same manner: 'of course,' I would think, 'I already know that. How could I ever have forgotten!'

Indeed, it appears that all that happens is for a purpose, and that purpose is already known to our eternal self.

In time the questions ceased because I suddenly was filled with all the being's wisdom. I was given more than just the answers to my questions; all knowledge unfolded to me, like the instant blossoming of an infinite number of flowers all at

111

once. I was filled with god's knowledge, and in that precious aspect of his beingness, I was one with him. But my journey of discovery was just beginning.

Now I was treated to an extraordinary voyage through the universe. Instantly we travelled to the centre of stars being born, supernovas exploding, and many other glorious celestial events for which I have no name. The impression I have now of this trip is that it felt like the universe is all one grand object woven from the same fabric. Space and time are illusions that hold us to our physical realm; out there all are present simultaneously. I was a passenger on a divine spaceship in which the creator showed me the fullness and beauty of all of his creation.

The last thing that I saw before all external vision ended was a glorious fire—the core and centre of a marvelous star. Perhaps this was a symbol for the blessing that was now to come to me. Everything faded except for a richly full void in which that and I encompassed all that is. Here, I experienced, in ineffable magnificence, communion with the light being. Now I was filled with not just all knowledge, but also with all love. It was as if the light were poured in and through me. I was god's object of adoration, and from his/our love, I drew life and joy beyond imagining. My being was transformed; my delusions, sins, and guilt were forgiven and purged without asking; and now I was love, primal being, and bliss. And, in some sense, remain there, for eternity. Such a union cannot be broken. It always was, is, and shall be.

Suddenly, not knowing how or why I returned to my broken body. But miraculously, I brought back the love and the joy. I was filled with an ecstasy beyond my wildest dreams. Here, in my body, the pain had all been removed. I was still enthralled by a boundless delight. For the next two months, I remained in this state, oblivious to any pain.

I felt now as if I had been made anew. I saw wondrous meanings everywhere; everything was alive and full of energy and intelligence.

Although it's been 50 years since my heavenly voyage, I have never forgotten it. Nor have I, in the face of ridicule and disbelief, ever doubted its reality. Nothing that intense and life-changing could possibly have been a dream or hallucination. To the contrary, I consider the rest of my life to be a passing fantasy, a brief dream that will end when I again awaken in the permanent presence of that giver of life and BLISS."

12. DANNION BRINKLEY'S NEAR-DEATH EXTRACT

Dannion's story is certainly unique and inspiring. Prior to his near-death experience, he was a Vietnam government paid assassin. By his own admission, he wasn't a *very nice guy*.

What happened in his NDE? He saw and felt the repercussions of all his actions and all the people his actions affected, not a pleasant experience. Naturally, due to what he experienced during his NDE he returned a completely different man with a whole new outlook on life. A wonderful example of why we, as humans, should not judge our fellow man as we never know what that person has chosen or why. His Father/Mother God and Dannion, were able to mold precious gold from cold steel as he played back Dannion's life to him in honesty and free of judgment.

In 1975 Dannion's heart stopped and he died. Thousands of volts of electricity had coursed through his head and body when lightning hit the telephone line he was talking on. In Dannion's words *"he was burnt from the inside out."* However, while his horrendously burnt inert body was being transported to the hospital, and then to the morgue, Dannion was very much alive experiencing a life-changing and extremely illuminating, near-death experience.

The following is an extract from his wonderful book *Saved By The Light* by Dannion Brinkley and Paul Perry.

"And that was it. The next sound I heard was like a freight train coming into my ear at the speed of light. Jolts of electricity coursed through my body, and every cell of my being felt as if it were bathed in battery acid. The nails of my shoes were welded to the nails in the floor so that when I was thrown into the air, my feet were pulled out of them. I saw the ceiling in front of my face, and for a moment I couldn't imagine what power it was that could cause such searing pain and hold me in its grip, dangling over my own bed. What must have been a split second seemed like an hour.... From immense pain I found myself engulfed by peace and tranquility. It was a feeling I had never known before and have not had since. It was like bathing in a glorious calmness.... I had no idea what had happened, but even in this moment of peacefulness, I wanted to know where I was.

I began to look around, to roll over in mid-air. Below me was my own body, thrown across the bed. My shoes were smoking, and the telephone was melted in my hand. I could see Sandy run into the room. She stood over the bed and looked at me with a dazed expression, the kind you might find on the parent of a child found floating facedown in a swimming pool

I must be dead, I thought. I could feel nothing because I was not in my body. I was a spectator of my final moments on earth, as dispassionate about watching my own death as I might be if I were watching actors re-enact it on television. I felt sorry for Sandy and could feel her fear and pain, but I was not concerned about that person lying on the bed.

Tommy showed up in less than ten minutes. He knew something was wrong because he had heard the explosion over the telephone .... I watched as Tommy held me and cursed the slowness of the ambulance, which we could hear approaching in the distance. I hovered above the three of them—Sandy, Tommy, and myself—as the medical technicians loaded me onto the stretcher and wheeled me to the ambulance.

From where I hovered, about fifteen feet above everyone, I could see the pouring rain hitting my face and drenching the backs of the ambulance crew . . . .

The perspective I had was that of a television camera. Without passion or pain, I watched as the person on the stretcher began to twitch and jump . . . . All of a sudden it hit me: That man on the stretcher was me! I watched as the technician pulled a sheet over my face and sat back . . . . I am dead! I thought. I was not in my body and can honestly say that I didn't want to be. If I had any thought at all, it was simply that who I was had nothing to do with that body they had just covered with a sheet . . . .

I looked toward the front of the ambulance to a spot over my dead body. A tunnel was forming, opening like the eye of a hurricane and coming toward me . . . . I actually didn't move at all; the tunnel came to me.

There was the sound of chimes as the tunnel spiraled toward and then around me. Soon there was nothing to be seen—no crying Sandy, no ambulance attendants trying to jump-start my dead body, no desperate chatter with the hospital over the radio—only a tunnel that engulfed me completely and the intensely beautiful sound of seven chimes ringing in rhythmic succession.

I looked ahead into the darkness. There was a light up there, and I began to move toward it as quickly as possible. I was moving without legs at a high rate of speed. Ahead the light became brighter and brighter until it overtook the darkness and left me standing in a paradise of brilliant light. This was the brightest light I had ever seen, but in spite of that, it didn't hurt my eyes in the least. Unlike the pain, one might feel when walking into the sunlight from a dark room, this light was soothing to my eyes.

I looked to my right and could see a silver form appearing like a silhouette through a mist. As it approached, I began to feel a deep sense of love that encompassed all of the meanings of the word. It was as though I were seeing a lover, mother, and best friend multiplied a thousandfold. As the Being of Light came closer, these feelings of love intensified until they became almost too pleasurable to withstand . . . .

The Being of Light stood directly in front of me. As I gazed into its essence I could see prisms of colour, as though it were composed of thousands of tiny diamonds, each emitting the colours of the rainbow . . . .

I felt comfortable in his presence, a familiarity that made me believe he had felt every feeling I had ever had, from the time I took my first breath to the instant I was sizzled by lightning. Looking at this being, I had the feeling that no one could love me better, no one could have more empathy, sympathy, encouragement, and non-judgmental compassion for me than this Being.

The Being of Light engulfed me, and as it did, I began to experience my whole life, feeling and seeing everything that had ever happened to me. It was as though a dam had burst and every memory stored in my brain flowed out . . . . This life review was not pleasant. From the moment it began until it ended, I was faced with the sickening reality that I had been an unpleasant person, someone who was self-centered and mean . . . .

. . . I was hit by a rush of emotions and information. I felt the stark horror that all of those people felt as they realized their lives were being snuffed out. I experienced the pain their families felt when they discovered they had lost loved ones in such a tragic way. In many cases, I even felt the loss their absence would make to future generations . . . . .

Now, in the life review, I was forced to see the death and destruction that had taken place in the world as a result of my actions. 'We are all a link in the great chain of humanity,' said The Being. 'What you do has an effect on the other links in that chain.'

When I finished the life review, I arrived at a point of reflection in which I was able to look back on what I had just witnessed and come to a conclusion. I was ashamed. I realized I had led a very selfish life, rarely reaching out to help anyone. Almost never had I smiled as an act of brotherly love or just handed somebody a dollar because he was down and needed a boost. No, my life had been for me and me alone. I hadn't given a damn about my fellow humans.

I looked at the Being of Light and felt a deep sense of sorrow and shame. I expected a rebuke, some kind of cosmic shaking of my soul. I had reviewed my life and what I had seen was a truly worthless person. What did I deserve if not a rebuke?

As I gazed at the Being of Light, I felt as though he was touching me. From that contact, I felt a love and joy that could only be compared to the nonjudgmental compassion that a grandfather has for a grandchild.

'Who you are is the difference that God makes,' said the Being. 'And that difference is love.' There were no actual words spoken, but this thought was communicated to me through some form of telepathy . . . . Again I was allowed a period of reflection. How much love had I given people? How much love had I taken from them? From the review I had just had, I could see that for every good

event in my life, there were twenty bad ones to weigh against it. If guilt were fat, I would have weighed five hundred pounds.

As the Being of Light moved away, I felt the burden of this guilt being removed. I had felt the pain and anguish of reflection, but from that, I had gained the knowledge that I could use to correct my life. I could hear the Being's message in my head, again as if through telepathy: 'Humans are powerful spiritual beings meant to create good on the earth. This good isn't usually accomplished in bold actions but in singular acts of kindness between people. It's the little things that count because they are more spontaneous and show who you truly are.'

I was elated. I now knew the simple secret to improving humanity. The amount of love and good feelings you have at the end of your life is equal to the love and good feelings you put out during your life. It was just that simple.

'My life will be better now that I have the secret,' I said to the Being of Light.

It was then that I realized that I wouldn't be going back. I had no more life to live. I had been struck by lightning. I was dead . . . .

What happens now that I'm dead? I wondered. Where am I going? I stared at the beautiful Being of Light who shimmered before me. He was like a bagful of diamonds emitting a soothing light of love. Any fear I might have had at the notion of being dead was quelled by the love that poured from the Being before me. His forgiveness was remarkable.

Like wingless birds, we swept into a city of cathedrals. These cathedrals were made entirely of a crystalline substance that glowed with a light that shone powerfully from within . . . . I was awestruck. This place had a power that seemed to pulsate through the air. I knew that I was in a place of learning. I wasn't there to witness my life or to see what value it had had, I was there to be instructed . . . .

In the next moment, the space behind the podium was filled with Beings of Light. They faced the benches where I was sitting and radiated a glow that was both kindly and wise.

I sat back on the bench and waited. What happened next was the most amazing part of my spiritual journey.

I was able to count the beings as they stood behind the podium. There were thirteen of them, standing shoulder to shoulder and stretched across the stage. I was aware of other things about them, too, probably through some form of telepathy. Each one of them represented a different emotional and psychological characteristic that all humans have. For example, one of these beings was intense and passionate, while another was artistic and emotional. One was bold and energetic, yet another possessive and loyal. In human terms, it was as though each one represented a different sign of the Zodiac. In spiritual terms, these beings went far beyond the signs of the zodiac. They emanated these emotions in such a way that I could feel them.

Now more than ever, I knew that this was a place of learning. I would be steeped in knowledge, taught in a way that I had never been taught before. There would be no books and no memorization. In the presence of these Beings of Light, I would become knowledge and know everything that was important to know. I could ask any question and know the answer. It was like being a drop of water bathed in the knowledge of the ocean, or a beam of light knowing what all light knows.

The Beings came at me one at a time. As each one approached, a box the size of a videotape came from its chest and zoomed right at my face. The first time this happened I flinched, thinking I was going to be hit. But a moment before impact, the box opened to reveal what appeared to be a tiny television picture of a world event that was yet to happen. As I watched, I felt myself drawn right into the picture, where I was able to live the event. This happened twelve times, and twelve times I stood in the midst of many events that would shake the world in the future.

At the time, I didn't know these were future events. All I knew was that I was seeing things of great significance and that they were coming to me as clearly as the nightly news, with one great difference: I was being pulled into the screen . . . .

Much later, when I returned to life, I wrote down 117 events that I witnessed in the boxes. For three years, nothing happened. Then in 1978, events that I had seen in the boxes began to come true. In the eighteen years since I died and went to this place, ninety-five of these events have taken place."[30]

This short extract from the same book shows the depth of Dannion's courage and determination and what he went through during his paralysis.

"It was time to begin my own rehabilitation. I had decided to make my body work again, one muscle at a time. My brother brought a copy of Gray's Anatomy to the hospital. This book describes the workings of the human body, with detailed written explanations and a line drawing of each body part. My brother made me a headdress out of a coat hanger and a pencil so I could turn the pages with the eraser on the pencil by moving my head.

I started looking at every muscle in my hand, examining the picture in the book while I focused on the muscles and tried to move them one at a time. Hour after hour, I stared at Gray's Anatomy and then at my hand, talking to it, cursing at it, making it move. When the left hand worked, I did the same thing with the right

---

[30] Brinkley and Perry, Saved By The Light. (Piatkus Books Ltd, London. 2006), pp. 4-11, 18-21, 24, 26-31.

hand, and so on down my entire body. The greatest moments came when I was able to move a muscle, even as little as an eighth of an inch. When that happened, I knew my body was going to work again.

Still, no one else thought I was going to make it. The nurses had looks of despair when they came in to see me. I heard doctors in the hallway say that my heart was too far gone and that I was going to die. Even my family had its doubts. They saw me for breathe and struggling to move, and they thought it would be only a short time before I was dead. 'Oh Dannion, you look very good today,' my folks would say, but the look on their faces was one of utter horror, as if they were examining a cat squashed in their driveway.

Regardless of my condition, the experience gave me the inner strength to endure. In my worst moments, all I had to do was recall the love that I felt emanating from those heavenly lights, and I could press on.”[31]

Once again, we see that it was the remembrance of that divine, all-encompassing love that gave Dannion the will to live and the determination to heal himself. Today Dannion is alive and well—against all odds. He was struck twice by lightning and overcame paralysis, heart failure, open-heart surgery, ruptured subdural hematomas, brain surgery, and a massive grand mal seizure. Since then he has had two more near-death experiences, making a total of 4 NDE's that he has overcome. He is an International Speaker and Educator of life after death.

Dannion's fight to regain physical normality was monumental. Since his four NDE's Dannion has spent the last 30 years in service to humanity. He has written three bestselling books, *“Saved By The Light,” “At Peace In The Light' and “The Secrets Of The Light”* which have also been made into a television motion picture that has been seen in 30 countries.

Dannion is also the Co-Founder and Chairman of The Twilight Brigade/Compassion In Action[32], a trained corps of over 5,600 volunteers who visit patients in Veteran's Hospitals, Nursing Homes, Hospitals and Hospice facilities in the USA. The volunteers provide:

- Reassurance and human companionship to the dying.
- Relief and support to loved ones and caregivers.
- Compassionate 24-hour attention through the last hours, allowing people to die in peace and with dignity.

---

[31] Brinkley and Perry, Saved By The Light. (Piatkus Books Ld, London. 2006), pp. 56-58.
[32] For further information on this wonderful organization go to www.thetwilightbrigade.com

- No cost for services to either the patient or the family.
- Educate individuals about death and issues surrounding the dying process, dispelling common fears and myths.
- Raise awareness about volunteer service and the joy of serving.
- Inspire others to become more involved within their communities.
- Enhance healthcare professionals' skills in caring for dying patient.

In 2000, *The Twilight Brigade/Compassion In Action* was recognized by the United Nations as an outstanding volunteer organization. Amongst many other accolades, Dannion has been credited with initiating the insertion of more than one million dollars in the 2004 Defense Appropriations Bill, to further the study of Complementary and Alternative End-Of-Live care for Veterans.

Dannion's contribution to raising humanity's awareness of eternal life is amazing. He is dedicated to removing the fear of 'death' and dying by providing thousands of terminally ill people that precious peace of mind and knowledge of a forgiving God of love that awaits them with open arms.

13. REV. JULIET NIGHTINGALE'S NEAR-DEATH EXTRACT

In this NDE Rev Juliet Nightingale describes in detail what it means to enter into the twilight stage where one is able to see into both dimensions simultaneously. This is a common occurrence among those who suffer a longer terminal illness and might help explain the process and that what those people are experiencing is very real to them but may seem improbable to those around them.

Rev. Juliet Nightingale—a lifelong mystic and Seer from England—has been through a number of near-death experiences resulting from life-threatening illnesses she has had since childhood. One of them occurred in the mid-1970s while battling colon cancer which caused her to lapse into a coma. These experiences have had a profound and lasting effect on her life. Initially, she rarely spoke about them because, when she did, she felt grossly judged and misunderstood

Rev Nightingale continues.

"Herein, I will attempt to explain and recapture my experiences on the Other Side and how it affected me. I will humbly attempt to grasp the proper words for describing this loftiest experience that had a profound impact on me . . . and has changed my life forever."

The Experience

"In the mid-'70s, I was dealing with a terminal disease, colon cancer, where my life was ebbing away. I was bedridden for the most part but could sometimes manage to sit up for short periods. Being the contemplative that I was, I was always listening and observing—taking things in and trying to understand the deeper wisdom behind what was happening to me and where all of this was leading. As a result, I became more withdrawn and detached . . . as I observed everything round me starting to change. Solid matter became more translucent and fluid-like, colours became more vivid and vibrant, sound was more clear and acute . . . and so on. I could no longer comprehend anything printed on a page, because it no longer meant anything to me in my changed state of consciousness. It was like trying to read and understand a foreign language! I had already departed from the third-dimensional realm for the most part . . . and my awareness enveloped other things.

I was entering into what I later came to refer to as the 'twilight' stage. In this state, everything was altered. I got to a point where my consciousness was already making the transition from one realm to the other—being more aware of other realities on other dimensions. I was seeing and perceiving things and other beings inter-dimensionally—even though I was still somewhat conscious on the physical plane. I've since realized that this is what a lot of dying people go through . . . (such as those in hospitals, nursing homes or others in hospice care), while an observer might think that they're hallucinating or seeing someone or something that 'isn't really there.' In truth, this is a state where one, such as myself, is experiencing other dimensions simultaneously while still on the physical plane, because, in reality, we are multidimensional beings.

I finally lapsed into a coma on Boxing Day, 26 December, and, ironically, declared 'dead' on my birthday, 2 February! (Now I've got two natal charts!) As others observed that I was in a coma—which lasted over five weeks—I was having a completely different experience! One would look at my body and think that I was unconscious . . . asleep . . . with no awareness of what was going on . . . or anything. Yet, I was very conscious and profoundly aware, because, in truth, we never really sleep; only our bodies do. We are always aware . . . and active . . . on one level of consciousness or another. Just the fact that we dream while asleep is an indication of our consciousness always being active. And, indeed, our bodies need to rest, so that we can tap into . . . and experience other aspects of our consciousness and being!

The best way I can describe the transition from being 'alive' on the physical plane and the passage to the Other Side is like passing from one room to another. You do not cease to be or lose consciousness; your consciousness simply shifts from one vantage point to another. The experience changes; your outlook changes;

your feelings change. And the feelings I experienced were profound; for me, it most certainly became that peace that surpasses all understanding . . .

My transition was gradual as a result of having a terminal disease—as opposed to a sudden one incurred from accidents, heart attacks, etc. I became aware of a 'Being of Light' enveloping me. Everything was stunningly beautiful—so vibrant and luminous . . . and so full of life—yes, life!—in ways that one would never see or experience on the physical plane. I was totally and completely enveloped in divine Love. It was unconditional love . . . in the truest sense of the word. I was in constant communion with this Light and always aware of its loving Presence with me at all times. Consequently, there was no sense of fear whatsoever . . . and I was never alone. This was a special opportunity to experience being at One with the ALL—never separate . . . and never at a loss.

The colors were so beautiful—watching the Light whirl all round me, pulsating and dancing . . . making whooshing sounds . . . and being ever so playful at times . . . then very serious at other times. Many things would take on a luminous glow—a sort of soft peach color. Everything was so vibrant—even when I saw deep space! I was constantly in a state of awe . . . There were always beautiful beings round me as well—helping me . . . guiding me, . . . reassuring me . . . and also pouring love into me.

One of the first things I remember experiencing was the Life Review, which included everything that I'd experienced in my physical incarnation up to that point. It was like being at the cinema watching a movie of my life and everything happening simultaneously.

I think most NDE'rs will agree that the Life Review is one of the most difficult aspects of the NDE. Viewing your entire life before you—with every thought, word, action, etc.—can be most unsettling, indeed. Yet, what happened was the fact that no one passed judgment on me! I only felt the constant enveloping of divine love from the Being of Light that was always with me. What I came to realize, then, is that we judge ourselves! There was no 'he-god' sitting on some throne, passing judgment on me, (not that I even expected to see such a being in the first place). I never subscribed to such religious myths anyway. I seemed to be the only one who was uncomfortable and most critical of myself. Yet, having stated that, I also realized that I wasn't coming from a vantage point of the 'ego self' but, rather, from my Soul Self that was much more detached and having no feelings of being emotionally charged, etc. I was no longer identifying with the personality of the physical self. Therefore, what I felt was very different—coming from a completely different perspective as the Soul Self . . . or my true identity.

Even though I was no longer in my physical body, I did have form—a body of sorts. The best way I can describe this is that I felt like a bubble—floating and moving about effortlessly—sometimes very fast . . . or gently drifting about. I felt

121

hollow inside and so clear, even having a sensation of a breeze blowing inside of me. There was never any sense of hunger, thirst, weariness or pain. Such things never entered my mind, in fact! Alas, I was pure consciousness, embodied in a light and ethereal form, travelling about . . . or being still and observing intently . . . and always in a state of awe. It was such a glorious sensation where I experienced such calm and a profound sense of peace and constant trust. I also experienced no blindness, (as I do with my physical eyes being legally blind), and what a sense of awe and wonder to be able to see!

At one point, I perceived myself as being on a guided tour, as it were, visiting and observing different places, beings and situations—some very pleasant and some very painful. The best way I can describe this 'tour' was like being in a circular enclosure of windows, each pane revealing something different . . . but when I'd focus on one particular pane, I'd suddenly see the pane become full size (much like a 'window' on your computer monitor becoming full screen), and I stood still, just watching . . .

One pane revealed a scene that one might interpret as a 'hell' or 'purgatory' where faceless, grey colored entities moved about aimlessly and moaned. They were clearly suffering and in great agony and anguish. I saw these souls as damaged souls, ones who had committed unspeakable atrocities during their previous incarnations. I have used the analogy of a soul being 'retrograde'— much in the way a planet will have the appearance of going backwards. The prevailing feeling that I had whilst observing these souls was one of deep compassion and a yearning to comfort them. I wanted so much to see them relieved of their horrible suffering. But, alas, as painful as this scene was, I was reassured that these souls were here only temporarily and that they, too, would heal and move back in a forward direction and ultimately return to the Light. All souls, without exception, eventually return to the Light . . . according to what was revealed to me.

The above scene led to another scene where I saw images of people I knew in my present life—obviously those still incarnate on the physical plane, but my viewing them from the Other Side in a scene that would take place in future. (Again, everything experienced on the Other Side is always in the 'Now', even 'past' and 'future'.) These were individuals who'd also committed atrocities in one form or another—individuals who had severely violated me, or people I love. But the scene I beheld was one where they were suffering . . . as a result of what they'd done— that, most likely being the karmic result of their decisions and actions, etc. Again, I felt a deep sense of compassion for them . . . and feeling sad that they had to endure such suffering, yet realizing that it was also unavoidable. Never once did I feel any sense of anger or hostility towards these individuals . . . but only wanting to see them healed . . . so that they, too, would come to know love.

122

Another scene I remember was that of finding myself observing a realm that constituted water. I beheld all its beauty and splendor, and it was teaming with life. Then, before I knew it, I found myself under water and not having to worry about breathing! I was moving about effortlessly and mingling with everything that I'd first observed from without. The same thing happened to me when I moved through space . . . and danced and flowed with all the heavenly bodies and lights. There were lots of times for play and buzzing about with all the light beings, moving all round me like comets. This was an opportunity to experience great joy and feeling so light and completely void of worry or fear. I could move effortlessly . . . and adapt to any environment I happened to be in at any given moment. I would simply think about something and it would instantly manifest . . . or I'd think about a place and there I'd be! Oh, what a sensation to experience such power—to be anywhere I wanted to be and to create anything I wanted to . . . and to feel so totally free!

After experiencing the 'tour,' adventures and times of play and creation, etc., things became more serious . . . and I was again in direct communion with the Being of Light. I was now being asked to 'help' or 'assist' in some way. . . in creating and determining the outcome of certain events, situations or even things affecting others! Me? Just little me. Oh my, I thought. That's a grave and serious responsibility. I felt so honored . . . and so humble . . . being asked to participate in such a feat . . . but what if I failed to do my part as needed, I wondered. Then, I was assured that everything would work out exactly as it should—even if I couldn't complete things as desired. It seemed that the point in all this was the fact that we co-create with the Light . . . and we are also part of the Light. Furthermore, no matter what happens . . . the Light Source will always be in control . . . and be there to see things through . . . despite any shortcomings on our part as souls. How auspicious it is, then, to realize that as souls, we are a part of all creation and take part in the actual creative process thereof!

This very thought of being asked to help—to co-create with the Light—made me feel profoundly special and important in the greater scheme of things, but by no means from an egotistical point of view. As stated above, I felt so deeply humble and a serious sense of responsibility for every thought and action I made. My only thought was that I wanted to do what was right. How important it was that I am very loving and creative . . . and never damaging in any way . . . and that's the gift. I realized at that point, how totally connected with all life . . . through all the Universes . . . I Am. I felt one with the All—never separate, never apart. Still, there was no fear. Still, there was only love. Forever and for always I could never be alone . . . because I would never be alone. It's impossible to be alone, because life is everywhere; love is everywhere . . . and this is what carried me and has stayed with me.

I so cherished this communion with the Light. Everything was communicated telepathically, whether with the Light or other beings, friends, or loved ones. It didn't matter. It was always honest, open and real . . . and it was always done with love. There's no such thing as 'putting on airs' and no need to hide on the Other Side. No one is there to hurt you in any way—not in the least—because there is no sense of lack . . . or the need to 'steal' someone else's power or energy. You are operating as a Soul, not centered in ego or personality. It's nice to realize that you will have whatever you need, because you've got the capacity and power to create it instantly!

As the mood seemed to shift . . . I felt as if there was something serious that was just about to befall me. I was now being told that I was going to have to return to the alien (physical) world I'd left behind—that I was needed there for something very special and significant. I needed to go back to share what had just happened to me . . . and to let others know that life is, indeed, eternal and that death is an illusion. On a personal level, I was told that I needed to experience great love and joy in that world . . . and finally I would be able to return Home. I was, then, assured that I was real . . . and that I could believe in what I'd come to know in this glorious realm—not only about myself . . . but also about all life. I was also told, however, that the world I was returning to was an illusion and that I wasn't to identify with it or be involved—to be in it but not of it—and that I was only passing through . . .

To say that my heart sank would be an understatement. This was the first time that I had the true experience of a broken heart while on the Other Side. The very thought of leaving this sacred realm where I was in constant communion with the Light and other beings . . . crushed me in ways I could never describe. I knew how dark and foreboding that strange, illusory world that I was being asked to return to was . . . and it is, indeed, a world I've never identified with! However, I was, once again, reassured that the Light and other loving beings would be with me at all times . . . and to remember that I'd never be alone. Gratefully, there was still no sense of fear—only sorrow now, but realizing that I had to honor the Divine Will, making this request of me.

As I reluctantly accepted this mission, I suddenly beheld before me, a most beautiful being who appeared in front of me—pouring tremendous love into me and filling me to overflowing. It was as if this was my gift . . . for accepting the painful request to leave my home on the Other Side and return to a world so alien to me. This being loved me very deeply and stayed with me, continuing to radiate love and sound . . . and it was made clear that he'd be with me always.

I started moving back into this world in much the same way that I had left it. It was a very gradual transition. I was, now, more aware of my body laying in hospital intensive care, hooked up to a life-support system, but it was still so separate from me and the vantage point I was experiencing, from the Other Side. It was like being a newborn baby when I finally regained consciousness on this plane. Everything was so strange and new! I had just come from another world— literally—and this world appeared so much darker and void of color by comparison. Everything was drab and appeared flat to me. I didn't feel the life-force I experienced on the Other Side . . . but I was resolved to honor the will of the Light I'd been sent back to fulfil. I had a mission . . . and there was a special promise that was made to me in return.

Even in the hospital, I was aware of the Being of Light still with me . . . and communicating with me. I was also still aware of other beings with me—beings that I came to realize, later, only I could see and hear. Finally, one day, the Being of Light disappeared from view of my mortal awareness . . . and I knew, now, that I was fully back in this world. Again, I was broken-hearted, but still free of all fear . . . and believing and trusting in the promise that I'd never be alone . . . and so it was . . .

This near-death experience (or what I prefer to call an Eternal Life Experience) left me feeling such a profound sense of triumph and awe. Something else I learned, too, is that fear is an acquired state, not a natural one. It is something that you learn. Love is the prevailing force at all times . . . no matter how things may appear in this world of duality and illusion. It's merely a hologram—created by the collective consciousness—for the sake of growth and evolution. Therefore, what occurred on the Other Side, for me, was a special opportunity to experience . . . and know—with total certainty—that everything was evolving exactly the way it should . . . and that the ultimate destiny for every living being is to return to the Source, The Light of . . . Pure Love."

14. ELIZABETH KUBLER ROSS' NEAR-DEATH EXTRACT

Elisabeth Kubler Ross had an *"out of body"* experience that parallels a near-death Experience. In fact, her passion and drive to experience what her hundreds of patients had experienced, probably created it. She too experienced the sublime all-consuming love emanating from the Light and saw everything is vibrating energy in its various forms.

"But it was, and the more I observed my own body lying there, the more amazed I became. Whatever part of my body, I looked at began to vibrate with the same fantastic speed. The vibrations broke everything down to their most basic structure so that when I stared at anything, my eyes feasted on the billions of dancing molecules.

At this point, I realized that I had left my physical body and become energy. Then in front of me, I saw many incredibly beautiful lotus blossoms. These blossoms opened very slowly and became brighter, more colourful and more exquisite, and as time passed, they turned into one breathtaking and enormous lotus blossom. From behind the flower, I noticed a light—brighter than bright and totally ethereal, the same light that all my patients talked about having seen.

I knew that I had to make it through this giant flower and eventually merge with the light. It had a magnetic pull, which drew me closer and gave me the sense that this wonderful light would be the end of a long and difficult journey. Not in any hurry, thanks to my curiosity, I indulged in the peace, beauty and serenity of the vibrating word.

My vision, which extended for miles and miles, caused me to see everything, from a blade of grass to a wooden door, in its natural molecule structure, its vibrations. I observed, with great awe and respect, that everything had a life, a divinity. All the while, I continued to move slowly through the lotus flower, toward the light. Finally, I merged with it, one with warmth and love. A million everlasting orgasms cannot describe the sensation of the love, warmth, and sense of welcome that I experienced. Then I heard two voices.

The first was my own saying, 'I am acceptable to Him.'

The second, which came from somewhere else and was a mystery to me, said, 'Shanti Nilaya.'"[33]

Later after sharing her experience at one of her 'Death and Dying' seminars, a monk clad in orange robes came up to her and told her what Shanti Nilaya meant. It is the Sanskrit way of saying, *the final home of peace.*

Elizabeth Kubler Ross researched life after death for over thirty years as a result of Mrs. Schwartz's NDE below. Mrs. Schwartz explained her experience to Elisabeth's astonished and disbelieving medical students at one of Elizabeth's controversial and innovative *Death and Dying* seminars (This was before books had been published on Near-Death experiences).

15. MRS. SCHWARTZ'S NEAR-DEATH EXTRACT

Mrs. Schwartz was dying, but a part of her did not want to go until after her son *"came of age."* At the point where she clinically died, she found herself floating out of her body towards the ceiling. She watched the resuscitation team frantically attempt to save her life. She noted every word spoken and every event. She felt calm without fear or pain. She could not understand why they weren't listening to her, telling them she was okay.

---

[33] Elisabeth Kubler Ross, The Wheel of Life (Bantam Books, London, UK, 1998) Pg 225

Frustrated, she eventually went down and *"poked one of the residents,"* but to her amazement *"arm went right through his arm."*[34] Her last recollection of being in this state was when they pronounced her dead, covered her, and one of the residents told some jokes.

Many hours later, a nurse came back to remove the body and to her utter amazement found Mrs. Schwartz very much alive. Part two of Mrs. Schwartz's story can be found in the After-Death Communication section.

Defying the Physical

Kenneth Ring was the first President of IANDS twenty—two years ago and is considered an International authority on NDE research. As Bruce Greyson M.D. says, *"If anyone has interviewed more NDErs than Ken-and I don't know that anyone has-then surely no-one has done it with as much depth, open-mindedness, and insight as he."*

In his book *Lessons From The Light,* Kenneth Ring interviews an extraordinary woman who has been blind since birth and who was able to see normally during her NDE. Kenneth Ring continue.

"When we first talked with her, Vicky Umipeg was forty-three years old, married, and the mother of three children. She was born several months premature, weighing only three pounds at birth. In those days, oxygen was often used to stabilize such babies in their incubators, but too much was given to Vicky, resulting in the destruction of her optic nerve. As a result of this miscalculation, she has been completely blind from birth.

Vicky earns her living as a singer and a keyboard musician, though, of late, because of illness and family problems, she has not worked as much as in the past. She has had an enormously difficult life, full of hardship, abuse, and tragic loss, and it is a wonder to me, and I know, to Clark and others who have heard her speak, that she has been able to endure it with such grace and courage."

16. VICKY UMIPEG'S NEAR-DEATH EXTRACT

As I shared previously, Vicky has had two NDE's. One occurred when she was twenty, as a result of an appendicitis attack; the other, and the most vivid of the two, took place when she was involved in a car crash after she had finished performing, at a local night club one evening. She was twenty-two at the time of her second NDE. The following is an interview conducted by Kenneth Ring.

---

[34] Elisabeth Kubler Ross, The Wheel of Life (Bantam Books, London, UK, 1998) Pg 178

"If any one person can claim to be an authority on near-death experiences (NDEs) without having had one, that person must surely be Kenneth Ring." After Raymond Moody sowed the seeds of modern near-death research by coining the term *"NDE"* in his 1975 *Life After Life*, it was Ken who watered and nurtured them till they grew into a self-sustaining phenomenon.

Kenneth Ring continues.

"At one point during her second NDE, she told me, she found herself out of her body at the hospital. I asked her to tell me more about that.

VU: The first thing I was really aware of is that I was up on the ceiling, and I heard this doctor talking-it was a male doctor-and I looked down, and I saw this body, and at first, I wasn't sure that it was my own. But I recognized my hair. (In a later interview, she also told me that another sign that had helped her become certain she was looking down upon herself was the sight of a very distinctive wedding ring she was wearing.)

KR: What did it look like?

VU: It was very long . . . and it went down to my waist. And part of it had had to be shaved off, and I remember being upset about that. (At this point she overhears a doctor saying to a nurse that it is a pity, but because of an injury to Vicky's ear, she could end up deaf as well as blind.) I knew, too, the feelings that they were having. From up there on the ceiling, I could tell they were very concerned, and I could see them working on this body. I could see that my head was cut open. I could see a lot of blood,(though she could not tell its colour-she still has no concept of colour, she says). She tries to communicate to the doctor and nurse but cannot, and feels very frustrated.

KR: After you failed to communicate to them, what's the next thing you remember?

VU: I went up through the roof then. And that was astounding!

KR: What was that like for you?

VU: Whew! It's like the roof didn't . . . it just melted.

KR: Was there a sense of upward motion?

VU: Yes, um-hmm.

KR: Did you find yourself above the roof of the hospital?

VU: Yes.

KR: What were you aware of when you reached that point?

128

VU: Lights, and the streets down below, and everything. I was very confused about that. (This was happening very fast for her, and she found seeing to be disorientating and distracting. At one point, she even says that seeing was 'frightening' to her).

KR: Could you see the roof of the hospital below you?

VU: Yes.

KR: What could you see around you?

VU: I saw lights.

KR: Lights of the city.

VU: Yes.

KR: Were you able to see buildings?

VU: Yeah, I saw other buildings, but that was real quick, too.

In fact, all of these events, once Vicky begins to ascend, happen with vertiginous speed. And as Vicky goes farther into her experience, she begins to feel a tremendous sense of freedom, (a feeling of 'abandon,' she called it), and increasing joy in this freedom from bodily constraint. This does not last long, however, because almost immediately, she is sucked into a tube and propelled toward a light. In this journey toward the light, she now becomes aware of an enchanting harmony of wood-chime-like music. Throughout all of this, of course, she reports being able to see.

Now finding herself in an illuminated field, covered with flowers, she sees two children, long deceased, whom she had befriended when they were all in a school for the blind together. Them they were both profoundly retarded, but in this state, they appear vital, healthy, and without their earthly handicaps. She feels a welcoming love from them and tries to move toward them. She also sees other persons whom she had known in life, but who have since died, (such as her caretakers and her grandmother), and is drawn toward them, too.

But before she can move to make closer contact with them, a radiantly brilliant figure-much brighter than the others, she says-interposes himself and gently blocks her way. This figure Vicky intuitively understands to be Jesus, (and she was able to give a detailed description of his face, especially his eyes, and his clothing). In his presence, she is enabled to have a total review of her life and she sees this review, too, including of course images of her family members and friends and then is told that she must return in order to bear her children. On hearing this, Vicky becomes tremendously excited because she had long cherished the dream of becoming a mother and now has the inner conviction that this will, in fact, be her fate when she returns.

Before leaving this realm of light, though, she is also told by the figure that it will be very important for her to learn 'the lessons of loving and forgiving,' (and, as Vicky has told me, these did indeed prove to be prophetic words and a touchstone for her life following her NDE).

At that point, she found herself back in her body, which she entered almost as if slamming into it, she said, and experienced once more the heavy dullness and intense pain of her physical being.

Even from this brief description, you can appreciate that Vicky, though blind from birth, has had the same kind of classic NDE as do sighted persons. Furthermore, during it, she seems to be able to see both things of this world and the other-worldly domain, just as most NDErs report. In fact, apart from the feelings of visual disorientation Vicky felt at first, (which disappeared as she found herself in the later stages of her NDE), and her inability to discern colors as such, there is nothing in Vicky's account of her NDE that would give an uninformed reader any hint that she is blind. As far as her NDE goes, in her own understanding, she was in fact not blind then.

. . . . If the NDE is like a dream, blind persons like Vicky, should notice at least some general similarity between the two. Wondering about this, I brought up this issue with Vicky toward the end of our interview.

KR: How would you compare your dreams to your NDE?

VU: No similarity, no similarity at all.

KR: Do you have any kind of visual perception in your dreams?

VU: Nothing, No colour, no sight of any sort, no shadows, no light, no nothing.

KR: What kinds of perceptions are you aware of in your typical dreams?

VU: Taste-I have a lot of eating dreams (she laughs). And I have dreams when I'm playing the piano and singing, which I do for a living, anyway. I have dreams in which I touch things . . . I taste things, touch things, hear things, and smell things that's it.

KR: And no visual perceptions?

VU: No.

KR: So that what you experienced during your NDE was quite different from your dreams?

VU: Yeah, there's no visual impression at all in any dream I have.

KR: Is it correct to say, then, that you don't think your NDE was dream-like in nature?

VU: No, it was not at all dream-like in nature. It was nothing like that.

Vicky's story-both her life story and the story of her NDE's-is unusual. Her life itself, as I have intimated, has been so full of trauma, illness, and other ordeals that it is astonishing to me that Vicky has survived to tell it. And because she is so articulate, her NDE's are remarkable for the clarity of their details. (I have more than 100 pages of transcripts of interviews with Vicky about them, in addition to the one I personally conducted)."[35]

17. JAYNE SMITH'S NEAR-DEATH EXTRACT

Jayne smith's NDE reaffirms the experience of so many that God's plan is perfect. We are living out what we have chosen and that our essence, our core, our spirit and Soul, is pure love. As we are a part of God, and God is love, so are we. Our Soul is only this.

A Moment of Truth

Sixty-five years ago, Jayne Smith was in the hospital in labor with her second baby. In the process, she experienced clinical death and had a near-death experience. The following is taken from her video entitled, *A Moment of Truth* where she describes her near-death experience.

"I was totally aware. I was in blackness. I couldn't see anything. I was thinking to myself, 'This isn't the way it is supposed to be. I'm not supposed to know anything, and I do. What on earth has happened?'

At that point, I felt something leave my body. It was a whoosh. It went up through the top of my head. I could feel it, and I could hear it. Just a gentle whoosh. At that point, I found myself standing in a kind of grey mist. Then I knew I had died.

The memory of this experience is seared into my very Soul.

When I found myself standing in this grey mist with the realization that I had died, I remembered feeling so overjoyed, so thrilled, because I knew that even though I was what we call 'dead,' I was still very much alive. Very much alive. I was totally aware. I began to pour out these feelings of thanksgiving. I wasn't doing it verbally, but it seemed that the very essence of me was saying 'Thank you, thank

---

[35] Kenneth Ring, Lessons From The Light. (Moment Point Press, M.A. 2000). Pgs 74-79).

you God, for setting it up this way, that I really am immortal. I was not annihilated.'

I was involved in this tremendous pouring forth of gratitude and joy, and as that was going inside me, this white light began to infiltrate my consciousness. It came into me. It seemed I went out into it. I expanded into it as it came into my field of consciousness. There was nothing I was aware of except this brilliant white light. The light brought with it the most incredible feeling of total love, total safety, total protection. I was just enveloped in it. I remember feeling almost cradled by it. It was so dynamic it was almost palpable.

As I existed in this white light, in this incredible love, I began to be rapturous. The rapture built. The bliss built. My consciousness began to expand with the bliss of it all. Suddenly, there came into my field of consciousness an entire field of knowledge It was like a whole block of knowledge that just simply came in and settled itself on me. What normally takes several sentences to tell came all in one piece. What I knew was that I was immortal, that I was eternal, that I was indestructible, that I always had been, that I always will be, and that there was no way in this world I could ever be lost.

It was impossible for me to fall into a crack in the Universe somewhere and never be heard from again. I just knew that I was utterly safe, and I always had been forever and ever.

When that block of knowledge was digested by me, as it were, another block of knowledge came in. A whole field of knowledge came into my being and what I knew then was that the Universe runs according to a perfect plan. I knew that the plan was perfect. Everything that we think about as being hard to understand or unfair or cruel or whatever that was really all without meaning. I know that it is very difficult, but I knew this. I understood it. I comprehended it in a way that when I came back from the experience, I really couldn't comprehend anymore. I understood that all of the things that we worry about and concern us, we really don't have to worry about at all. There is a perfect plan, and the plan is working itself out in its perfection.

Then I simply remember I became more blissful, more rapturous, more ecstatic. I was just filling and filling with this light and love that was in the light. The dynamics of this light are not static at all. They are so dynamic and so much going on in there of love and joy and knowledge. As you take it into yourself, or as it goes into you and you receive it, your ecstasy level just becomes tremendous.

I knew that I had lost all sense of having a body. It was just my consciousness, sort of pure and free-floating, and I did not think at all during this part of the experience. I had no thoughts. I was a receiving station. I merely felt and absorbed and took in and did not think at all. I reached the point in the rapture of it all where I thought to myself suddenly, the first thought.

I wonder how much more of this I can stand before I shatter?'

With that thought, the light began to recede. So, the Universe will not let us shatter. We cannot take in more of this bliss and joy than we are able to handle at a time.

As the light began to recede, the rapture that I had built up also began to dissipate. For a couple of seconds, I could not remember what was going on. I remember thinking to myself, 'I don't know how I got here. I can't remember what's going on.'

I didn't know if I had been in that light for a minute of a day or a hundred years. I think the force of all that energy just produced a condition in me of amnesia for a couple of seconds. But that was not allowed to last very long either.

Within a second or two, I found myself standing in an absolutely beautiful green meadow. I knew then what was going on. I knew once again who I was, that I had died. My amnesia period was over with. I stood there in this gorgeous meadow, and I remember that the light there was different from the light here on earth. Though it was not that brilliant white light in which I was involved, it was a more beautiful light. There was a goldenness to this light. I remember the sky was very blue. I don't recall seeing the sun. The colours were extraordinary. The green of the meadow was fantastic. The flowers were blooming all around, and they had colours that I had never seen before. I was very aware that I had never seen these colours before, and I was very excited about it.

I thought I had seen all colours. I was thrilled to death of the beauty that was incredible. In addition to the beautiful colours, I could see a soft light glowing within every living thing. It was not a light that was reflected from the outside from a source, but it was coming from the centre of this flower—just this beautiful, soft light. I think I saw the life inside of everything.

When I finished looking at this exquisite beauty, I started to walk. I had only taken a few steps before I saw that there was in front of me a hill, a low hill. There were perhaps 18 to 20 people standing on the hill. They were dressed in robes, very simple, and I suppose Grecian type robes. They were also in all these beautiful colors. There were men and women—more men than women. I don't know why. I thought about this a little bit, but there were both men and women there. There was no one that I knew, but then I had no close emotional ties on the other side, so it is not surprising that there was no one there that I knew. I felt to myself, 'Oh, I want to talk with them.' It seemed that immediately I was there on the top of the hill. I don't know whether I was able to just glide there effortlessly or whether I

133

only had to think I wanted to be there and I was there. What I do remember was that I did not have to climb the hill. There was no effort involved in this.

As I found myself at the top of the hill, I saw that over on the horizon and just a little bit lower on the horizon, there was a city. I realized in some way that this was more than just a city, that what I was seeing actually represented a world. I wondered, 'Was that the world I just came from, or the one I am going to?' I never had a chance to find out because right at that moment, three or four of the men that were in this group of people over on the hill, came to me and we met.

I said to them, 'I know what has happened. I realize that I am dead. I know what's going on.'

One man in the group did all the talking to me. He was quite tall, taller than the rest. I remember the robe he was wearing was purple. He had a white fringe of hair that went around his head. The top of his head was bald. He had an absolute marvelous face. It was very noble, very kind, what we would think of as a very spiritual face. He also had about him a great deal of authority, so that I felt I was talking to someone that I could trust completely.

When I said to him, 'I know what's going on. I know that I have died,' he said, 'Yes, that's true, but you are not going to be staying here. It isn't time for you to be here yet.'

I must tell you that when we talked, we did not move our mouths. I can remember that I only had to have the impulse that contained the things that I wanted to say, and he would immediately be able to get that and answer me. Even though he was not moving his mouth when he talked with me, I could hear the sound of his voice in my inner ear. I know what he sounded like. It was a mental transmission, yet I could hear what he sounded like. For a long, long time, I could remember the sound of his voice. I said to him again, 'Everything that has happened to me since I crossed over is so beautiful. Everything is so perfect. What about my sins?'

He said, 'There are no sins, not the way you think of them on earth. The only thing that has any meaning here is what you think.'

Then he asked me a question. 'What is in your heart?'

Then in some incredible way that I don't understand at all, I was able to look deep inside myself, really into the very core of me to my Essence. I saw that what was there was love, nothing else. My core was perfect love, loving perfection. I had complete love and acceptance for everything. I saw my own gentleness, tenderness, harmlessness. I simply was perfect and loving.

I said to him, 'Of course!' I felt I was connecting with knowledge that I had known before. I wondered how on earth had I forgotten anything that important. I have known that.

I said, 'Can you tell me what everything is all about—the whole world—everything?'

He said, 'Yes.'

He told me in only three sentences at the most. It was so simple. I understood that immediately. I had total comprehension of what he was saying to me. I remember again saying to him, 'Of course!' Then there was that feeling again of connecting with the knowledge I had once had. I wondered how on earth did I forget that. I said to him, 'Since I am not going to be able to stay, there are so many people I want to take this back to. May I take this all back with me?'

He said, 'You may take the answer to the first question back, the one about sins. But the answer to the second one, you are not going to be able to remember.'

The next thing I knew, there was a tremendous banging in my head. It was loud, it was fast, and it was extremely irritating. It went on for just a few seconds—a loud bang, bang, bang, bang. Then that was over, and there was a sort of electronic click in my ear. I will never forget the sound of that click, because I remember thinking that it sounded almost like a tape recorder. When the click clicked, that was it, I was back, and I opened my eyes. My doctor was standing over me, and he was doing something that was extremely uncomfortable.

After the experience, I have never been able to remember the specific two or three sentences I was told. I have tried and I have tried for years after this experience to make a concerted effort to try, especially after I went to bed at night when I would be lying there in that not quite asleep state. And I never could. Finally, I just stopped trying to do that.

But I do think I know what he was telling me even though I cannot recall the actual two or three sentences. I know that it has to do with love. I believe it has to do with what I was enabled to see when he said, 'What is in your heart?' I looked inside myself and saw that I was perfect love. Now this does not apply to just me. It applies to all human beings. That is what we are. That is our core. This love, this perfection, this God-ness. I believe that what it is all about is that the world will keep turning and we will have all these experiences and it will go on forever and ever and ever.

As we bring that into our consciousness and have it remain there all the time, our connection with God will be there, not somewhere in our unconscious. We will be consciously aware of who we are all the time. I think that's what the journey is.

135

18. Josiane Antonette's Near-Death Extract
Vision of Two Different Worlds

In Josiane's NDE she is shown two starkly different worlds; one devoid of love, light and freewill and the other one full of love, joy and beauty and she is told that it will be whatever we choose to create. That we are all interconnected by a transparent *web*, each strand shining with great radiance—all connected to the One Source of *Light* or love.

1966 when she became aware of her ability to *"communicate with the other side."* For over 30 years, she has worked with the dying and the living, in hospitals as a chaplain, universities as a teacher, as a spiritual counsellor, healer and ceremonial leader. Her understanding of living, dying, and the spiritual realms has touched many people.

The following are short excerpts from her book, *Whispers of The Soul*.

"My near-death experience shattered my world. It shook me back to remembering spirit and other dimensions of life, which I had known as a child but had forgotten so that I could fit into society.

I feel the jerking of the ambulance as it rushes me through the dark streets of Marseille to the hospital. Twenty-four hours have passed since my underground abortion with a feuseuse d'anges, an 'angel maker.' Abortion is illegal in France now, and many women die because of the unsanitary conditions of the procedure. I am only twenty-four years old, a young nurse. Am I dying? Am I outside myself observing? I see my body and its pain. I look at my feet; they are pale and lifeless. My legs cannot move. My face is white and drawn.

I watch as the walls of the ambulance dissolve. I see the lights of the city speed toward me. I can see the stars! What am I doing up so high? Why does everything look so small all of a sudden?

Memories pass before my eyes as in a movie.

(She momentarily returns to her body)

I see family members at the foot of my bed through a haze. Suddenly they disappear. From where they stood I see faces rushing toward me with incredible speed. They race toward my face, expanding then dissolving. Face after face washes over me! I am terrified. I'm drifting. I'm unable to keep my eyes open.

Who are these people? Some I recognize as people I've known who have died. Others I do not recognize.

'Stay away! Where is my family?'

136

Now the whole room is filled with spirits! They hover near me and look into my eyes. I try to push them away. I fight them. The experience seems to go on forever. These are spirits who are restless. Their faces are twisted with pain. They seem lost. It's frightening to see them walking back and forth around my bed. And now spirits with glowing faces come close to me. They reflect a gentle and powerful light, reminding me of the pictures of beautiful angels that I love so much. I feel nurtured and loved by them, and enveloped by their luminescence. These beings are made of light, and even though their brilliance is intense, I am not blinded. Tremendous compassionate love surrounds me!

Now – I am filled with the essence of love and compassion. This magnetic power is filling every atom of me. I have never before experienced such depth and power of love. I am the power of love! Merging into an intimate dance wherein all boundaries have disappeared, I feel myself one with these beings of compassion.

No words or sounds are being exchanged, and yet communication is happening.

A strong presence assures me, 'Yes, you are dying to the world of men. But to us you are being born. Do not be afraid. You have always been with us; we have always been with you. We know you. You just fell asleep during your time on earth and forgot who you are. Now you are remembering.'

Revelation fills my awareness – of course, yes! I am of the Beings of Light, and they are of me! What is this new surge of energy? It begins as a very gentle vibration rising through the length of my body, from my feet to the top of my head, but now my whole self is vibrating. I hear buzzing. It is growing louder, and now the vibration and the buzzing are becoming one.

I feel such a wonderful release! I'm free! I can't resist this new and wonderful tide of energy sweeping my body upward. Now I'm on the hospital room ceiling gazing down! Everything appears so small: I see my bed; my body looks small and colorless; the people around the bed are tiny. Overwhelming grief and sorrow fill the room, and yet I feel completely disconnected from the scene below me. I hover nearer and look at the strange form lying on the bed. I feel compassion beyond words. I understand everything, but I have no feeling of attachment to anyone.

I look at each person standing at the bedside and feel tremendous love.

I want to say to them, 'I'm all right. You don't have to worry. I'm all right. Look at me! I'm fine!'

I am love; I am understanding; I am compassion!

My presence fills the room. And now I feel my presence in every room in the hospital. Even the tiniest space in the hospital is filled with this presence that is me. I sense myself beyond the hospital, above the city, even encompassing earth. I am melting into the universe. I am everywhere at once. I see pulsing light everywhere. Such a loving presence envelops me!

I hear a voice say, 'Life is a precious gift: to love, to care, to share.'

Questions race through my awareness: Why is there so much pain in the world? Why are humans made of different colors? Why with different creeds? Why with different languages?

A vision appears. I see our world from the vantage point of a star, or another planet. Earth appears as a sphere cut in half. The surface of the planet is flat and colorless. The ground is bare. No living plant grows from the earth. Tree branches are naked. There are no fruits, no flowers, no leaves. The barren hills are obscured behind a grey veil. It is a passionless place where no one rejoices at the sunrise, and no one knows when night comes. Naked phantom-like people stand on what seems to be a stage. All the actors are puppets animated by an invisible force. They move in unison and stop all at once.

On one side of half of the sphere, a sun attempts to shine upon the stage, but no one pays attention or makes a sound. Even the birds in the dead trees are silent and motionless. The other side of the half-sphere is in darkness. I watch as the darkness grows with frightening speed and covers the whole planet. No one pays attention. Now the darkness covers the sunlight, and now it covers all the bright planets in the universe.

'This is the world with the absence of light, love, and free will,' the voice states. 'It is the people's choices that created the world you have just seen.'

With these words, the nightmarish world begins to dissolve and is replaced by the other half of the planet – a place of vibrant, breathtaking beauty. I perceive how the earth, the sun, the moon, the darkness, the light, the planets, and all forms of life – plants, rocks, animals, people – are interconnected; they come from the same source of light. Everything is united by a transparent net, or web, and each thread shines with great radiance—everything pulses with the same luminosity – a magnificent light of unparalleled brilliance.

'From the light, we have come, and to the light, we all shall return,' continues the voice.

I realize now I have been standing in the middle of the two worlds. And with this understanding, an image of the path I have been walking appears. It is narrow and rocky; I have the sensation of losing my balance. I grow afraid of falling into the darkened planet. Free will! With remembering, I gaze at my invisible feet. The narrow path changes into a wide road. The darkness is replaced by light.

'Never, never forget.' I hear the voice say.

Merging with the light, I am so overcome with gratitude and overwhelmed by the love that fills me that I cry.

Suddenly, time and space are different again, and I am momentarily aware of my body.

I am aware that the window to the left of my bed is filled with a vibrant, powerful light. It seems to be calling me and pulling me toward it like a magnet. I hear the buzzing again, and . . . Whoosh! I'm zooming through the window! I merge with the light! I am the light, and the light is me.

'From the light, we have come, and to the light we shall all return,' repeats the voice.

What a joy to bathe in this incredible all-knowing, all-loving . . .

I can travel through walls, ceilings, and space at amazing speed! I visit my son, Philippe, who is only four.

A tremendous power moves me. I am boundless, formless, no longer controlled by my emotions. I am everything. Everything is me!

I'm back in the hospital room. A mist coming from the door facing my bed attracts my attention. In the middle of the vapor is a being with the most heavenly smile. Jean Pierre! It is my cousin, Jean Pierre! I am overwhelmed with joy. As I gaze at Jean Pierre, the hospital room disappears. We are suspended in mid-air. There are no windows or doors, no ceiling or ground. A brilliant radiance fills all space. He slowly approaches my bed and bends to kiss me. I feel the moisture of his lips on my face, the weight of his body against mine, the gentle touch of his hands on me.

Jean Pierre is the brother I never had. After a long and painful battle with lung cancer, he died two years ago when he was only twenty-two. I am still grieving his passing. How wonderful to see him again! And what is this? He is wearing his butterscotch jacket. This jacket has been the subject of many discussions. He loves it; I hate it.

'How did you know I was here?'

My question is a thought not yet put into words as Jean Pierre answers, 'We know everything about you, and we welcome you.'

Such a warm feeling of peace! I am complete – whole! I am free of pain and fear. There is no past or future – everything is! There is no need to speak to be understood or to communicate. I feel serenity beyond anything I have ever known.

139

And joy of joys: I can fly! I swirl easily and with great speed around my cousin in a playful way, expressing the ultimate joy that is me. Everything is the way it should be. Never have I felt so clear, so complete, so loved. I gaze at myself: I am whole and healed! I can interact and play with Jean Pierre with my natural vigor. Familiar Beings of Light are here, too. I immerse myself in their loving presence. It's as if they are protecting me and carrying me. We are all interconnected. I relax into the timeless joy. What a glorious feeling! I want to be here forever. Jean Pierre is gazing at me now as the other beings begin to depart. His dark eyes are filled with great tenderness and purity. He turns to leave with the others, and I plead with him to take me with him. His eyes fill with sadness.

'Not now,' he responds. 'There is much, much work for you. You have to go back and tell them life is a precious gift. Each moment is filled with great opportunities. Don't waste your time on earth. Spread love and understanding. We will always be with you – guiding you, protecting you, awaiting the time when we will be reunited – when your work on earth is over.'

I watch as Jean Pierre dissolves into the same brilliant light with which he had entered. The light is fading away, too.

The room is empty now. My grief is intense. I start to cry out of desperation and loneliness.

Suddenly, I'm back in the hospital in bed. I am fully aware of my surroundings and my physical state of being. Tubes are implanted in my body. The pain is overwhelming. My sadness is intense. I am so weak I cannot speak. I have lost my voice, and the doctors are alarmed by the tears which are using up the strength I need to recuperate. Crying is all I want to do! My body feels like a suit that is too tight; the room is confining; the smell of sickness surprises my senses; the human condition saddens me.

'Josianne, you're back!' I recognize my sister's voice. I see her careful gaze. 'You've been in a coma for three days. We didn't know if you were coming back.'"

Josiane's NDE is extremely powerful in the simplicity and potency of the message given to her to share. Her chosen time to depart the life as Josiane hadn't come and she returned to her broken body that felt too tight to fit into. On a soul level, she had chosen to spread the message that we never die, that we are all interconnected by a radiant web of our Creator's love that immerses every particle of our being in unconditional love if we would but allow ourselves to believe and feel it.

On one hand, she saw the world devoid of light, love and free will where everyone walked around like robots on a planet that was 'flat and colorless' created by a mass consciousness of people that did not think for themselves, that were selfish and self-centered. On the other hand, she was shown a planet that was breathtakingly beautiful where the mass consciousness was aware that they were all interconnected parts of their divine Creator and as such they were aware that what one does affect the whole. A planet where the people give, share, and love unconditionally in support of one another. She was shown that which planet we are 'on' is purely a matter of our own free-will choice, determined by our own predominant thoughts, beliefs, and actions.

GROUP NEAR-DEATH EXPERIENCES
19. JAKE'S NEAR-DEATH EXTRACT

The following NDE's we look at are a rare type of NDE called the *"group near-death experience"*. This is an amazing phenomenon where a whole group of people have a 'shared' NDE at the same time and location.

In 1996, Arvin Gibson, a prominent near-death researcher, interviewed a fire-fighter named Jake who had a most unusual near-death experience while working with other fire-fighters in a forest. What makes it unique is that it happened at the same time as several co-workers also had a near-death experience. During their near-death experiences, they actually met each other and saw each other above their lifeless bodies. All survived, and they verified with each other afterwards that the experience actually happened.

Jake's near-death experience is an incredible example of the awesome power of God's protection as when Jake returned to his body he noticed some of his metal tools had melted from the intense heat of the fire, but he was still able to walk up the hill, (as he said as if in some sort of protective, invisible bubble), with only singed hairs to show for it!

What follows is an excerpt of Jake's near-death experience from Arvin S Gibson's book, *The Fingerprints of God*.

"Jake was a member of an elite fire-fighting group called the 'Hotshots;' a crew whose job it was to be dropped into particularly troublesome forest fires and bring them under control.

During a wilderness fire in 1989, a helicopter dropped Jake, as crew boss, and two 20 person Hotshot crews onto a fire at the top of a steep mountain. The fire was burning below the crews in thick Ponderosa Pine and Oak brush . . . .

141

The slope of the hill the men and women were working on was about 40 degrees. They worked their way down the steep slope, when, part way down, to their horror, the wind changed to an upward direction. The trees in front of the men and women travelling down the hill erupted into flames with explosive force.

Jake explained how fire-fighters have a fire-resistant pack that is carried on their web gear. The pack includes an aluminium foil-type material which they can throw over themselves as they crouch to the ground in an emergency. These foils are only effective if the people can deploy the shelters after properly preparing the ground by reaching mineral soil with no residual flammable organic materials. The problem, in this case, was that the enormous winds caused by the inferno erupted all around them and the immediacy of the crisis made the shelters useless.

The panic-stricken crews started to try and go back up the trench trail they had built. Trees exploded and fire engulfed the immediate area, and oxygen feeding the conflagration was sucked from near the ground where the people struggled to breathe. One by one, the men and women fell to the earth suffocating from lack of oxygen. They were reduced to crawling on their hands and knees while they attempted to get back up the hill to a safer area.

Suddenly Jake had the thought: This is it. I am going to die. And with that thought in mind, he found himself looking down on his body which was lying in a trench. The noise, heat and confusion from the inferno surrounding them were gone, and Jake felt completely at peace. As he looked around Jake, saw other fire-fighters standing above their bodies in the air. One of Jake's crew members had a defective foot which he had been born with. As he came out of his body, Jake looked at him and said: 'Look, Jose, your foot is straight.'

A bright light then appeared. Jake described the bright light in this manner: 'The light—the fantastic light. It was brighter than the brightest light I had ever seen on earth. It was brighter than the sun shining on a field of snow. Yet I could look at it, and it didn't hurt my eyes.'

Standing in the light was Jake's deceased great-grandfather. His great-grandfather acted as Jake's guide throughout his near-death experience. Jake met with others of his ancestors and had extensive experience. Only the portions pertinent to this discussion are repeated here.

His great-grandfather ultimately communicated by mind thought to Jake that it was Jake's choice whether or not he should return to earth. Not wanting to come back from a beautiful and peaceful place that he was in, Jake argued with his great-grandfather. Explaining that it would be devastating to return to a horribly burned body, Jake pled with his great-grandfather to remain. Jake said that all of this communication was by questions he would think of and have instantly answered in his mind. Jake was informed that neither he nor any of his crew who chose to return, would suffer ill effects from the fire. This would be done so that: 'God's power over the elements would be made manifest.'

Returning to his body was one of the more painful events of his life. When I asked Jake why it was painful, he said: 'When I was there, everything was so perfect, and my spirit body, it . . . it was so free. It felt like everything was limitless. When I came back, well you know, there's always something plaguing you, like arthritis, or sore muscles, not there. Getting back into my physical body felt cramped—held back. For example, when I used to play football for a few days after a game or hard practice, I was always sore. The same thing was true after coming back into my physical body. I hurt and felt constrained, and it was hard to get used to for some time.'

Finding himself, again, in his body, Jake looked around and noticed that some of the metal tools they had used to fight the fire had melted. Despite this intense heat, and the fire still raging around him, he was able to walk up the hill in some sort of protected bubble. He did not hear nor feel the turbulence around him. Upon reaching the relative safety of the hilltop, the noise of the fire was again evident, and he saw other members of the crew also gathered there.

The entire happening was so profound that upon escaping from what they had supposed would be sure death the group of saved people knelt in prayer to thank the Lord for their deliverance. All of the crew escaped, and the only visual evidence on them of what they had been through was a few singed hairs.

Jake said that in comparing accounts of their different episodes, the men and women were astonished that they had each undergone some type of near-death experience. And this happened to a diverse ethnic and religious group of Hispanics, Caucasians and American Indians.

Throughout the summer as the crew worked together, they continued to discuss the miraculous adventure which they had lived through. Other members of the crew confirmed that they also felt the ill effects of returning to their physical bodies. They, too, had met with other members of their deceased families and were given the choice of remaining where they were or of returning to earth."[36]

20. RASHAD'S NEAR-DEATH EXTRACT

The following group NDE appears in the *International Association for Near-Death Studies* publication *Vital Signs* (Volume XIX, No. 3, 2000) This powerful

---

[36] Gigson, Fingerprints Of God. (Horizon Publishers, U.T.,1999, pp. 129-131.

group NDE is both real and symbolic. The three friends were connected arm in arm when they were electrocuted, and they were able to observe heaven and stayed connected while their angels explained to them that this was also symbolic of how we are all connected one to the other as the children of God that we are. The following is May's near-death experience as described to Dr Stephen Hoyer.

"During the fall of 1971, when I was 22 years old, I shared a near-death experience with my cousin, James, and his best friend, Rashad, who was from India. Both young men were on a break from school and were staying with my family on our farm. One afternoon the three of us went to the cornfield to cut fodder. To get to the field, we had to go through a metal gate, and we took turns climbing down to open and shut it. By late afternoon a storm started brewing in the west, and we decided to quit for the day. It was James' turn to open the gate, and as he did so, he reached up for my arm to climb back up onto the wagon. I was leaning the wrong way, and his weight pulled me toward him. Rashad grabbed my other arm to steady me, and we were in just this position when the lightning hit us.

I saw the lightning sparkle along the top of the gate. The next thing we knew, we were in a large room or hall made of dark stone. The ceiling was so high, and the gloom was so thick we couldn't see the top. There were no furnishings or wall hangings, just cold, black stone all around. I knew I should be afraid, but I just felt peaceful, floating along there in the gloom with my two friends in the great, dark hall. The stately walls of this place loomed above us and seemed to radiate both great power and also great masculinity. I remember thinking it would have suited King Arthur. It was at that point that I realized that the three of us were united in thought and body. Images of Arthur came to me from James and Rashad. James saw only a cosmic version of the king. Rashad seemed to [be] envisioning himself in the time of Arthur. As we all became conscious of each other's thoughts, I suddenly knew James and Rashad better than I have ever known anyone else.

We realized there was light coming into the chamber from an archway at one end. It was more than just light. It was a golden, embracing warmth. It gave off a feeling of peace and contentment more intense than anything we had ever felt. We were drawn toward it. We weren't talking, but we were communicating with each other on some other level, seeing through each other's eyes. As we came to the archway and passed through, we entered a beautiful valley.

There were meadows and tree-lined hills that led to tall mountains in the distance. Everything glistened with golden sparks of light.

We saw that the sparkling lights were tiny, transparent bubbles that drifted in the air and sparkled on the grass. We realized that each tiny sparkle was a soul. To me, the valley appeared to be Heaven, but at the same time, I knew that James and Rashad were seeing it differently. James saw it as the Gulf of Souls. Rashad saw it as Nirvana, and somehow we knew all this without speaking. The light began gathering at the far end of the valley, and slowly, out of the mist, a pure white being began to materialize. I saw an angel with a strong, bright face, but not like you'd usually imagine. She was closer to a strong, Viking Valkyrie. I knew she was the special angel that watches over the women of my family, and I perceived her name to be Hellena. James saw this same being as his late father, a career Naval officer, in a white dress uniform. Rashad perceived the being to be the Enlightened One, or Buddha.

The being spoke first to Rashad and welcomed him. He said that Rashad's time on earth was done. He was worthy now of Nirvana. Rashad asked why James and I were there and was told that we were part of the reason why he was worthy of Nirvana. His two great friends loved him so much that they had willingly accompanied him on his last journey. At the same time, however, James received a different message. He had been worried about what his father would think about his anti-war protest activities, and his father told him he was proud of him for standing up for what he believed. He knew he was not a coward because a coward would not have made this journey with Rashad. I received yet another message in which Hellena told me she was glad I had remembered the example of strength, honesty, wisdom, and loyalty taught to me by my family.

We spent what seemed like an eternity in this place as we talked to our separate, yet joined, entities. They said they appeared to us in this way because back in the real world, we were physically joined when the lightning struck us. They said it also symbolized the joining of all religions and doctrines. They said I would live to see a new age of tolerance, that the souls and hearts of humanity would be joined as the three of us were.

The guides taught us that doctrine and creed and race meant nothing. No matter what we believed, we were all children joined under one God, and that the only rule was God's true law—do unto others as you would have them do unto you. We should treat all people as if they were a part of our soul because they were. All living things in the universe were connected to one another. They said that soon humanity would mature enough to assume a higher place in the universal scheme of things, but until then we must learn acceptance and tolerance and love for each other. They said there would come a new age when people would not be able to endure seeing others homeless and hungry. We would realize that only by helping each other could we truly help ourselves.

Eventually, we were told that it was time to go. We would not be allowed to stay longer because it was not yet time for me or for James, only for Rashad. The enlightened one told Rashad he would have a little time before he returned to take care of his worldly affairs. James' father told him he would return to this place soon after Rashad, but the two of them had to go back for now so that I could. I said I would willingly stay here in this valley with them, but Hellena told me that I had not fulfilled my destiny; that I had children yet unborn.

We drifted slowly toward the archway. The pull became stronger and we were literally thrown back into the world. We floated for a while there, hovering above our bodies. Some of my cousins had been in the next field and had seen what had happened. We saw them all come running to where we lay. James and Rashad's hands were still stuck to my arms. We saw my cousins pry their fingers loose so they could turn Rashad over to help him.

When our hands were pried loose, James and I re-entered our bodies. We felt as if we were on fire, but it turned out that we had only minor injuries. Rashad, it seemed, being on the end, had taken most of the charge. The doctors said that the lightning had caused damage to his heart, lungs, and liver. He remained in the hospital for several weeks. During that time, tests revealed that James had a brain tumor that would eventually claim his life.

As soon as Rashad could travel, James took him home to India. He offered to stay, but Rashad told him that he wished solitude for his final time. Rashad took on the life of the Ascetic, in the Vedic tradition. He asked his wife to stay with her family because he wanted his last days to be spent in spiritual awakenings. About a year and a half later, on a cold day in January, Rashad returned to Nirvana. James and I knew when his soul left the world without being told.

James lived about three years after he found out he had the brain tumor. He gave most of his considerable inheritance to a charity that educated young people in India. I, on the other hand, have survived for another thirty years (so far) with the knowledge that this experience which I shared with my closest friends has been a guiding force in my life. I strive every day to meet my destiny, whatever it may be, with the same quiet dignity and resolution they showed when they met theirs. They have truly been my pathfinders, and I know that the connection I shared with them so long ago is the same connection we all share. We just sometimes fail to realize it."

May finally made the transition into spirit on February 19, 2002, due to complications following a surgical procedure to repair one of her heart valves. She was 52 years old.

Like May, Arthur Yensen was also shown how we are all interconnected with one another as Children of God however, at the time he had his NDE, in the year 1932, it met with so much controversy that he didn't publish it until 1955.

21. ARTHUR YENSEN'S NEAR-DEATH EXTRACT

A Man Ahead of His Time

Arthur Yensen was another near-death experiencer who received the knowledge of reincarnation. In August of 1932, Yensen, a university graduate, geologist, and staunch materialist-turned-syndicated-cartoonist, decided to take some time off to research his weekly cartoon strip, 'ADVENTUROUS WILLIE WISPO.' Since his main character was a hobo, Yensen became a hobo for a time, blending in with the over sixteen million unemployed at that time in our nation's Great Depression. He bummed rides from Chicago through Minnesota, until a young man in a convertible coupe picked him up on the way to Winnipeg. Going too fast for the road conditions, the car hit a three-foot-high ridge of oiled gravel and flipped into a series of violent somersaults. Both men were catapulted through the cloth top before the car smashed into a ditch. The driver escaped unharmed, but Yensen was injured, losing consciousness just as two female spectators rushed to his aid.

After seeing the afterlife during this near-death experience, he later learned that telling others about his NDE often brought criticism, especially from the church, remembering it was the 1930's. But there were those who would listen, and as time wore on, more and more people would ask him about it. Finally, in 1955, Arthur Yensen published a report of his near-death experience after much public interest[37].

The following are some excerpts from his booklet, where Arthur Yensen recounts his journey.

"I felt as if I were coming loose from my body! While I believed that my body was me, I knew instinctively that if I separated from it, I'd be dead! My soul and body started separating again and continued to separate until I felt a short, sharp pain in my heart, which felt as if something had been torn loose. Then slowly and softly, I rose out through the top of my head.

Gradually the earth scene faded away, and up through it loomed a bright, new, beautiful world—beautiful beyond imagination! For half a minute, I could see both worlds at once. The earth is fading away, and the other world looming up brighter, and brighter, and still brighter! Finally, when the earth was all gone, I stood in a glory that could only be heaven.

In the background were two beautiful mountains similar to Fujiyama of Japan. The tops were snow-capped, and the slopes were adorned with foliage of

---

[37] His booklet is titled, I Saw Heaven. It is now out-of-print, but a photocopy of the booklet is available from his son Eric Yensen, at eyensen@collegeofidaho.edu

indescribable beauty. Since there was no pollution, haze, or other obstructions to mar one's vision, all the details were sharp and clear. The mountains appeared to be about fifteen miles away, yet I could see individual flowers growing on their slopes. I estimated my vision to be about 100 times better than on earth . . .

While I stood there marveling, I saw twenty people beyond the first trees, playing a singing-dancing game, something like 'Skip-to-my-Lou.' They were having a hilarious time holding hands and dancing in a circle—fast and lively. Their singing, their laughter, and even their shouting were melodious.

As soon as they saw me, four of the players left the game and joyfully skipped over to greet me. As they approached, I estimated their ages to be: one 30; two 20; and one 12. Their bodies seemed almost weightless, and the grace and beauty of their easy movements were fascinating to watch.

As the heaven-people gathered around, the oldest, largest and strongest-looking man announced pleasantly, 'You are in the land of the dead. We lived on earth, just like you, till we came here.'

With unbounded enthusiasm, I shouted, 'This is wonderful!'

'It's marvelous!' they answered. Then with delight, they told me how I could swim around in the lake as long as I pleased, and when I came out, I'd be dry! Another one said, 'You can run, jump, dance, sing and play as much as you want to, and you'll never get tired!' . . .

Then I noticed that the landscape was gradually becoming familiar. It seemed as if I had been here before. I remembered what was on the other side of the mountains. Then with a sudden burst of joy, I realized that this was my real home! Back on earth, I had been a visitor, a misfit, and a homesick stranger. With a sigh of relief, I said to myself, 'Thank God I'm back again. This time I'll stay!'

Then the oldest man, who looked like a Greek God, continued to explain. 'Everything over here is pure. The elements don't mix or break down as they do on earth. Everything is kept in place by an all-pervading Master-Vibration, which prevents aging. That's why things don't get dirty or wear out, and why everything looks so bright and new.' Then I understood how heaven could be eternal.

Next, I noticed that I was loving everything and everybody and that it was making me intensely happy. Apparently, only the good in me had survived. Without the bad, which is discord, I was happy beyond anything I had ever known.

My next question was, 'How do you explain this intense happiness?'

'Your thoughts are vibrations which are controlled by the Master-Vibration. It neutralizes all negative thoughts and lets you think only the good thoughts, such as love, freedom and happiness.'

'Then what becomes of the old grouches?'

'If they are too bad they go to a plane of lower vibrations where their kind of thoughts can live. If they came here, the Master-Vibration would annihilate them after death, people gravitate into homogenous groups according to the rate of their soul's vibrations. If the per cent of discord in a person is small, it can be eliminated by the Master-Vibration; then the remaining good can live on here.'

'For example, if a person were 70% good and 30% bad, (I'm not sure of these percentages), the bad could be eliminated by the Master-Vibration and the remaining good welcomed into heaven. However, if the percentage of bad were too high, this couldn't be done, and the person would have to gravitate to a lower level and live with people of his own kind. In the hereafter, each person lives in the kind of a heaven or hell that he prepared for himself while on earth.

'If you threw a small pebble into a threshing machine, it would go into the box— not because it is good or bad, but because of its proper size and weight. It's the same way here. No one sends you anywhere. You are sorted by the high or low vibrations of your soul. Everyone goes where he fits in! High vibrations indicate love and spiritual development, while low vibrations indicate debasement and evil.'

When I asked what a person should do while on earth to make it better for him when he dies, he answered, 'All you can do is to develop along the lines of unselfish love. People don't come here because of their good deeds, or because they believe in this or that, but because they fit in and belong. 'Good' deeds are the natural result of being 'good', and 'bad' deeds are the natural result of being 'bad'. Each carries its own reward and punishment. It's what you are that counts!'

While we talked, my mind, or whatever I had to think with, became crystal clear. Instantly and without effort, I could remember everything I had ever known. I seemed to understand the earth and all about it. The whole scheme of life was plain as day. Everything on earth has its purpose. It all fits into a pattern which will, in the end, work out for justice and good. People worry because of their incomplete viewpoints. They don't realize that trouble is nature's way of teaching lessons that won't be learned otherwise. If we'd only learn from other peoples' troubles, we could avoid most of our own.

While we were still talking, and I was enjoying the ecstasy of heaven, my friend gently announced, 'You can't stay here any longer. You have to go back to earth.'

149

'Back to earth! Oh, no, not back to that horrible place!'

But already I was leaving this beautiful land and slipping back into my body—still enough in heaven to have no inhibitions, and yet far enough back into my body to have terrible thoughts. Like a kid having a tantrum, I kicked and screamed, 'Let me stay! Let me stay!'—But all my protesting did no good.

As I moved farther back into my body, there was a painful, prickly feeling all over, similar to a foot waking up. Also, a crowded feeling as if the real me was having to compress itself to get back into its hateful prison.

The last thing the strong man said to me was, 'You have more important work to do on earth, and you must go back and do it! There will come a time of great confusion, and the people will need your stabilizing influence. When your work on earth is done, then you can come back here and stay.'"

Arthur Yensen's near-death experience continued for a few more paragraphs as he returned to his body. What follows are answers to questions people frequently asked him (13 of the 46 in the booklet).

Can You Tell Us A Little More About Heaven?

"Heaven is really hard to describe in earth language because our words aren't adequate to describe things beyond our imaginations. However, the heaven I saw is characterized by its vivid greenness, its crystalline cleanliness, its newness, its all-pervading music and its overall beauty—all of which are maintained by the Master-Vibration.

It's a vigorous, lively place with an outflowing happiness that's uncontainable. It's an 'over-answer' to everything we should have, and so far as I know, it's a final home for the soul.

It's not a place of rest, as so many tired people picture it, because no one there gets tired. It's more like a new lease on life. No one could possibly use all the bubbling energy that wells up from his diaphragm. It's a lively hilarious place that's unbelievably sweet, serene and melodious. The people there reminded me of uninhibited, carefree children—before well-meaning adults work them over.

In heaven where all people really love each other, there are no inhibitions or need for them. Everyone does exactly as he pleases. This works out well because only the best in each person survives, and good is all anyone wants to do. This allows freedom and happiness that people on earth can't imagine."

How Does A Person Get Ahead In The Next World?

"You don't. There is no place in heaven for discontent or personal ambition.

150

If everyone completely understood the afterlife, they'd quit trying to keep up with the Joneses and start learning how to love unselfishly. Here we can change ourselves quite easily and should use this life to make ourselves into the kind of people we want to be in the hereafter. This world is a miserable place for anyone who hasn't learned internal harmony—characterized by unselfish love. Mankind is like a chain. What one does affects us all. We should try to strengthen our weakest links. In heaven, as far as I could tell, all people do is enjoy themselves. They're like children who don't demand work in order to be happy."

What Is Success And What Is Failure?

"We came into this world to have trouble and to learn from it. Unfortunately, many people don't realize this and complain about their bad luck and spend their lives chasing pleasure, fame and money. Then they die without making any spiritual progress. And so, they waste life after life.

It should be obvious that all we'll take with us is our character, our karma and our abilities, and that we'll have to live with people like ourselves.

Therefore, our highest success would be to rise into the highest heaven through unselfish love. And our most dismal failure would be to hate ourselves out of existence—if that is possible."

If You Saw Heaven, Why Didn't You Mention God And Salvation?

"I didn't omit them intentionally. It's only that I didn't see God, Christ, or hear anything about salvation. However, I do consider the Master-Vibration as part of God because it controls the universe and seems to regulate everything.

To understand God, I believe one would have to be almost as Great as He is. Or at least be like Christ, who was in harmony with God. On the other hand, salvation is simple. All one has to do is to love so unselfishly that his soul-vibrations will rise high enough to fit him into heaven."

What Is Sin?

"Sin is anything that stops spiritual growth. The three great sins are: Not learning from experience, letting leadership turn into tyranny, and letting selfishness turn into greed.

Everyone should constantly check themselves for developing greed, tyranny, fear, worry, anger, hate, jealousy, and especially guilt. By conquering these harmful traits, we keep in tune with our Oversouls (Guardian Angels), God and the Universe. Sin is anything that causes us to lose this contact. When the subconscious mind feels guilty, it is ashamed to face its Oversoul and builds up barriers to shut it out. Without the Oversoul to guide it, such a person is like a child lost in the dark. The only hope it has is to get rid of its guilt and re-connect with its Oversoul."

How Are We Saved?

"By unselfish love. When we love unselfishly, our vibrations are so high that the only place we'll fit into is heaven. There is no other place we can go if we want to. This is divine justice because it gives all the people who ever lived, as well as all the higher animals who know right from wrong, an equal chance to eventually attain internal harmony which will fit them into some kind of heaven—regardless of their intelligence, education, indoctrination, ignorance, wealth or poverty."

Explain The Trinity

"The Father, of course, is God, or Infinity, who Created and still controls the Universe.

The Son is an individualized portion of God who has attained a perfect Oneness with God—which is also our goal.

The Holy Ghost, or Holy Spirit, would be the Master-Vibration which flows into us as freely as the barriers we have built up against it will allow."

Do You Believe In The Devil?

"No, but if there is one, he would have to be an insane angel who was crazy enough to fight with God, which would be as futile as for us to try to stop the sunrise. I believe the devil is a mythological character, invented by humans and used for a scapegoat. Grown people with immature minds like to blame the devil for their misdeeds instead of acting like people and taking the blame themselves.

However, there may be earthbound spirits of low vibrations, whom we may regard as devils because they annoy us through mental telepathy. These demons tune in on us through our low vibrations of hate, fear and greed. They can be tuned out with unselfish love, or if necessary, be chased away by the stronger spirit of Jesus Christ.

There's an old saying, 'Birds of a feather, flock together.' The way to be rid of the 'devil' is not to be like him."

Which Do You Believe In, Predestination Or Free Will?

"Both. Since they told me I had a destiny, why wouldn't everyone else have one? Obviously, our brains can only know what we've recorded in them, but our Oversouls know all about us. That's why they try to guide us and keep us in our bodies until our life's work is finished—just like we try to stay in our cars until we reach our destinations.

Yet, we all have free will. Any of us can get drunk and drive into a telephone pole."

What Is Wrong With Fixed Beliefs In The Hereafter?

"On the other hand, if we have no fixed beliefs about anything, we'd be free to adapt to the new surroundings and fit in where we belong with no unusual difficulty.

Everything has its place. Fixed beliefs are useful in prayer where doubt is fatal. Yet doubt is always useful in sizing up the religious dogma, reading junk mail, listening to commercials, and the promises of politicians."

Why Are People Turned Off by Religion?

"Any complete body of knowledge is like a spoke in a wheel—pointing to the centre of ultimate truth. Science, art, music, philosophy and religion run into trouble because they are not yet complete bodies of knowledge even though religion is advertised and sold as such.

Many religionists think they have the whole truth and the only short-cut to heaven. And in their well-meaning zeal to rescue wayward humanity, they argue, persuade and even go to war to force non-believers to accept their formula for getting into heaven.

Outsiders are turned off mostly because the churches can't agree among themselves. Some churches have even resorted to torture to force their particular brand of God's love on people who were perfectly satisfied and who were on good terms with God already.

But even though the churches have abused religion, and the beliefs of some churches are ridiculous to other churches, I believe everyone should have some kind of religion, or philosophy, to encourage them to think and grow spiritually."

What Is God Like?

"I don't know. I didn't see him. But I did feel a Master Vibration which must be a part of God because it kept everything in good order and controlled the Universe. Maybe it was the Holy Spirit.

People differ a great deal in their ideas of what God is like. Little children imagine him to be a grey-haired old man with a long white beard.

One religious denomination believes there is a Mr and Mrs God. Other churches consider God to be a universal spirit that created and rules the Universe, while the atheists say there is no God at all—until they get in a jam. Then they pray like there really is one!

Under self-hypnosis, I once asked what God was like. I saw a huge mountain almost covered with clouds. Here and there were small peepholes through which I could see lightning and great activity. Then a voice from somewhere said, 'To fully understand God, you'll have to be almost as great as He is!'

This put me in my place. But for reasoning purposes, I had to have some kind of a mental image of what God is like. To me now, after many years of thought, He's a combination of many things such as the known and unknown laws of nature, light, electricity, gravity, time, space, infinity, love and life itself—totally incomprehensible! But since we have life, we must all be a small part of Him.

That's probably why we call Him Father and consider ourselves his ornery kids— who always need forgiveness."

What Is Karma?

"Karma is the totality of all our actions—good and bad—which determine our fate, or destiny.

If we do only good things we will eventually run out of bad karma, and only good things will happen to us, and vice versa.

Between lives, with the great knowledge of our Oversouls, we choose the next life we are going to live and how much karma we are going to meet and settle. For example, if you abused animals or people, in one life you would be likely to reincarnate into a situation where you'd be abused to make you realize the misery you've caused others. The only way to bypass karma is to develop so much unselfish love that paying for bad karma will serve no purpose—much like a college student challenging a course he already knows."

Do You Believe in Reincarnation?

"'Except a man be born again, he cannot see the kingdom of God,' John 3:3. Reincarnation certainly explains a lot of things that would be hard to account for otherwise. From my experience, I'm convinced we have all lived and died many times. The reason we don't remember our former lives is that our vast soul memories are not transferred to our baby brains at birth. What we know in this life is what we learned in past lifetimes. That would be the reason why some things are so much easier for us to learn than others. For example, Mozart didn't have to learn music because he already knew it. One of the good things about reincarnation is that at the beginning of each lifetime we are cleared of all past prejudices, learning blocks and wrong teachings, and are ready for a fresh start— just like a new term at school—and, like school, when we have learned enough of life's lessons, we graduate and don't have to come back to this earth anymore, except as volunteers to teach stragglers.

154

Since our opportunities for spiritual growth on this planet are probably limited time-wise, we should realize that in dealing with children, the learning value of any incarnation can be spoiled by indoctrination before the child is old enough to reason. In some cases, this is worse than murder because it may waste a whole lifetime instead of just a few years. Some scholars say that in the Dark Ages the Church had all references to reincarnation deleted from the Bible, so as to better control the people by threatening them with hell fire. But they didn't get rid of every passage that refers to reincarnation because there are some that could hardly mean anything else, such as: 'He that overcometh, I will make a pillar in the temple of God and he shall go out no more . . .' Rev. 13:12'"

Kevin Williams, through his lifetime of work studying NDE's on the internet, discusses Arthur Yensen at length,

"More about Arthur Yensen. Born on a Nebraska sandhill during a blizzard in 1898, Yensen recalled being force-fed religion as a youngster. Not only did he turn against it, but he started challenging his parents at every turn—including questioning the way they ate. He observed that their farm animals did just fine on a diet of fresh greens and whole grains, yet family members were always suffering indigestion and constipation from the white flour, sugar, and grease they consumed. Behind his parents' back, he cured himself by eating bran flakes. He continued to defy the conventions of his day, switching from atheism to mysticism after his near-death experience at the age of thirty-four, marrying afterwards, and built his own home in Parma, Idaho, from blocks of 'tuff,' (water-deposited volcanic ash), he and his sons quarried. At various times in his life he was an educator, public speaker, active in politics, specialized in historical sculpture (his work adorns Parma's city park), was a movie extra in several Hollywood films, an authority on organic gardening and nutrition, and was singled out as one of Idaho's 'Most Distinguished Citizens.'

Although Yensen later became a public figure, at the time of his NDE he was frequently at odds with the school boards where he taught: opposing any procedure that capped a child's creative drive; speaking out against the incarceration of American citizens of Japanese ancestry during World War II, and ignoring school rules by sharing his near-death experience in class as proof to his students that morality matters and life really has a purpose. Ironically, Yensen was still questioning whether or not he had fulfilled his life's work when he returned 'home' in 1992, the quiet benefactor of thousands."[38]

Arthur's son Eric kindly consented to my publishing the above account which he mentioned is an abridged version of his father's full account. Arthur Yensen was a wise man, very much ahead of his time, who challenged authority when his

---

[38] Extract taken from www.near-death.com

consciousness dictated him to do so. He had the courage of his convictions, and he indeed left his mark.

22. FREDERIC DELARUE'S NEAR-DEATH EXTRACT

Frederic's remarkable NDE poignantly illustrates what can happen when a person is in a deep coma, having left their physical body, but who is still intensely aware of the sounds and happenings all around them. In Frederic's case he was able to see into two dimensions simultaneously. For a time he was able to feel the inert heaviness of his body, without feeling any pain, and the emotional turmoil that surrounded him, (initially the sounds of which were amplified greatly), and yet, also leave his body at will and 'fly' freely without the confines of his dense earthly body. Like so many NDE'ers, when he was out of his body, Frederic observed the emotional chaos that was taking place around his battered body devoid of emotional attachment to it. His experience is indeed 'food for thought' and contemplation on how best to treat people who are in deep comas.

While those he loved were naturally in anguish over his potentially life-threatening injuries, he was very much alive, well, and in a tranquil, often blissful state of peace, love and Light, far removed from the *seeming* reality of that time. In fact, ironically it was Frederic, the seeming victim, who was busily doing his best to telepathically send love and endeavor to calm everyone down a little. *Nothing is ever as it seems* is so true for this world.

Imagine having this enlightening experience at age 12. Frederic went on to carry the priceless gems he had gleaned from his experience as his foundation for life. This experience showed Frederic that what many perceive as the only reality, (that is what we perceive through our five senses), is but a tiny part of the totality of the 'whole' in the heavenly 'unseen' spiritual dimensions that surround and sustain us.

Frederic continues his story.

So Light in the Light

"Ecrosnes, November 30, 1975. It was one of those winter afternoons in northern France when you get the sensation that the cold breeze is entering your entire body and freezing you, right down to the bone. My parents were about to drive me to a healer, a few hours away from home, in regards to a small growth on my right foot that I had gotten from the swimming pool lessons at school. My father, Georges, was driving the car. My mother, Claudine, was in the passenger seat. My little brother, Fabrice, who was 5 at the time, was sitting in the back seat

behind my dad, and myself, age 12, was behind my mom. My sister, Brigitte, was not part of the trip.

Chartres is a charming touristic town located fifteen minutes west of my parents' farm. It is world-renowned for its majestic gothic Cathedral, its sacred Labyrinth, and its pilgrimage. Chartres is my place of birth, and as I also announce, my place of rebirth. It's as if I was born twice in 12 years periods. You will understand this better after reading my experience in this chapter.

To go to the healer's home, we had to pass through the outskirts of Chartres by crossing a national road, equivalent to an interstate highway in the US. This road was feared by many as car accidents were common in that location. It was about 3 o'clock in the afternoon. The sun was extremely bright and low, which was making it difficult for anyone to see. The police were at the intersection to help people cross. I remember hearing the policeman tell my dad to go, but because he did not go right away, the policeman waved agitatedly to signal him to move faster. While crossing this national road, my eyes were suddenly captivated by a car, a Citroen DS that I could see from very far away, moving closer and closer so rapidly, that before I could even say anything, struck head-on at the door where I was sitting.

At that time in France, back seat belts were not required, so my brother and I did not have one. The extreme brutal shock of the collision ejected me a few feet above the car before my body crashed like a rock in the middle of the road. My parents' car, a Renault 16, was still spinning in a circle from the accident. Finally, it stopped, by a miracle, at my right ear. My brother was thrown out of the car and, thanks to the flexibility of his youth, gently rolled onto a grass area on the side of the road which protected him from being hurt. My mom had some minor chest contusions due to the seat belt, but she was OK. My dad was unhurt.

As for myself, my body was badly damaged. My face and ears were bleeding, and my left eye was out of its socket. I sustained many contusions and serious cranial fractures, leaving you to imagine the horrific vision for those who witnessed the scene.

However, for me, who experienced it with my heart and soul, it was one of the most beautiful, powerful, empowering and meaningful moments of my life. It taught me that there is definitely much more out there than what I could ever be able to see or experience with my eyes.

The day that changed my life had finally come. Lying in the middle of the road, I was in a deep coma. My body felt extremely heavy, yet I was feeling so light. Even though it may sound paradoxical, there is no other way to describe this feeling. Heavy, as my body felt like a mountain and I could not physically move or vocally respond, and light, because I was free to spiritually move out of my body and fly

157

anywhere I wished to as if infinity was the limit. It was definitely an unusual yet magnificent experience.

Here is a way that can help you to understand this sensation. For those of you who may have had anesthesia before surgery, do you recall when your body suddenly warms up a few seconds after the injection? As the anesthesia progresses through your body, you have the sensation that your head becomes heavier, and just between the moment when this is occurring, and before you find yourself deeply asleep, your body and head feel extremely and densely heavy, so that you cannot move or vocally find the energy to respond anymore. This is that very moment that corresponds best to the description of how it felt to be in the deep coma. However, in the coma, you stay in that state until you either go further in the coma, having a Near-Death Experience (NDE) or until you come back to your living loved ones, on earth.

In this extra-sensitive state, I was able to hear everything without being able to respond to anything. Every whisper, word, cry, and scream from anyone at the scene, felt amplified ten or twenty times, sometimes accompanied by echoes. I also could hear someone throwing up, and learned afterwards, that it was a woman who had been behind our car and saw the accident as it happened. She was emotionally traumatized from seeing how high I was thrown out of the car before my body crashed onto the road. When I heard her, I wanted to give her a big comforting hug. I did not want her to be traumatized for me, because I was just fine where I was at. She was still being treated for emotional trauma after I left the hospital approximately three weeks later.

This paradox of heaviness and lightness was a present part of the moment I was experiencing that lasted many seconds, minutes and hours. This time allowed me to encounter this amazing, brilliant and unforgettable journey in the Light.

Most importantly, I was feeling wonderfully well. In contrast to that, hearing and feeling the pain, the sorrow, and the great suffering from all the people around me, including my parents and especially my dad, who was very loud in despair, was almost unbearable. I remember very well that I could not understand why people were experiencing so much pain? For whom were they going through this emotional agony? Was it for me? How could it be for me? I was in the most beautiful place I could have ever imagined or could ever be. I was in Heaven! A place of light, of peace, of a love that cannot be found on earth, a love that is not human, a love that embraces you totally and unconditionally, a love that sets you free! Why would they feel this misery? I felt sorry for all of them, for that great suffering state they were in because I was feeling the greatest. I was already in the highest vibrations, and because they were not conscious of it, they were still living the misery of the lowest vibrations that are so common on earth.

I was so light in the Light. If only they could have been with me, I mean, if only they could have felt my feelings, my wellbeing, my heart, my soul, instead of focusing on the 'material' pain of the 'physical' me, they would have then felt my happiness and my peace in their hearts. I felt no pain whatsoever, and I wished they could have caressed that feeling of me soaring in that Light. However, a silence within would have been required for them to grasp that sensation, and they were unfortunately way too busy going through the torturing feelings of pain. In order for them to hear and/or feel me, they would have needed to be calm, serene, centred, grounded, in silence, to enter in contact with me this way. And this was very far away from the reality of their moment.

My mom knelt at my side and was softly talking to me. It felt good to hear her voice and to feel the loving presence of my mother, but I was unable to acknowledge her with words. I could only communicate mentally by telepathy.

Different perceptions of the same moment, same scene; one of freedom, for me, and one of painful emotional attachment, for them!

My dad was crying and screaming, taking all the blame and guilt for doing this to his own son. Many other people were expressing their saddened feelings, for being emotionally moved by the vision of the bloody scene that my body was in.

I felt so much compassion for all of them. Let your imagination go for a moment and see yourself being in a peaceful, serene, soothing, comforting dreamy state. And then suddenly, have an angry crowd, screaming, yelling and crying, with the sounds being amplified ten to twenty times in your ears, into your head that had already suffered from contusions and fractures. Imagine how you would feel? Even a whisper yards away, could be heard very distinctly, as if it was next to your ears.

Those sounds containing the vibrations of agony were very heavy on me. If only they could have felt how I was feeling! I only wished they would have taken a moment to be with me, lovingly, purely and simply, instead of yelling and begging for my return. I was sending light to everyone to calm down their suffering and mentally talking to them, but everyone was too busy in their own experience of the pain to hear or feel me communicating in a way they were not even aware that could exist.

The deep coma I was in leads me to demonstrate to all of you something that I find essential. Of course, this was my own experience, and I cannot speak for everyone who has been or is still in the coma at the time you are reading this. But I believe that if I experienced it, others might be in the same situation. I offer it to you as my perspective/perception of this incredible experience from someone who has lived through it.

In the deep coma, I was leaning towards the beautiful Light. On the other hand, I had people like my dad, who was begging me to come back to him, who was in need of having the 'physical' me back. He was crying, screaming, giving me the palette of suffering on earth. Let me ask you this question. "If you ever had the choice to decide between a beautiful Light of pure welcoming unconditional love, and the earthly human suffering, which one would you choose to go towards to? The answer comes by itself. If you had to choose between a beautiful place where you feel embraced by a totally pure bright light with love or a place where you feel the pain and suffering of people's neediness, the attachment of their emotions to the 'physical' as if you are only a body or nothing at all, what would you choose? You would choose the Light, of course!

Back at the scene, I then heard the sounds of the ambulance arriving. I was blessed to have the best nurse I could have ever got for the situation. After being transported into the ambulance, my dad came in, totally out of control, living in a state of constant folly where you do not even remember who you are, and what you are doing. Needless to say, it was not feeling good to hear as it was pushing me out of this world to go towards the garden of stars on the other side. I mentally communicated with the nurse and told him to get my dad out of here, which he sensed right away. How fortunate I was to have had a nurse to understand the power of mental communication. Or was he a human-angel on my path to protect me? He told my dad that I wanted him to leave the truck. My dad refused and aggressively responded (while crying) 'Excuse me, I am his dad! So I can stay here. How can he ask something, he cannot talk? The accident is all because of me, and I need to be with him.' The 'human angel' had to be firm enough to ask him to step out. My dad felt so out of hand. It was sad for him, but at the same time, almost emotionless, I knew I needed to be alone, in the silence of my own Self, to live what is to follow. Again, try as much as you can to be aware that when you are in the Light, you do not have any more emotions of attachment. Those are simply earthly ties. Once we were both in the ambulance, the nurse whispered to me 'Now you are OK. Don't worry. You can rest now'. And it felt so good and peaceful. The ambulance left the scene.

I remember that I could see myself from above. I could fly. I could not see any of the horrific physical details, as if the physical being was not the most important. I could fly. I was free and out of the body. This was pure Joy!

Suddenly, I slipped into another world. It felt like being inhaled into another dimension where silence was king. A world of silence! Floating, feet forward, going at a fast pace in a totally dark tunnel shaped like a big tube, which would sometimes be slightly rounded and move upward. A bright light was at the end of that tunnel, and I was going towards it. I was going faster and faster. I was coming closer and closer to this overwhelming beautiful, loving Light. The Light was so bright, a little like the brightness you may experience on earth when your eyes are

160

facing the sun. It felt as if this Light was opening its arms to welcome me with all its Love. It felt so good, so welcoming, so free, so peaceful, and so heavenly.

I was surrounded by 'Beings of Light', shaped like small kidney pools. They were everywhere, made of pure love. They all had various density and variations of white and grey. They looked like a substance made of cotton mixed with light. I was told that they are 'Beings of Light' and that they are everywhere around us, even on earth, at all times. They are part of our living system, they said. They are used as a gap between our negative emotions and pure love. The Light became so close now and was so white and bright. It was a color and a brilliance that you would not be able to find on earth. I had never seen such a bright light before. It was so crisp and bright, yet it would not hurt any eye because it was made out of pure love. It was just magical, fairylike, hypnotic, enchanting and fascinating. I was admiring it and overwhelmed with pure joy. It was calling me. I felt so light in the Light. I was experiencing the real unconditional love, and how more exciting could it be? Little did I know that it would become even more awe-inspiring, astonishing and empowering as the Angels magically appeared out of nowhere inside the tunnel and said to me 'You are okay. Everything is okay. We are with you. We love you'. These words felt like a mother comforting her child with a rainstorm of pure unconditional love. What intrigued me, thinking about it, is that because I felt so small compared to the immensity of this tunnel, and because the Angels were so huge, so tall and big, the ratio of speed seemed different. While I felt like I was going so fast, the Angels did not seem to move as they covered more space in the tunnel hardly. It was amazing. It felt like floating while being transported in the Angels' heavenly arms.

The Light became so close that I finally entered into it.

The day that changed my life had finally come, and I will always cherish that moment with all my heart.

During this time, the ambulance arrived at the hospital, which found me between dimensions for a while; one where I was in the Light, and the other where I was able to hear people talking about me inside the hospital. I remember hearing the nurses distinctly yelling 'Hurry up. Hurry up. It's serious here. He is dead, I think.' I immediately flew outside the ambulance, looking below at the scene, and could see the nurses running towards the ambulance in a state of panic. It took no effort to fly. It happened the very instant I thought of doing it.

They took me inside the hospital while I was looking over the scene from above as we arrived in the emergency room. They prepared me briefly and injected me with something. I don't remember anything, until suddenly, the same way you wake up in the middle of the night before going back to your dream. I went back to my new world in the Light.

161

In this world of silence, I could feel and hear the vibrations of pure love and some delightful melodies, voices with such purity and clarity, like nothing we can hear on earth. Again, you can notice another paradox here where I talk of silence and hearing vibrations at the same time. This is what was so fascinating and so empowering to live. The lesson is, in order to hear clearly and purely, I had to be in a state of complete silence where I could finally find my Self. Here, no one was crying. Every Being knew that I was protected and loved, in the Light. It felt so good. Everything was on such a High Vibration. It is difficult to explain how I knew it was a high vibration, but I just knew it. It is like you just know it is, without having any doubt. It just is. That is what made it so peaceful because every experience I caressed and felt, was so pure, and crystal clear. I was just breathing in the moment!

I was left alone for quite some time in my room at the hospital, floating above myself and was quite enjoying it. I felt so free, and so light with no boundaries, no limitations nor restrictions. It was a piece of Heaven. Next, I remembered that it was time to come back and that I had things to do on earth. It was time to get ready to come back. I suddenly felt like I was slowly re-entering, re-adjusting into my body, and the experience was not pleasant at all. Feeling the heaviness, the gravity of the body, which triggered to feel the pain all over again, was like living hell after Heaven. It felt so limiting, like being confined in a small cell in prison. It felt like freedom was over and I did not like it at all.

A nurse came to check me out and screamed of excitement as if seeing me alive could have caused her a heart attack. She left the room while yelling 'He is alive, he is alive. It's a miracle!' The surgeon came into the room, accompanied by his assistant nurses and said 'What do we have here. It is impossible he is alive.' As if something went wrong for me to be alive. I could not talk yet, but I could hear everything. I could feel his sceptical emotions about the reality I was for him. I could even see at times, even though everything seemed blurry. He did not seem to be very happy that I was alive. It may have disturbed his belief about death. Who knows! Then he talked to me, and I was able to start answering a little. He then left the room, and I heard the nurses repeatedly saying that it was a miracle!

The surgeon did a wonderful job putting my left eye back in its socket. He later acknowledged to my parents that I was a total miracle, and the fact that I did not lose my eye was another miracle in itself. The eye popped out of its socket from the brutal force of the accident. Yet, a tiny filament was still attached to it, and I remember him saying that it was impossible otherwise, that something or someone must have held that little tiny filament so they were able to fix it properly after putting in a few stitches. Without it, I would have lost my eye for good. I said while smiling 'Thank you, my Angels.' I knew they held it, so I would not lose my vision. It was such a powerful and overwhelming feeling. I stayed in the hospital for 3 weeks before I was released.

162

After I arrived home, every time I had to stand up or sit down, I would feel as if my head was spinning, which would make me feel dizzy. It was impossible to take any kind of elevator for many years afterwards. But I was home, alive, with my eyes seeing normally and I was on the mend.

This experience was one of the most beautiful moments of my life. It helped me to understand that I am never alone and that there are many Angels out there, whose mission is to help me on earth. It also taught me that what I am able to see with my eyes is only about 10 to 15% of what is in this world. This day changed my life forever, as it has expanded the vision and the perception of my life and life in general. This is a good lesson for everyone.

Now I would like to share some personal insights about what I have learned from having had this NDE experience. Our perception of things, of life, of people, and the events we go through, can either have a negative effect or empower our lives. Every time we go through an event in our life, we are faced with making a choice, in terms of perceiving this event as bad or negative, or by choosing to see the positive side in every experience we have.

Because I chose to see the positive side of this event, this car accident has inspired my entire life, and I will keep cherishing it with the grace that it deserves. It has taught me that no matter how tough episodes of our life may be, or may sound, we have the free will, the free choice to perceive them, as a victim or as a blessing in disguise. When you choose the latter, it changes your life forever and for the better as you allow yourself to accept the bigger picture of that event, even if it does not make any sense right away. When we can accept it as truth, as Godly, it can bring forth an outcome that is bigger than you can ever imagine. I call it blind faith. From that moment on, I blindly trust my intuitions and all that is happening in my life, as I know that, if they are happening to me, it is only a goal to teach me something and empower me. If I believed in the bad, and in the negativity of events, then it would simply mean that I do not believe in God. When I use the word 'God' throughout this book, I am referring to the Divine Source, The Universal Light, or whatever you choose to label it as.

My experience has also taught me a lot about death. We all know of someone whom we loved and who passed away. When that moment occurred in your life, how did you react? Did you find yourself crying? Crying for whom? Crying for them, or for losing the comfortable illusion of attachment, of you being able to touch them? There is a high probability that they were just fine, by reaching to the magnificent Kingdom of the Loving and Embracing Light. So, you may have simply ended up not crying for them after all, but to the illusion, you had about the event or life itself. Life never ends. We are spiritual beings having a physical experience on Earth and not the opposite way around. By acknowledging that, we never die as the soul never dies. The body may die, but the soul continues on its journey, and eventually, if it chooses to, will explore a physical life in a different body later on.

After this near-death experience, I was reborn at the age of 12, in a new me, for a new life. I will never be afraid of death as I have caressed it, as I have tasted its marvelous colors and flavors. Death is just a beautiful place where freedom and being limitless is king. I like to call it 'infinitude of expressions'.

Another immensurable blessing, I invite you all to cherish every day of your life. To find a moment to stop your busy life. To stop running everywhere as if life was going to end in the next minute. And to trust and practice, as often as it may be, the power of silence.

It is only in the power of silence within that you hear God, your inner voice, receive clarity on the many events you went through, or you are currently going through and may find who you truly are.

It is important to share with you, my personal insights about people in the coma and what to do, how to react, when you are faced with the situation in order to help to welcome the one in the deep coma, into your world.

While being in the deep coma, I would have loved to been talked to from the heart, very calmly, gently, softly, mentally, or a soft whisper and being shown the love that is awaiting me back on earth, surrounded by genuine human love. That would make me want to return to my loved ones on earth. Wouldn't you feel the same way? If people in the deep coma had to choose between the love in the Light, and the love on earth from people who can demonstrate to them sincerely that they love them unconditionally, and convince them of the abundance of love awaiting them on earth, I believe they would choose to come back in an instant. Only most people are unaware of this, and therefore, by expressing their raw, painful emotions of attachment, which triggers the vibrations and sounds of pain and suffering, they may unconsciously persuade the one in the coma to make the decision to go towards the Light.

Additionally, be open to the many different ways of communicating your love and thoughts to the ones you love and to the world. We have learned ways to communicate, in person or not, with our voice, with a gesture, with writing, using the phone, and via e-mail. I would like you to consider other options, such as mental telepathy, that can be so important and the only way to communicate with those in the coma, or those experiencing a NDE or may I even dare to say, those who have already passed away to the radiance of the Light.

Love has no limits. Love has no boundaries. Love has no barriers. Love is infinite. Love can only be found in the mysterious and beautiful kingdom of infinitude, and this world can only be felt from within, from a calm and positive state of being.

164

The illusion made out of selfishness and ownership is not part of this beautiful world of peace.

The beautiful soul that you are, who came to earth for a mission, and finds a home within a physical body, never dies. Your physical body dies as it is a temporary home to be able to experience life on earth, but your soul is always alive as it is eternally free."

The last extract and the following one were taken from Frederic's enlightening and inspiring book, *Eyes Of Your Heart*. In the following extract, we see that what appeared to be disastrous medical negligence resulting in complete paralysis, turned out to be a *blessing in disguise,* as it enabled Frederic to face his fears, learn the power of listening to his own heart, and follow his own divine guidance to utilize his *"giftings"* that God had endowed him with to the extent that he could then go on to help heal multitudes around the world through his *magical music* for the soul.

Frederic shares his story.

"At the age of 13, a year after my first Near-Death Experience when I encountered Angels and Beings of Light in the tunnel reaching to the Bright Warm Light, I was guided to start playing people's soul songs.

I knew this was very powerful and could change people's life. However, it scared me as I was unable to share this experience and feeling with anyone, in France at the time. It is only at the age of 30, after being temporarily paralysed, that I got it and surrendered on the spot and forgave myself for not sharing this gift earlier. I strongly believe this has helped me to walk again, as I felt a 'Breath of Life' being released from my solar plexus at the time of total forgiveness."

The Wake-Up Call

"Also, at the age of 19, I wanted to find my musical identity, so I started by composing a few songs, singing while creating music, and then began to combine original instrumental music with the sounds of nature. I went to Paris and met with many different artistic directors and producers. I met with them gifted with my natural innocence, as well as with a certain ignorance of their world. I was far from foreseeing what would happen next. They listened, and said while laughing at this music 'What's that? That's not what we're looking for. Do you really think this can be a hit? Do you ever listen to the radio? My advice to you: Go home. Listen to the radio and hear what's out there, so you know what we want, and then feel free to come back.' Sure, I thought. Should I already take a

ticket for my next humiliation? It felt so insulting and disrespectful to see them laughing at my creations, which was 'my world'.

Of course, my ego was hurt, but I was not aware of this at the time. I did not know that this hurtful experience would bring the best life lessons out of me. I did not realize it because I was living it and feeling those raw emotions. I did not know what the bigger picture was, yet.

This incident had set in motion the second major blessing in disguise, as I took the decision to listen to the producers, to work as hard as I could, to bring them what they wanted. I had thought that after I sign a contract with them, I could slowly go back to the unique creation of my true Self. My naïveté had cornered me in the inferno of sharks.

For four years, I worked arduously to give them what they wanted to hear. A signed contract was the compensation expected. My friends at the time, who were divinely guided to become my earthly messengers, and probably sent by the Angels, were warning me that this new 'pop music' that I was creating was not me and that it was just OK, as I was trying to copy what was already professionally done by others. The uniqueness and magical touch of my heart could not be heard in these copycat creations. However it annoyed me to listen to them destroy my new illusionary motivation, and like any human being with a free will, I made a choice to refuse their advice, which also altered some of my friendships with them. However, my determination was such that nothing could have ever stopped me. Well, that's what my ego thought. I believe that God loves us unconditionally and always gives us the comfort and support that we need, by guiding us, sending us emissaries, Angels or human messengers, to bring us back to our path in the event we let our 'Self' be distracted from it. I was running away from the path of my true Self.

One day, a week before going on a leisure trip to Singapore, I started to feel sick. I went to the doctor and he diagnosed something and reassured me it would need a minor surgery that only required a local anaesthetic and that I would be home one hour later, so I said OK.

On the morning of the surgery, I had an odd feeling that pervaded my entire being attached to the outcome of the surgery. Should I cancel it? What should I do? It felt inappropriate to cancel with such short notice, so I went to the private hospital located in a town just east of Paris. Before the surgery, the nurse prepared me and injected the anesthesia shot into my lower back. The surgeon waited a little bit and then started to make an incision. I began shouting as I could feel the excruciating pain. He ordered the nurse to add some more liquid into my lower back. I could unmistakably sense the product being packed up somewhere, and it was not feeling right. I told the surgeon that it was hurting, but his annoyed sigh made me think that he was not taking my request seriously. He probably thought

166

I was just a wimp. He ordered the nurse to add more of that substance. And this little game continued until I told him that I really was not feeling well. He looked at me and said in a panic to his assistant while I was leaving my body 'Merde, on est en train d' le perdre' ('F.ck, we're losing him.') His sudden fear made him add some other big words. I then lost consciousness.

When I woke up in the hospital, an unknown amount of hours later, I attempted to sit up and quickly realized that something was abnormal. I had no strength, so I touched my legs and realized that it felt like touching air. I touched my legs again, and the same sensation occurred. It was like touching nothing. The physical legs that I could see with my eyes felt like air on the contact of my hands. I could not understand. I tried to move my toes, with no success. I touched my hip and felt nothing. I immediately grasped that I was paralysed. It was just like acknowledging it with no emotions attached, what had just happened so vividly, made perfect and whole sense to me, which allowed my acceptance to luminously envelope my entire body, heart, and soul.

With the loss of use and feeling of my legs, I felt the peace of God with the pure consciousness of surrender. The intense fear I felt previously had given way to a sacred sense of Divine Presence, a deep serenity, and complete freedom. It was a blissful acceptance and understanding. For me to explain this, I will need to go backward a little bit in time.

A year after my near-death experience, at the age of 13, I was watching a variety show on French television when the singer, Dalida, was on. I suddenly felt driven to play her name on my piano, by attributing a note to each letter, such as A for letter A, B for letter B, and so forth. Playing her name for about 7 minutes, I unexpectedly found myself seeing as if peeking through a window that just opened like a multidimensional part of the Universe, another Realm. I could clearly perceive her distress, her call for help, her true feelings, which were drastically different from the appearance we had of her on television. This shocked me vividly. It also scared me as I did not understand exactly what had happened. I did not know whether I caused this to occur, and if so, did I have the right to do it and see? What if I had violated a Universal Law, I wondered.

Without knowing it, I had experienced for the very first time, my main musical gift. I repeated the formula a few more times, with other celebrity names, and it would always instantly open up like a window of another dimension where the true feelings of that person could be perceived. It was fun and scary at the same time. The more I was practicing it, the quicker I would be able to perceive.

Lacking the opportunity to talk about it to anyone, I preferred to shut it off and refused it for many long years. There would not be a single day that passed by, without this haunting my thoughts. I was wondering: 'Even if I had the right to do it, what use can I do with it, how could I ever help this singer from her distress?'

It felt worthless and was causing me a lot of stress. Eleven years later, when I was 24, the Medias announced the death of Dalida, by committing suicide. This is the day when I understood a gift that I was able to perceive things, and it felt peaceful that I probably did not do anything wrong. I deeply knew, as my own truth, that one day would come when I would have to face the fear-based on this unknown world of perception of my gift. If it's a God-given gift, how can I escape by not honoring it?

I had heard of some healers or mediums giving workshops and classes, but again, I was cautious not to fall on some charlatans that do that for the sake of piling up the money. I knew of some of them who were misleading people, in the name of God, Jesus, the Angels, etc. So without knowing, I refused a little bit longer to develop my gift and tried as much as I could to avoid it. As the proverb says 'You can run, but you cannot hide', this is exactly what I did to myself for seventeen years. I tried to run away from my path, from fear based on the unknown, and something had to stop me.

When I woke up in the room of the private hospital, understanding that I was paralysed, it made a total complete sense. I had been running away from my path, first, from my gift to create music based on someone's name, and second, running away from creating the soothing instrumental music, in order to please the French producers. Friends as messengers tried to save me by warning me that they could not recognize me in this 'pop' music I was creating, but I chose to lose myself in it, by refusing to listen. In other words, nothing could stop me unless God had some better ideas for me.

Being paralysed was, therefore, the second huge Blessing in disguise of my life, as I could not escape anymore. I was face to face with the reality that I had co-created for my highest good. Instantly, I went into prayer, and I said to God, the Angels, and to myself 'Oh! God, I just got it. Oh! I am so sorry for being so stubborn and for not listening sooner. I could have done better, but I was afraid of everything. I ran away from what I am supposed to do. I promise you God, I promise you, the Angels, and I promise myself, that I will not be afraid anymore, and that I will be doing my life's work from now on, even if that means doing it from a wheelchair.' This commitment was real. It was expressed with such sincerity that I felt some energy being released from the solar plexus area. I felt calm and serene.

A nurse came in, and I told her the reason I became paralysed. She was rude and told me 'No, you are not paralysed. You are just waking up. Your body is still numb, maybe, but it's going to come back. You are leaving soon, anyway.' I asked her 'How could I leave soon, I cannot walk?' Then she said while leaving the room that she would send the doctor to me. The surgeon arrived and totally denied the fact that I was paralysed. They all deliberately chose not to pay attention to this fact. They knew that if they acknowledged an eventual mistake on their part that they could be sent to trial. So the best way was to continue denying it. They would rather consciously lie than deal with a lawsuit.

The day of my release had arrived. The doctors ignored the fact that I could not walk. But I just had to get out as they needed the room for somebody else. They released me with no word, not even a simple goodbye from anyone. A friend of mine came to pick me up, and with much difficulty, finally succeeded to get me into his car and brought me to my apartment, located rue de Rochechouart, in the 9th district of Paris. My friend sat me on the couch, and after a while, he left. Alone at home, I realized that I could not do anything. I tried to get a glass of water, as the kitchen was about 2 feet from the couch I was sitting on, and I fell. I started to sob and shed tears, as I understood that my independent life was over, at least for now. I finally succeeded to crawl to the phone with the help of my arms and dialled the number of my parents. I did not know how to announce to them my news. When I heard the voice of my mom, no words could come out, and only tears could be heard. My mom, not understanding why I was crying, said 'What's going on? Why are you crying? Tell me!' No words could flow. After a few minutes like that, my mom was stunned to hear me say, while sobbing 'Mom, I am paralysed.' About two hours later, my brother and my dad were at my house and drove me to their home.

Even though I could not walk, the reality of life made me weep in despair. I was thinking of the job I loved so much. I was currently working for a dubbing company in the Champs Elysées. We would dub into French all the US soap operas, and series.

My parents called their family doctor the next morning. He was the same doctor I used to have since I was a child. He was a nice man who always took the time to listen to his patients. They all comforted me a lot, with positive thoughts, saying that maybe I will be able to walk again with a good attitude. It felt good to hear that. However, my new reality was to accept being totally dependent on my family after enjoying being independent.

My friends and family tried to convince me to sue the doctors of the private hospital. But my major focus was to be able to walk again. I knew why this episode had occurred as I was the co-creator of it, but how could I ever reveal that to anyone, including my parents? I did not want to be judged. I decided not to pursue the idea of a lawsuit. Even if I did not appreciate the cowardly behavior of the doctors, I knew, most importantly, that God had certainly guided them to act upon the lesson I had to learn, which triggered to return to my path. I never believe in mistakes or coincidences because I know there is always a bigger picture than what we can see or feel at the time of an occurring event.

I had given my power away to the French Producers that convinced me to change my Self. And I was happy to be back to my true Self. Everything was so clear in my mind.

Every single day saw a little progress, from slowly feeling my toes, my legs, and then begin learning to stand up without falling. My lower back was so swollen from all that liquid they injected, which made it almost impossible to stand straight for a long time.

I finally finished my recovery by travelling to my favorite Greek island, Amorgos. I loved to travel to Greece. This would be my #1 destination as I loved the people and the experience there, especially in the less touristic islands. I wondered whether it was reasonable to plan for a recovery in Greece as I could not even walk perfectly yet. But my mom, with a genuine attitude, told me that she intuitively felt that because I loved Greece that much, it would bring my strength back, which did happen as she had foreseen it.

This episode taught me a lot about our judgments, why we sue, who we dare to blame, and so forth. Blaming or suing seems easier as it makes the other person the bad guy, instead of learning to be responsible. I believe in God; therefore, I cannot blame somebody else. It would then make me a victim that judges, and I do not think this feeling comes from a loving Godly nature. I also find amusing, the fact that in America, a nation that is so fundamentally based on Christian roots is also a nation that uses blame, judgments, wrong or right, and that practices lawsuits towards anyone so easily for the greed of money. It seems to me that there is a gap of misunderstanding somewhere.

I have learned through my own experiences that it is never too late to be aware of what we could have done better, and reverse, by going forward with more clarity and gratitude between ourselves. "[39]

I could not agree more with Frederic when he says that too often we try to apportion blame onto someone else for things that we have elected to experience at a Soul level, which are potentially our greatest times of change, growth and awareness - then they become the 'gifts' that help shape us for the development of compassion, humility and understanding of self and others.

Frederic has gone on to write some breathtakingly beautiful music that does speak to the Soul, that I have personally found to be is uplifting, healing, de-

---

[39] Frederic Delarue, *Eyes Of Your Heart*

stressing,(my word), peaceful, help raise your vibration and so much more. One of his greatest contributions to the musical healing of humanity is a channeled piece entitled, *Musical Rapture.*

Frederic continues.

"On December 29, 2010, Joao Cota-Robles made his transition to the Light, from sudden pneumonia. I did not know him personally, but I did know his dad, Dick and his mother, Patricia Cota-Robles, who have invited me to perform my music for four years in front of a big Spiritual Conference she organizes in places of high frequency, or 'vortexes'. When I learned of his transition, I felt immediately compelled to drive from Palm Springs, CA to Tucson, AZ, for his Celebration of Life. In the meantime, Joao seemed to communicate with me and ask for me to create the 'Music of his Soul' CD, as a legacy of him for his family. But after being at the Celebration, it felt like he wished that this CD to be 'A Gift to Humanity', a music that can bless with comfort anyone who is dealing with any form of cancer, music that helps you raise your vibrations.

It took several months for this idea to be totally clear and ready to blossom. In the middle of April 2011, I suddenly felt and heard (inner voice) that I should go to France immediately, which I did. In France, besides visiting my family, I went to Rennes-le-Chateau to film 2 DVDs with Debowska Productions. There, at the location of the filming, I had the strong feeling that Mary Magdalene had walked on that field, feeling her blueprint. Then when visiting the Church of Rennes-le-Chateau, I went to pray at Marie Madeleine statue, and I had the incredible, surreal, paranormal experience, to feel her face moving, and speaking to me. I will never forget that moment ever!

Back in California, Joao seemed to urge me to do the CD and to communicate with his mother, that she would know better than me, how to share it with the World. I called Patricia right away and told her about it.

Patricia shared with me that her son seems to wish the CD to be made the next day, which was on Pentecost Sunday as a honor to Mary. In the meantime, Dr Florence Phillips, wife of Dr Ernest Phillips and ministers for a long time in Hemet, CA then Palm Springs, CA passed away from cancer. She was the only Minister in Palm Springs to welcome me to do my meditation work, without any conditions attached. She was an Angel. Passing on early Pentecost Sunday gave me one more validation that the CD had to be made that day, and I strongly feel Dr Florence was with me during the creation of this music and I honour her for that.

Before and while creating the CD, I felt enveloped with intense and profound vibrations and frequencies, and I had a hard time to stand up at the end of this divine creation. It was THAT beautifully overwhelming!

Joao seemed to say that this CD should NEVER be bought or sold by anyone. It shall be given away, free of charge, and 'dare anyone who tries to make a penny out of this divine project!'

The frequency of this Celestial Music communicates with the Divine Intelligence of the body at a cellular level raising the consciousness of each cell. As the music soothes and comforts the cells, the body's natural ability to heal itself is enhanced.

This sacred music is compatible and works in harmony with every healing modality or medical treatment a person may choose to experience. The music resonates with an additional blessing for everyone who is dealing with any form of cancer."[40]

I had been thoroughly enjoying Frederic's CD's and *Musical Rapture* for a few months while completing the first edition of this book. It was at the second-to-last interior book proofing stage–right near the end–when I felt my intuition prompt me to include Frederic's story in this book. Up until then, I had no idea he had even had an NDE, and when I started reading about his remarkable journey, I could see and feel why he needed to be included. I have since been in touch with Frederic who graciously consented to my printing some excerpts from his book. He is truly a beautiful, humble, gracious and very gifted soul. It is my honor to be able to present his story and music to you all. I will close with his summation.

"My mission is to share my musical gift in order to help anyone to feel embraced by heartfelt musical vibrations of pure love, and help you to re-connect with who you truly are.

My goal is to be able to perform FREE CONCERTS for people in great need of feeling embraced by inner-peace, unconditional love and comfort, which is why in 2007, I founded a non-profit organization called 'Cathedral Of Angels.'

I have learned in the 3 major events of my life (NDEs and from being paralysed) that Miracles happen, and they happen every day for many of us on this planet. When you are in tune (resonate) with a 'vibration' that feels comfortable (home, familiar) to you, (whether it is touching a sacred cloth, grotto, statue, photo, or feeling overwhelmingly embraced by pure love through music, and any other type of vibrational art,) then a miracle can take place as you surrender, and for some, even as you start releasing all unnecessary sufferings. Instead of giving your power away to anger, suffering, a distraction by feeling home at all levels, you are taking your Power back, and this is when the process of healing gets activated.

---

[40] You can download this *"music for the soul"* (and cells) for free at Frederic's website www.fredericdelarue.com and purchase his other wonderful CD's if desired.

For this goal to happen, I am calling for your help, for all ideas and suggestions."

Whether you are or know of potential Sponsors, Donors, or Benefactors. Whether you have a large outdoor ranch or large room in the Palm Springs area, (or anywhere else in the country), where you can provide the space for an ongoing concert. Another Vision would be to perform for thousands in Lourdes, France. Whether you have media connections and want to help to promote this healing endeavor. I also accept your heartfelt monetary contributions to continue this mission..[41]

I thank you from the bottom of my heart for taking the time to read this. Your help is precious to all on the living world who are currently suffering. Know that spreading the word out to your friends, relatives and sharing this page with them, is one of the most powerful tools one can use. I am very grateful to you for doing that.

Many Blessings of Unconditional Love and Gratitude to All of You.

Frederic Delarue

23. LAURELYNN MARTIN'S NEAR-DEATH EXTRACT

Laurelynn Martin was at the height of a promising tennis career when she had a routine surgical procedure that catastrophically sent her into an ecstatic world of light, beauty and love on the *"other side."* She was Home – Home in the Light!

The following are excerpts from her book, *Searching For Home*, which describes her near-death experience. Her book is a powerful story of a young woman's love, hope and healing after a near-death experience. She discovered that life is not about what we do but about how we do it. She realized that she had been using what she did as the means to seek approval and love from people instead of giving love unconditionally to those around her and in so doing she would then receive that love and validation back ten-fold. She discovered that when she had forgiven herself for doing this, she received love in abundance. She realized that our experiences that we would rather forget about, where we may have judged ourselves for behaving in the way that we did, happen to bring us to places of awareness and compassion for others. Like so many other NDE'ers she observed the scene below where medics were frantically working to save her, without

---

[41] Frederic can be contacted at - info@fredericdelarue.com

emotional attachment and wanting to let everyone know she was in a wonderful place and still very much alive.

"She helped me slide onto the operating table and gave me a motherly look. 'Don't worry. We know it's your first time. We'll make this a most pleasant experience for you.'

With those reassuring words, I drifted off to sleep. I awakened and found myself floating above my body, off to the right side, looking down, watching the attempts of the medical team trying to revive the lifeless form below. I viewed the scene with detachment. The surgical team was frantic. The colour red was everywhere, splattered on their gowns, splattered on the floor, and a bright pool of a flowing red substance, in the now wide open abdominal cavity. At that moment, I didn't make the connection that the body being worked on was my own! It didn't matter anyway. I was in a state of floating freedom, experiencing no pain and having a great time. I wanted to shout to the distressed people below, 'Hey, I'm okay. It's fantastic up here,' but they were so intent on their work, I didn't want to interrupt their efforts.

I had travelled to another realm of total and absolute peace. With no physical body, my movement was unencumbered. Thought was the avenue for travel. I floated up through blackness where there was no fear, no pain, no misunderstandings, but instead a sense of well-being. I was enveloped by total bliss in an atmosphere of unconditional love and acceptance. The darkness was warm and soft, a blanket of velvety love, stretching endlessly. The freedom of total peace was intensified beyond any ecstatic feeling I've ever felt on earth. In the distance, a horizon of glorious white, golden light beckoned me forward.

As the brilliance increased and the encompassing rays stretched to meet me, I felt that time, as we know it, was non-existent. Time and existence were a blending and a melding of the past, present and future into this one moment. A sense of all-knowing enveloped me. Every part of my being was satisfied with an unconditional love beyond description. All questions were answered. An inner peace without striving or achieving was created and understood.

It flashed in my mind; this was the pleasant experience the nurse had spoken about. I understood why she didn't elaborate. Words and descriptions somehow lost the essence of the experience.

As I admired the beauty of the light, I was drawn closer, feeling the radiant warmth, infinite love and lasting peace. I felt as if I were home – home in the light. Before I became further engulfed in the light, I became aware of many spirits. They surrounded, embraced and supported my journey with their gentleness, knowledge and guidance. I felt one of them approach from my right upper side. This familiar presence came forward, and my feelings changed to sheer joy when

174

I discovered my thirty-year-old brother-in-law, the one who had died seven months earlier from cancer. My essence moved to meet his essence.

I couldn't see with my eyes or hear with my ears, yet I instinctively knew that it was 'Wills.' I heard his smile, saw his laughter and felt his humor. It didn't make sense, but it made complete sense. We were separate, but we were also one. It was as if I had come home, and my brother-in-law was there to greet me. I instantly thought how glad I was to be with him because now I could make up for the last time I had seen him before his death. I felt sad and a bit guilty for not taking the time out of my busy schedule to have a heart-to-heart talk with him when he had asked me to. I realized I was not being judged by him but by myself. I was in his position – dying, wanting to say goodbye to those I loved, and then meeting people like myself not 'getting it' – not getting that all the achievement, money or recognition in the world cannot be taken with you when you die. The only thing you take with you is the love you give away.

Wills gave love away his whole life. In a sense, he was ready to leave our physical world and continue his work in the spiritual world. People, like my sister, who was left behind without their beloved, sometimes didn't understand. I would have to remember to tell Gwen about my discovery.

The ones who depart are in a loving space with much guidance, understanding and purpose. Their wish upon departure is not to bring sorrow and grief to others but to honor the divine plan. It is their time for transition, for the continued development of their soul. Many times, the departed loved one will work in ways to help, serve and guide others.

Wills' gentle guidance allowed me to view my innocence. I understood, instantly, life was about people, not pursuits. I was putting pursuits first as a means to seek approval and love from people. Once I understood, I forgave myself for my actions and in the act of forgiving, I received love in abundance.

By giving love, one receives and experiences a tremendous love from the universe.

Wills was like the 'Spirit of Christmas Past.' By reviewing my past, I was brought to new places of discovery within myself. Many events were shown simultaneously. I recalled two examples. When I was five years old, I teased Tammy Fowler, another five-year-old girl, to the point of tears. I was now in a unique position to feel what Tammy felt. Her frustration, her tears, and her feelings of separateness were now my feelings. I felt a tremendous amount of compassion for this child. I was Tammy and needed love, nurturing and forgiveness. My essence gave love to both of us – a love so deep and tender, like the love between a mother and child. I realized by hurting another, and I was only hurting myself. Again, I was experiencing oneness.

The next incident was similar. I had made fun of Billy Bradley, a scrawny, malnourished asthmatic kid. He died when he was seventeen years old from a cerebral aneurysm. He seemed to be in the realm of existence I was in. Yet, still, I was not sure where I was. When Billy was twelve, he had written me a love letter that I rejected. I was experiencing his pain which became my pain. At the same time, I felt a tremendous amount of love for this boy and myself. My contact with him went beyond the physical, and I felt his soul. He had a vibrant, bright light burning inside of him. Feeling his spirit's strength and vitality was an inconceivable moment, especially knowing how much he physically suffered when he was alive.

The message was clear. The message was – LOVE.

Above and beyond anything else, one must first learn to love oneself non-judgmentally and unconditionally. Then one will actually love all people and all things the same way.

I realized how important people were in life, how important it was to accept them and love them. And I finally understood the old Mohegan Indian saying I had heard when I was in Girl Scouts, 'Never judge another squaw until you have walked a mile in her moccasins.'

As I reviewed my life with Wills, my judgment prevailed, and I remember thinking, 'I've done worse things in my life.' My question was answered before I finished my thought.

All events in your life are significant. To bring an understanding of all things, even the experiences which you consider insignificant will bring you to places of great awareness and compassion.

By the time my review was finished, I had understood. I was aware of an almost cathartic release. I experienced emotion without the physical signs of tears. It brought me to a deep place of understanding and compassion. I never took the time to think about how my actions affected others or how I treated myself. I felt a grieving for all my unconscious actions. With awareness of my unaware state, I released all the grief I had ever caused and joyfully moved into forgiveness.

Other thoughts were conveyed, and I remember thinking, 'Wow, now I get it. Everything about our existence finally makes sense.' I had more questions for Wills. The transference of information was immense and reassuring. He kept saying, 'All is known. You have simply forgotten.'

I didn't feel like I knew anything; yet, there was a place in me that knew everything. I asked Wills if I could stay. He said, 'It's not your time yet. There's been a mistake. You have to go back.'

I remember thinking, 'Okay, I'll go back, but I can get back up here.'

At that same instant, his thoughts were mine, 'You can't take your own life. Suicide, for you, isn't the answer. That won't do it. You have to go back and live your life's purpose.'

I responded, 'I understand, but I don't want to go back.'

Wills' thought came to me again, 'It's okay. We're not going anywhere. We'll be here for you again.'

His last communication was, 'Tell your sister, I'm fine.'

With those final thoughts, I felt myself going back, dropping downward through the darkness. I was not afraid. Instantly, I felt myself slam into my body."[42]

24. DOUG MCMENAMIN'S NDE & ADC

The following NDE was given to me by Doug's wife Carol. It illustrates the power of prayer and that nothing is ever as it seems.

Angelic Choirs And Christ's Intervention

"Unfortunately, Doug's memory had deteriorated and he was unable to remember the fuller version of his Near-Death Experience which he told when he regained consciousness after being in a coma for 3 months and being kept alive by a ventilator as his intercostular muscles had completely collapsed. He was then kept in a semi-anesthetized state for a further five months because of the trauma of being so paralysed.

Doug's story is truly remarkable. He defied physicality many times and left his Doctors and nursing staff bewildered, but knowing something very special was taking place. He proved that people in a coma are still very much alive and often aware of what is being said and done around them. They are just in a different state of consciousness and unable to communicate through their normal five senses. This also illustrates the importance of loved ones, carers and medical staff being aware that people in a coma can often hear what is being done and said around them and that compassionate respect for the patient is wise.

Originally Doug was not expected to live long, however, he lived on a ventilator breathing for him for many years, while in ICU for an unprecedented two years. He was very much aware of his surroundings and ultimately, together with his extraordinary Doctors and specialists, found ways to communicate by blinking.

---

[42] Laurelynn's website is www.laurelynnmartin.com

His selfless, adoring wife, Carol, never gave up and helped him to live as long as he possibly could.

Just before passing Doug entered 'The Twilight Stage,' when loved ones, (and sometimes pets), who have passed over often come close and the person soon to pass over can see and interact with them.

Doug also showed us how loved ones could communicate after their so-called 'death' in the remarkable After Death Communications he was able to orchestrate.

Doug's first recollection was 'waking up' and finding his bed surrounded by water that he could trail his hands in! Standing next to him was a Monk and a family friend, Fr Borello, who was praying for him. Then Doug found himself out of the ICU room in the corridor listening to the Specialist telling Carol to contact the family as they were losing him fast. He said he saw that his wife was very upset. Next, he found himself in a room with the Monk, he cannot recall what was said, but he remembers him being very friendly.

Then he found himself in the most beautiful Spring field. There were flowers everywhere, and the colors were exquisite. Doug said it was like a warm Spring day. All the time, beginning in the room, Doug heard Angelic choirs singing, the like, Doug said, he would never hear again on Earth. His favorite song was 'Bread Of Angels'.

Doug then remembered talking with someone who gave him a choice to come back as he had unfinished business to take care of.

For three months after that happening to the time of becoming semi-conscious, he had the Monk with him and he heard the choirs all the time."

His wife Carol had a 'spiritual' experience two weeks after he was admitted. She tells the story:

"I was called to the hospital as he was having a very bad day, and the doctors were worried they were going to lose him. Walking down the corridor, I became panicky and could not go through the locked door of ICU. I said a prayer, 'Lord, I cannot go through that door without you. I will not cope on my own.' With that, I rang the bell of ICU, and the sister came to open it. As the door opened, I saw someone walk through, out of the corner of my eye ahead of me. Actually, he didn't wait for the door to open he walked right through it! It was a figure in a white robe with a cord around his waist. I dismissed it immediately and hurried to Doug's room. He was very bad – then the strangest thing happened; His breathing monitor rang off the wall to say he was now breathing on his own, (up until then a ventilator was doing all the breathing for him). The excitement from the nursing staff was radical as no one could see how it could be possible that he had come

from death's door to breathing on his own in the condition he was in. This lasted for 15 minutes, and then he was back on the ventilator, which kept him alive for the next four and a half years. I knew then it was our Lord; he had walked in ahead of me and shown me that God had everything under control and that Doug wasn't going to die. It remained a complete mystery to the staff!

I experienced another spiritual happening, this time with our Neurologist. He was a man of great faith, and if he felt worried about his patient, he would go down to his study and pray for them in the small hours of the morning. He was despairing of Doug's condition, as it was the worst he had seen and when they are that severe their life expectancy is never longer than six months. He was due to go on holiday that Friday and Doug was completely paralysed, he hadn't moved a muscle or blinked an eye. He didn't want to go on holiday and leave Doug without a diagnosis or some form of recovery. It was already seven weeks into his coma. He prayed for Doug early that morning and later did his rounds before being due to go on holiday. He examined Doug and found no movement at all, and he felt very despondent. He did the rest of his rounds and went back to Doug, and in that completely paralysed state, while he was re-examining him, Doug moved his Big toe on his right foot! (Which never moved again up to his death, four and a half years later) The Neurologist remembered the passage he had read that morning from the Bible that had said to keep believing and having faith. He rang Carol all excited to say that God had given him a sign that Doug wouldn't die and that God was in control, and he now felt he could go on holiday. For the next seven months, Doug was unable to move anything!

He remained in ICU for two years; the longest stay the hospital and ever had.

His paralysis was so bad that the only movement he could make when he came out of the coma three months later was to blink one eyelid.

The tragic thing was that his mind was still intact – as the one doctor said it is like being buried alive in a body that could not move. He could not talk or flinch one muscle during that time-- the doctors explained that they had to make two-hourly decisions to keep him alive as he contracted one superbug after another, which were totally resistant to antibiotics.

In that state, living at deaths door continually, they used to turn on the TV as some stimulation for his brain. The Physiotherapist used to come in and move his arms and legs to give him some exercise. On one of these occasions, he became very, very agitated and she called in the specialist, Dr Ian Finlay, who suggested that they devise an alphabet and point to a letter for Doug to spell out what was agitating him by blinking once for a correct letter and twice for a full stop. As I mentioned the TV was on, and he must have seen the date, 12 December, which was the date of the first time he brought me roses, and I used to get roses on that

179

date every year after that! To the amazement of the surrounding medical staff, Doug managed to spell out -- Carol must have roses today.

As fate would have it, Doctor Ian Finlay was head of the rose society, and unbeknownst to me, he had gone straight home and picked 12 of his best Vera Johns roses. The nursing staff got a bottle from the kitchen to put the roses in, and they put Doug in the lazy-boy chair and propped him up with at least 20 cushions. They wrapped his arms around the bottle with the roses propped up with more cushions. You can imagine how amazed I was when I arrived for my daily visit to find my beloved sitting up in a chair holding twelve beautiful roses on that auspicious day. When our eyes met, I could see his eyes were brimming over with love and joy, and tears began to roll down his cheeks. It wasn't long before my tears matched his. What the hospital staff could not get over was that in his critical state in Intensive Care, being fed intravenously attached to drips and monitors, he could still find it in him to think of someone else. They still speak about it today!

What wonderful medical staff to do this for them. I don't know about you the reader, but this made me cry – the author- If there are any medical staff reading this or people with loved ones in comas and the patient's brains are still functioning okay maybe this could be a methodology to trial to see if communication can be established. I can't think of anything worse for a patient who can hear and understand everything that is going on around them but is unable to communicate with those they love and the medical staff attending them.

Doug remained in ICU for 2 years, and then I took over the nursing for the next two and half years. His speech never really came back as he had a permanent 'trachy' until he died. However, I learnt to lip-read, and we could understand each other perfectly.

He loved gardening. When our house was being built, while he was in the hospital, my first thought was how I am going to get a garden going, as he was the gardener. I did my best and obviously put in loads of roses. He used to love to sit outside in his wheelchair and watch me prune the roses and always used to say the same thing, 'Chippy, (his pet name for me), you have such a beautiful garden.'

I always replied, 'It is OUR garden NOT mine,' to which he used to reply, 'NO I could never do a garden like this.' The complex we used to live in used to run a Garden of the Year award and that year they got in a horticulturists to do the judging. I won second place in the garden awards.

That was Doug saying to me 'Now do you believe me?'

Another experience Doug had just 11 months before his death.

Eleven months before he passed away we were saying good night and I was at home with 24-hour nursing and a special bed. We had a hoist to lift him out of bed, (he was a total quadriplegic), and he had an apparatus that helped him breathe. As he had no cough reflex we had to suction him hourly; otherwise his lungs would have filled up with fluid, and he would have drowned. He could not go a full day without being on the machine, as his intercostals had not fully returned from paralysis.

I was standing at the foot of his bed, and I could see that he was looking straight through me. When I questioned him, he mentioned that he was in a field with the most beautiful daffodils of which the vibrant colour yellow he had never seen before. Then he mentioned that he was walking and could feel the grass under his feet, which got him quite excited, and then he mentioned that our Old English sheep, Thumper, was with him and that they were now running. The excitement and happiness on his face were so special to see. When I asked him if he wanted to go to that field, the vision seemed to fade, and he looked straight at me and said, 'Chippy I am already in that field.'

Doug passed away on 05/11/2008, and of course, he knew even down to the time. On Monday 03/11/08, he got very agitated and asked his visitors to leave the room as he wanted to speak to me in private. When we were alone he said to me, 'Chippy, you know I am dying.' I said, 'Yes, why don't you go and be at peace.' His answer was, 'Because it is the hardest thing I have ever had to do because I don't want to leave you.' I gave him permission, and he just said, 'Thank you.'

On Tuesday, he called in a friend to keep an eye on me to advise him if I needed any help. The friend asked me when the other children were coming out, and I said tomorrow around noon. Doug's reply was 'Too late.'

Later that afternoon, he started smiling and greeting people that we could not see. When I asked him he told me it was his mom and other family members who had gone before. But most amazing was all of a sudden excitedly he said to me, 'At the bottom of my bed, at the bottom of my bed, standing next to you.' I could not get out of him who it was, but his face just shone. Eventually, I asked him if it was his mom and he answered no.

It turned out to be Mary, and when I asked what she was like all he could answer was, 'She is BEAUTIFUL, BEAUTIFUL.'

The family managed to fly the other two children down earlier, and they arrived at 10 pm that evening. They came in and said hello, spent a few minutes with him and promised to see him tomorrow. They were whacked as one had just flown in from Australia and they had managed to get onto the last connecting flight down to Cape Town from Johannesburg.

We all went home, and the hospital phoned at 11 pm and said there was no need for concern as there was no change in his condition, but they could not settle him as he was asking to see me. The children came and hugged him then left the room, as he wanted to speak to me. He said to me, 'I just want to tell you how much I love you and to say thank you for all you have done for me, now I want you to go home and get as much rest as possible as you are going to need it.'

The following morning at 5.30, the hospital phoned again and said we had better come as he was in a coma. When we arrived, the nursing sister in charge said to me, 'I have never seen anything like this in my entire nursing career, you guys were not even in the car park after leaving last night, and he just slipped into a coma.'

Two most amazing things happened. He had the most horrible cancer sores across the top of his head, red and oozy, but when I went in to see him there was not a mark on his face! I have never seen anyone look so peaceful, and I could not believe how young he looked?

The second thing was I was standing at the foot of his bed when all of a sudden, I said to my son, 'Brett Dad has just gone.' Brett was a paramedic in the Army; he felt for a pulse; there was none. He rushed out to call the Sister. On examination, she said she could just hear the last fluttering of the heart. There was no movement, no sound. I cannot explain it, but I just knew he had gone.

He passed away at 7:30 am -- so the kids would have been too late if they had arrived that afternoon as originally planned.

He planned his own funeral. He said he did not want a mournful service but one of celebration, something that celebrated his life, as in his words, 'I have had such a good one. I cannot complain about anything.'

He died very peacefully with his entire family around him, the two children from Australia, Carey & Craig, Brett from Johannesburg and Gary from Cape Town. Of course, he chose 'Bread of Angels' as one of his hymns, his other favorite was 'Make Me an Instrument of Your Peace,' he loved that.

Later on, I had the most vivid dream where he showed me where he was and how happy he was. We were walking in the same field that he had described several times before. I could not get over how well and young he looked. We arrived at a door that he proceeded to open, and I presumed that I could walk through with him.

He turned around and said, 'Chippy, you cannot walk through this door yet.' I walked away, feeling very sad and then all of a sudden he was walking next to me. He was dressed in white and seemed taller than I remember him. Suddenly there was a very bright light that lit up the entire garden that we were walking in. There were people in the light, and they all seemed so happy.

Doug turned to me and said, 'Do you see the light?'

By the time I answered 'yes,' he was gone. I knew he had gone to the light.

I walked down to the end of the garden, where there was another door that was opened for me. On the other side of the door, I felt Doug's presence. I couldn't see him. He then gathered me in his arms like a child, and we seemed to be travelling at such great speed. It was so exhilarating. The next minute I found myself on a regular street with cars and people. I knew that I had been shown a very special place-it was a gift to know where he is and that he is healthy and happy.

I have had several dreams; another one was at Christmas, which was always a big thing in our house. I did not think I could put up the decorations that year, as it was too painful.

That night I had a dream and Doug said to me, 'Chippy don't you know it is time you got out the tree and put up the Christmas decorations.'

I did, and I knew he was with me.

He always used to say to me, 'I will never leave you. I will be in you hear. You just have to look and have faith.'

Last year after chatting to him, (which I do all the time and he always answers me), it was near my birthday, and so I said to him, 'If you are really around and it is not my imagination, I want just one rose for my birthday.'

Well, I got a few rose type emails, and I said to him 'They don't count, I want a real one.'

The night before my birthday I said to him, 'Well, you are running out of hours.'

Well, I could not believe it. By the end of the day of my birthday, I had received 53 roses! Every person almost to the person had a few roses attached to their presents. My apartment was full of them-everywhere you looked!

I was so privileged to have experienced his illness through his eyes, and if anyone asks me if I would do it all over again, the answer is yes."

Wow, is all I could say when Carol sent me this. What an amazing and totally inspiring couple. That is unconditional love in action on all levels of their life together. It is a privilege to be able to honor and acknowledge *both* of them, their selfless journeys together coupled with their faith, strength and perseverance through so much adversity. What wonderful illustrations of the reality and potency of After Death Communications, which we will look at in the next chapter.

Since writing this originally in 2011, the book you are reading has been republished as a new, revised and expanded edition in 2020. Carol has also passed over to be reunited with her precious Doug. What a wonderful reunion that would have been!

CHAPTER FIVE

DETAILED EXPERIENCES FROM ONE LIVING IN THE SPIRIT WORLD

Introduction

I have discovered on numerous occasions now, while revising this book for the second edition, that I would be guided to new information that would add a whole new dimension to its contents. This particular discovery led to my adding a new chapter as this extraordinary material is so enlightening and gives us even greater detail from a man who passed over quite some time ago and who actually lives in these marvelous realms. This chapter contains excerpts from two books by the same author, Anthony Borgia, *Life In The World Unseen* and *Here And Hereafter*. All the extracts from these two books are in italics.

The real-life experiences of life after death in the first edition of this book were from people who had clinically died and returned to Earth to recount their experiences of their brief sojourns to the Spirit World. They still retained amazing details and perspicuity for their brief stays as you will see. However, the excerpts in this chapter are from Anthony Borgia's good friend Robert Benson, who resides in these dimensions, and who gives us gloriously detailed accounts that could only be given by someone actually living there.

Robert Hugh Benson was born in 1871 and died in 1914. Robert was a supernumerary private chamberlain to the then Pope in 1911 and thus gained the title of Monsignor. He was a prolific author of religious works.

In 1909 Anthony Borgia met Monsignor Robert Benson, son of a former Archbishop of Canterbury and a friendship blossomed. The Monsignor, as he was known to Anthony, died unexpectedly at age 42 from an illness. Robert contacted

Anthony some time after his passing and asked Anthony's permission to act as his channel to transcribe information about the spirit realms he now lived in. Robert had felt the necessity to 'put right' the 'untruths' he had written in his books whilst alive as a prominent Minister of religion. Although Robert was very much steeped in orthodox religion in his capacity as Montsignor he had had some personal psychic experiences in his life which he had twisted the truth of to fit what he believed acceptable within his Church's dogmas and creeds.

Anthony recalls.

"We are old friends, and his passing hence has not severed an earthly friendship; on the contrary, it has increased it, and provided many more opportunities of meeting than would have been possible had he remained on Earth. He constantly expresses his delight upon his ability to return to Earth in a natural, normal, healthy and pleasant manner, and to give some account of his adventures and experiences in the spirit world, as one who 'being dead' (as many would regard him), yet 'he speaketh.'"

These were some of the first detailed books ever written on the subject of the 'Hereafter,' as it was known then.

Robert Passes Over

Naturally Robert describes his passing in a very similar way to those who had Near-Death Experiences mentioned in this book.

"I suddenly felt a great urge to rise up. I had no physical feeling whatever, very much in the same way that physical feeling is absent during a dream, but I was mentally alert, however much my body seemed to contradict such a condition. Immediately I had this distinct prompting to rise, I found that I was actually doing so. I then discovered that those around my bed did not seem to perceive what I was doing, since they made no effort to come to my assistance, nor did they try in any way to hinder me. Turning, I then beheld what had taken place. I saw my physical body lying lifeless upon its bed, but here was I, the real I, alive and well. For a minute or two I remained gazing, and the thought of what to do next entered my head, but help was close at hand. I could still see the room quite clearly around me, but there was a certain mistiness about it as though it were filled with smoke very evenly distributed. I looked down at myself wondering what I was wearing in the way of clothes, for I had obviously risen from a bed of sickness and was therefore in no condition to move very far from my surroundings. I was extremely surprised to find that I had on my usual attire, such as I wore when moving freely and in good health about my own house. My surprise was only momentary since, I thought to myself, what other clothes should I expect to be wearing?

186

I could not resist the impulse to turn and take a last look at the room of my transition. It still presented its misty appearance. Those who were formerly standing round the bed had now withdrawn, and I was able to approach the bed and gaze at 'myself.' I was not the least impressed by what I saw, but the last remnant of my physical self seemed to be placid enough. My friend then suggested that we should now go, and we accordingly moved away. As we departed, the room gradually disappeared."

Robert was able to make a smooth and quick transition due to his previous knowledge about transitioning into another dimension. He found himself very much alive and in radiant health in his new abode.

"Such knowledge of the spirit world as I had been able to glean from my own experiences instantly came to my aid. I knew at once of the alteration that had taken place in my condition; I knew, in other words, that I had 'died'. I knew, too, that I was alive, that I had shaken off my last illness sufficiently to be able to stand upright and look about me. At no time was I in any mental distress, but I was full of wonder at what was to happen next, for here I was, in full possession of all my faculties, and, indeed, feeling 'physically' as I had never felt before. Although this has taken some time in the telling, in order that I might give you as much detail as possible, the whole process must have taken but a few minutes of earth time.

As soon as I had had this brief space in which to look about me and to appreciate my new estate, I found myself joined by a former colleague—a priest called Edwin—who had passed to this life some years before. We greeted each other warmly, and I noticed that he was attired like myself. Again, this in no way seemed strange to me, because had he been dressed in any other way I should have felt that something was wrong somewhere, as I had only known him in clerical attire. He expressed his great pleasure at seeing me again, and for my part I foresaw the gathering up of the many threads that had been broken by his 'death'.

For the first moment or so I allowed him to do all the talking; I had yet to accustom myself to the newness of things. For you must remember that I had just relinquished a bed of final sickness, and that in casting off the physical body I had also cast off the sickness with it, and the new sensation of comfort and freedom from bodily ills was one so glorious that the realization of it took a little while to comprehend fully.

And here let me say that all ideas of a 'judgment seat' or a 'day of judgment' was entirely swept from my mind in the actual procedure of transition. It was all too normal and natural to suggest the frightful ordeal that orthodox religion teaches that we must go through after 'death'. The very conception of 'judgment' and 'hell' seemed utterly impossible. They were wholly fantastic, now that I found myself alive and well 'clothed in my right mind' and, in fact, clothed in my own familiar habiliments. Here I was standing in the presence of an old friend who

187

was shaking me cordially by the hand, giving me a greeting of good wishes and showing all the outward signs, and in this case genuine manifestations, of being as pleased to see me as I was to see him. He, himself, was in the best of spirits as he stood there giving me such a welcome as, upon the earth-plane, two old friends accord each other after long separation. That in itself was sufficient to show me that all thoughts of being marched off to some form of judgment were entirely preposterous."

Of course, the nearest we come to this is in our Life Review, as illustrated in the many NDEs, where we witness our entire life and become accountable for all our thoughts, words and deeds. Then we, *ourselves*, together with wise counsel from the Higher Realms decide what *we* want to *put right*.

"We both were too jolly, too happy, too carefree, and too natural, and I, myself, was waiting with excitement for all manner of pleasant revelations of this new world, and I knew that there could be none better than my old friend to give them to me. He told me to prepare myself for immeasurable number of the pleasantest of surprises, and that he had been sent to meet me on my arrival. He already knew the limits of my knowledge, so his task was that much the easier."

Robert explains a little of his former Earth life.

"My Earth life was not a hard one in the sense that I never underwent physical privations, but it was certainly a life of hard mental work. In my early years I was drawn towards the Church because the mysticism of the Church attracted my own mystical sense. The mysteries of religion, through their outward expression of lights and vestments and ceremonies, seemed to satisfy my spiritual appetite in a way that nothing else could. There was much, of course, that I did not understand, and since coming into spirit I have found that those things do not matter. They were religious problems raised by the minds of men and they have no significance whatever in the great scheme of life. But at the time, like so many others, I believed in a wholesale fashion, without a glimmering of understanding, or very little. I taught and preached according to the orthodox text books and so I established a reputation for myself. When I contemplated a future state of existence I thought— and that vaguely— of what the Church had taught me on the subject, which was infinitesimally small and most incorrect."

Some time later when Robert was settled into his new abode Edwin showed him a bookcase which contained many books. The information that Robert gave to Anthony to transcribe of his actual experiences whilst living in the Spirit World for his subsequent books, were the direct result of his original perusal of this bookcase. Robert continues.

"I was interested to learn what was the nature of these books and so I made a closer examination. I found that conspicuous among them were my own works. As

I stood in front of them I had a clear perception of the reason, the real reason, for there being there. Many of these books contained those narratives that I spoke of earlier, in which I had told of my own psychic experiences after giving them the necessary religious turn. One book in particular seemed to stand out in my mind more than the others and I came to the full realization that I now wished that I had never written it. It was a distorted narrative, where the facts, as I had really known them, were given unfair treatment, and where the truth was suppressed. I felt very remorseful, and for the first time since coming into this land I had regret. Not regret that I had, at last, arrived in the spirit world, but sorrow that, with the truth before me, I had deliberately cast it aside to place in its stead falsehood and misrepresentation. For I knew that so long as my name lived, that is, so long as it had any commercial value, that book would continue to be reproduced and circulated and read—and often regarded as the absolute truth. I had the unpleasant knowledge that I could never destroy what I had thus done. There was, at no time, any sense of condemnation over this. On the contrary, I could feel a distinct atmosphere of intent empathy and compassion towards me.

My first question was to ask my companion how I could put this matter right. He told me that there were several ways in which I could do so, some more difficult— but more efficacious—than others. I suggested that perhaps I could go back to the earth-plane and tell others of this new life and the truth of communication between the two worlds."

From that moment on this became Robert's mission and prayer as he vowed to make amends for misleading people, albeit unknowingly at that time, through his doctrine-based books. Robert was endowed with some psychic abilities whilst living amidst orthodox religion on Earth. This subject was frowned upon and considered *"work of the Devil"* by his church. Needless to say, Robert never told anyone in the church about this as he knew it was real and not of the Devil. He took this secret with him to the grave.

Soon after Robert had arrived in this new realm, he met a young lady called Ruth. Ruth was also on her own and she too had recently passed over. Subsequently she became a dear friend and Edwin took great delight in showing them both around their new surroundings.

Buildings for Those Who Passed from A Long Illness

Or From A Violent Passing

For those of you reading this book who have lost loved ones from long illnesses or violent passing's of some kind this will be of great comfort to you. You can replace the unknown and visualize them as they would have been; nurtured, loved and prepared with love and compassion for their exciting new life with loved ones, who had previously passed over, waiting to reunite with them.

189

"Ruth espied a rather stately building set among some well-wooded grounds, which also aroused my curiosity. On appealing to our guide, Edwin told us that it was a home of rest for those who had come into spirit after long illnesses, or who had had a violent passing, and who were, in consequence, suffering from shock. We wondered if it would be possible to peep inside, without appearing to be curiosity-seekers. He assured us that it would be quite in order to do so, as he had given his services there, and was therefore persona grata. Added to which was the fact that he knew we had that necessary sympathy which would banish any thought of inquisitiveness. As we drew nearer I could see that the building was in no sense a 'hospital' in outward semblance, whatever its functions might be. It was built in the classical style, two or three stories high, and it was entirely open upon all sides. That is to say, it contained no windows as we know them on earth. It was white in colour as far as the materials of its composition were concerned, but immediately above it there was to be seen a great shaft of blue light descending upon, and enveloping, the whole building with its radiance, the effect of which was to give a striking blue tinge to the whole edifice. This great Ray was the down-pouring of life—a healing Ray—sent to those who had already passed here, but who were not yet awake.

When they were fully restored to spiritual health, there would be a splendid awakening, and they would be introduced into their new land. I noticed that there was quite a number of people seated upon the grass in the grounds or walking about. They were relatives of those who were undergoing treatment within the Hall of Rest, and whose awakening was imminent. Although, doubtless, they could have been summoned upon the instant when necessary, yet, following their old earthly instinct, they preferred wait close at hand for the happy moment.

They were all supremely joyful, and very excited, as could be seen by the expressions on their faces, and many were the friendly smiles we received as we walked among them.

The floor was carpeted with some very soft covering in a sober design, and here and there a handsomely wrought tapestry was hanging upon the walls. Occupying the whole of the floor space were extremely comfortable looking couches, each of which bore a recumbent form, quite still, and obviously sleeping profoundly. Moving quietly about were a number of men and women intent upon watching the different couches and their charges. I noticed as soon as we entered this hall that we came under the influence of the blue Ray, and it's effect was one of pronounced energizing as well as tranquility. Another noticeable quality was the entire absence of any idea of an institution with its inevitable officialdom. There was no question of patronage, nor did I feel the least shade of being among strangers. Those in attendance upon the sleepers did so, not in the attitude of a certain task to be done willy-nilly, but as though they were performing a labour of love in the sheer joy of doing it. Such, indeed, was precisely the case. The glad awakening of

190

these sleeping souls was an ever-recurrent joy to them, no less than to the people who had come to witness it.

I learned that all the 'patients' in this particular hall had gone through lingering illnesses before passing over. Immediately after their dissolution they are sent gently into a deep sleep. In some cases the sleep follows instantly—or practically without break— upon the physical death. Long illness prior to passing into the spirit world has a debilitating effect upon the mind, which in turn has its influence upon the spirit body. The latter is not serious, but the mind requires absolute rest of varying duration. Each case is treated individually, and eventually responds perfectly to its treatment. During this sleep-state the mind is completely resting. There are no unpleasant dreams, or fevers of delirium.

While gazing upon this perfect manifestation of Divine Providence, the thought came to me of those absurd earthly notions of 'eternal rest,' 'everlasting sleep', and the many other equally foolish earthly conceptions. I wondered how this sleep I was now beholding had been distorted by earthly minds into a state of eternal slumber, whither all souls pass at dissolution, there to await, in countless years' time, the awful 'last day'—the dread 'Day of Judgment'. Here was the visible refutation of such a senseless belief.

The patients resting upon their couches looked very peaceful. Constant watch is kept upon them, and at the first fluttering of returning consciousness, others are summoned, and all is ready for the full awakening. Some will wake up partially, and then sink back again into slumber. Others will shake off their sleep at once, and it is then that those experienced souls in attendance will have, perhaps, their most difficult task. Until that moment, in fact, it has been mostly a matter of watching and waiting. In so many cases it has to be explained to the newly awakened soul that he has 'died' and is alive. They will remember usually their long illness, but some are quite unaware that they have passed over into spirit, and when the true state of affairs has been gently and quietly explained to them, they often have an urgent desire to go back to the earth, perhaps to those who are sorrowing, perhaps to those for whose care and welfare they were responsible. They are told that nothing can be done by their going back, and that others of experience will take care of those circumstances that are so distressing them. Such awakenings are not happy ones by comparison with those who wake up with the full realization of what has taken place. Were the earth more enlightened, this would be more often the case, and there would be a great deal less distress to the newly awakened soul.

...We were shown another large hall similarly appointed, where those whose passing had been sudden and violent were also in their temporary sleep. These cases were usually more difficult to manage than those we had just seen. The suddenness of their departure added far greater confusion to the mind. Instead of

191

a steady transition, the spirit body had in many cases been forcibly ejected from the physical body and precipitated into the spirit world. The passing over had been so sudden that there seemed to them to be no break in their lives. Such people are taken in hand quickly by bands of souls who devote all their time and all of their energies to such work. And in the Hall of Rest we could now see the results of their labors. Had so many of these souls had but a small knowledge of spirit matters, these awakenings would have been so much the happier. I do assure you it is not a pleasant sight to see these gentle, patient helpers wrestling mentally— and sometimes almost physically—with people who are wholly ignorant of the fact that they are 'dead'. It is a most saddening sight, which I can vouch for from first-hand evidence as I have seen it."

It is also comforting to know that anyone who had suffered disabilities of any kind whilst alive on Earth leaves those disabilities behind when they transition into the spirit realms.

Disabilities

"What effect, you might ask, does maiming of the physical body have upon the spirit body? None whatever, as far as the full complement of limbs and organs is concerned. ...The physical body is corruptible, but the spirit body is incorruptible. And what applies to the whole in the latter also applies to the limbs and organs; in fact to every part of the spirit body. The loss of one or more limbs of the earthly body, the possession of diseased organs, physical malformations, any subnormal or supernormal conditions of the physical body, any or all of these states leave the spirit body entirely unaffected. Whatever has happened to the physical body, the spirit body will always maintain its complete anatomy."

Edwin continued to assist Robert and Ruth to explore their marvelous new realm. Every place revealed a new wonder. This time they found themselves amidst a large number of people all moving towards the same place.

Visitation from The Higher Realms

"As we walked down the broad avenue of trees and gardens we formed part of a great concourse of people who were all proceeding in the same direction and obviously for the same purpose. Strange to say, that although we were among so many people, yet we never experienced the feeling, (so common on earth), of being amongst a large crowd. It was an extraordinary feeling which Ruth shared with me. We supposed that we had expected our old earthly sensations would have overcome us; the fear that in such an immense assembly of people there would be something of the confusion that one is accustomed to on the earth-plane; the jostling and the noise, and above all the sense of time passing, when our enjoyment would be over and passed. To have such ideas as these was quite ridiculous, and Ruth and I laughed at ourselves—as did Edwin—for expressing

such notions, or entertaining them for an instant. We felt—because we knew—that everything was in perfect order; that everyone knew what to do or where to go; that there was no question of another's superiority over ourselves for reasons of privilege. We felt that we were expected for the support we should give, and that a personal welcome was waiting for us. Was not this sufficient to banish all feelings of discomfort or uneasiness?

There was, moreover, a unity of mind among us that is not possible on the Earth plane even with those of the same religious beliefs. What Earthly religion is there where all its adherents are entirely of one mind? There is none. It has been thought essential on Earth that to offer up thanks and worship to the Supreme Being there must be a complexity of ritual and formularies and ceremonies, with creeds and dogmas and strange beliefs, over which there is as much diversity of views as there are numbers of different religions.

But we have our Temples where we can receive the Great Messengers from the highest realms, fitting places to receive the Father's Representatives and where such messengers can send our united thanks and our petitions to the Great Source of All. We do not worship blindly as on Earth.

As we drew close to the Temple we could already feel ourselves being, as it were, charged with spiritual force. Edwin told us that this was always the case because of the immense power, brought by the Higher Visitants, which remained undiminished within a wide circle of the Temple. It was for this reason that the Temple stood completely isolated, with no other buildings near it. Gardens alone surrounded it—a great sea of flowers, extending, it almost seemed, as far as the eye could see and presenting such a galaxy of brilliant colour in great banks and masses as the Earth could never contemplate. And arising from all this were the most heavenly sounds of music and the most delicate perfumes, the effect upon us being that of pure exaltation of the spirit. We felt that we were lifted up above ourselves right up into another realm.

The building itself was magnificent. It was stately; it was grand; it was an inspiration in itself. It appeared to be made of the finest crystal, but it was not transparent. Massive pillars were polished until they shone like the Sun, while every carving flashed its brilliant colours until the whole edifice was a temple of light. Never did I think such scintillations possible, for not only did the surfaces reflect the light in the ordinary way, they gave out a light of their own that could be felt spiritually.

Edwin took us to some seats which we knew to be our own—we had that feeling of familiarity with them as one does with a favourite chair at home.

Above us was the great dome of exquisitely wrought gold, which reflected the hundreds of colours that shone from the rest of the building. But the focus of all

193

attention was upon the marble Sanctuary—which word I must use for want of a better—at the end of the Temple. It had a shallow balustrade with a central opening at the head of a flight of steps leading down on to the floor. We could hear the sounds of music but whence it came I knew not, because there was no sign of any musicians. The music was evidently provided by a large orchestra— of strings only, for there were no sounds of the other instruments of the orchestra.

The sanctuary, which was of spacious dimensions, was filled with many beings from Higher Realms, with the exception of a space in the centre, which I guessed was reserved for our visitant. We were all of us seated and we conversed quietly amongst ourselves. Presently we were aware of the Presence of a stately figure of a man with jet-black hair, who was closely followed—very much to my surprise— by the kindly Egyptian whom we had met in Edwin's house on the boundary of our realm. To those who had already witnessed such visitations, their arrival was at once the indication of the coming of the high personage, and we all accordingly rose to our feet. Then, before our eyes, there appeared first a Light, which might almost be described as dazzling, but as we concentrated our gaze upon it we immediately became attuned to it and we felt no sensation of spiritual discomfort. In point of fact--as I discovered later—the Light really became attuned to us; that is to say, it was toned down to accord with ourselves and our realm. It grew in shade to a golden hue upon the extremities, gradually brightening towards the centre. And in the centre there slowly took shape the form of our visitant. As it gained in density we could see that he was a man whose appearance was that of youth—spiritual youth—but we knew that he carried with him, to an unimaginable degree, the three comprehensive and all-sufficing attributes of Wisdom, Knowledge, and Purity. His countenance shone with transcendental beauty; his hair was of gold, while round his head was a lustrous diadem. His raiment was of the most gossamer-like quality, and it consisted of a pure white robe bordered with a deep band of gold, while from his shoulders there depended a mantle of the richest cerulean blue, which was fastened upon his breast with a great pink pearl. His movements were majestic as he raised his arms and sent forth a blessing upon us all. We remained standing and silent while our thoughts ascended to Him Who sent us such a Glorious Being. We sent our thanks as we sent our petitions. For myself, I had one boon to ask, and I asked for it.

It is not possible for me to convey to you one fraction of the exaltation of the spirit that I felt while in the Presence, though distant, of this heavenly guest. But I do know that not for long could I have remained in that Temple while he was there without undergoing the almost crushing consciousness that I was low, yet very low upon the scale of spiritual evolution and progression. And yet I knew that he was sending out to me, as to us all, thoughts of encouragement, of good hope, of kindness in the very high degree, that made me feel that I must never, never despair attaining to the highest spiritual realm, and that there was good and

194

useful work ready for me to do in the service of man, and that in the doing thereof I would have the whole of the spiritual realms behind me—as they are behind every single soul who works in the service of man.

With a final benediction upon us, this resplendent and truly regal being was gone from our sight.

We remained seated for a while, and gradually the Temple began to empty. I had no inclination to move, and Edwin told us we could stay there as long as we wished. The building was, therefore, practically empty when I saw the figure of the Egyptian approaching us. He greeted us warmly and asked me if I would be good enough to go with him, as he wished to introduce me to his Master. I thanked him for his continued interest in me, and to my astonishment he led me into the presence of the man with whom he had entered the sanctuary. I had only been able to see him from my seat, but close to I could see that a pair of dark sparkling eyes matched his raven hair, which was made the more pronounced by the slight paleness of his complexion. The colors of his attire were blue, white, and gold, and although these were of a very high order, they were not of such intensity as were those of the principal visitor. I had the impression that I was in the presence of a wise man—which indeed he was—and of a man with a great sense of fun and humor.

The kind Egyptian presented me to his Master, and the latter took me by the hand and smiled upon me in such a manner as to take away, completely, any feelings of diffidence that I had. In fact, he simply diffused assurance in one's self, and he placed one perfectly at ease. One would, without disrespect, call him the perfect host.

When he spoke to me his voice was beautifully modulated, soft in tone, and so very kindly. His words to me filled me with joy even as they left me filled with wonder: 'My beloved Master,' he said, 'whom you have just seen, bids me tell you that your prayer is answered, (His prayers to make amends by communicating to the Earth plane the truth about life in the Hereafter), and that you shall have your desire. Fear not, for promises that are made here are always fulfilled. Then he told me that I should be asked to wait for a period before the fulfillment because it was necessary that a chain of events should take place before the right circumstances were brought about in which my desires should find fruition. The time would soon pass, he said, and I could, meanwhile, carry on with my intended work with my friends. If at any time I wished for advice my good friend Edwin would always be able to call upon our Egyptian friend, whose guidance was ever at my service. Then he gave me his blessing, and I found myself alone. Alone with my thoughts and with the abiding gap memory and the celestial fragrance of our resplendent visitants."

The Children's Sphere

The children's sphere, as witnessed and recounted by a soul actually living in these realms, will certainly provide enormous comfort to all those who have lost babies and young ones. Even stillborn babies and those who passed over with only minutes of Earth life are tended to and they grow up just as if they never died. Such a beautiful, **heavenly place for the young ones to continue to grow up** and be given everything they truly require.

Robert continues.

"ONE of the innumerable questions that I put to Edwin, shortly after my arrival in the spirit world, concerned the destiny of children who, as such, passed into spirit lands.

There is a period of our earthly lives which we are accustomed to call 'the prime of life'. There is also a prime of life here in spirit, and it is towards that period that all souls either advance or return, according to the age at which their transition takes place. How long it will take rests entirely with themselves, since it is purely a matter of spiritual progression and development, though with the young this period is usually much shorter. Those who pass into spirit after the prime of life period has been reached, whether they be elderly or extremely aged, will, in due time, become younger in appearance, although they will grow older in knowledge and spirituality. It must not be assumed from this that we all eventually reach a dead level of commonplace uniformity. Outwardly, we look young; we lose those signs of the passage of years which cause some of us no little disturbance of mind when we are incarnate. But our minds become older as we gain know ledge and wisdom and greater spirituality, and these qualities of the mind are manifest to all with whom we come into contact.

When we visited the Temple in the city, and, from a distance beheld the radiant visitor whom we had come to honor, he presented to the eye the appearance of perfect—and eternal—youth. Yet the degree of knowledge, wisdom and spirituality which he diffused and which we could feel with our minds, was almost overpoweringly great. It is the same, in varying degrees, with all those who visit us from the Higher Realms. If, therefore, there is this rejuvenation of fully grown people, what of the souls who pass over as children; indeed, what of those, even, who pass into the spirit world at birth?

The answer is that they grow as they would have grown upon the Earth plane. But the children here—of all ages—are given such treatment and care as would never be possible in the Earth world. The young child, whose mind is not yet fully formed, is uncontaminated by earthly contacts, and on passing into the spirit world it finds itself in a realm of great beauty, presided over by souls of equal beauty. This children's realm has been called 'the nursery of heaven', and surely

196

anyone who has been fortunate enough to have visited it will say that a more apposite term could not be found. It was, therefore, in response to my original question that Edwin proposed that Ruth and I should accompany him on a visit to the 'nursery of heaven.'

We walked towards the boundary between the Higher Realm and our own, and we turned in the direction of Edwin's house. Already we could feel the atmosphere more rarified though it was not sufficiently pronounced to cause us any inconvenience or discomfort. I noticed that this atmosphere had a great deal more colour in it, much more than in the depths of the realm. It was as though a great number of shafts of light were meeting and spreading their broad beams over all the landscape. These shafts of light were forever on the move, interweaving themselves and producing the most delicate and delightful blending of colors, like a succession of rainbows. They were extremely restful, but they were also filled with vitality and, as it seemed to Ruth and me, light-heartedness and merriment. Sadness and unhappiness, one felt, would be utterly impossible here.

The countryside took upon itself a much brighter green in its verdure, the trees were not so tall, but they were as shapely as every other tree in these realms, and they were growing as perfectly.

After we had proceeded a little distance the atmosphere became clear of the coloured beams, and it more resembled that of our own sphere. But there was a strange and subtle difference which was puzzling to the visitor upon his first visit, and it arose, so Edwin told us, from the essential spirituality of the children who live there. Something akin to this is to be encountered when one is privileged to journey to a higher realm than that in which one normally resides. It is almost as though there were a greater degree of buoyancy in the air, apart altogether from a noticeable effect of elevation of the mind.

We saw many fine buildings before us as we walked along the soft grass. They were not of any great height, but they were broad in extent, and they were all most pleasantly situated among trees and gardens. Flowers, needless to say, were growing prolifically everywhere, in artistically arranged beds, as well as in large masses upon the grassy slopes and beneath the trees.

....We could see delightful ponds and small lakes, upon the surface of which were flourishing the most beautiful water flowers in the gayest colors. In another direction we could see larger expanses of water like a series of lakes, with many small boats gliding serenely along.

The buildings were constructed of a substance that had all the appearance of alabaster, and they were all tinged with the most delicate colors, such as one is accustomed to seeing in the subtle blendings of an earthly rainbow. The style of architect resembled, for the most part, that of our own sphere; that is to say, some

197

of the buildings bore upon their surface the most exquisite carvings of such natural objects as abound in the trees and flowers, while others drew for their relief upon the known features particular to the spirit world.

But what gave us the most enjoyable surprise, was to see interspersed throughout the woods, the quaintest little cottages such as one was always inclined to believe only belonged to the pages of children's story books. Here were diminutive houses with crooked timbers—beautifully crooked—with bright red roofs and lattice-windows, and each with a charming little garden all their own surrounding it.

It will at once be concluded that the spirit world has borrowed from the Earth world in these fanciful creations for the children's delight, but such is not the case. In truth, this whole concept of miniature houses emanated, in the first instance, from the spirit world. Whoever the artist was who received our original impression, she has been lost to the Earth world through the course the years. That artist is known to us here, though, where she continues her work in the children's sphere.

These little houses were large enough to allow a grown person plenty of room in which to move without appearing to knock his head! To the children they seemed to be of just the right size without their feeling lost within them. I learnt that it was for this same reason that all the large buildings in this realm were without any appreciable height. By thus not making them too high, nor the rooms too large, they conformed with the child's mind, as yet not fully formed, where spaces seem greater than they really are and where buildings too spacious would have the effect upon the little mind of seeming to dwarf it.

Great numbers of children live in these tiny dwellings, each being presided over by an older child, who is perfectly capable of attending to any situation that might arise with the other residents.

As we walked along we could see groups of happy children, some playing games with their fellows, others seated upon the grass while a teacher was reading to them. Others again, were to be observed listening attentively and with marked interest to a teacher who was explaining the flowers to them and giving them something of a lesson in botany. But it was botany of a very different order from that of the Earth plane, in so far as the purely spirit flowers were concerned. The distinctions between the Earthly flowers and the spirit flowers were amply demonstrated by the two orders of flowers being separated.

Edwin took us to one of the teachers and explained the reason for our visit. We were instantly made welcome and the teacher was kind enough to answer a few questions. Her enthusiasm for her work added to her pleasure, she said, in telling us anything we wished to know. As to herself, she had been in the spirit world a goodly number of years. She had had children of her own when upon the Earth plane, and she was still keenly interested in their welfare, and that had led her to take on her present work. What she did not tell us—it was Edwin who later gave us the details—was that she had made such a success with her own children upon Earth, who now joined their mother in her work, that it had been obvious from the commencement just what her work would be in spirit lands. Needless to say it was the very work upon which she had set her heart—the care of children.

It needed no one to tell us that she was admirably suited for such work. She radiated that charm and confidence, kindliness and mirthfulness of nature that so appealed to the children. She understood the child mind—she was, in fact, just a grown-up child herself! She possessed a wide knowledge of the most interesting things, especially of those things that appeal most to children; she had an inexhaustible fund of capital stories for her small charges and, most important of all, she could be—and showed herself to be—at one with them. I do not think we had as yet seen anyone so superlatively happy as this gracious soul.

In this sphere, our new friend told us, there were to be found children of all ages, from the infant, whose separate existence upon the Earth plane had amounted to only a few minutes, or who even had had no separate existence at all, but had been born 'stillborn', to the youth of sixteen or seventeen years of Earth time.

It frequently happens that as the children grow up they remain in this same sphere, and themselves become teachers for a period, until other work takes them elsewhere.

And what of the parents? Were they ever the teachers of their own children? Seldom, or never, our friend informed us. It was a practice that would scarcely ever be feasible, since the parent would be more inclined to be prejudiced in favour of her own child, and there might be other embarrassments. The teachers are always souls of wide experience, and there are not many parents upon the Earth plane who would be capable of undertaking the care of spirit children immediately upon the transition of the former.

Whether the teachers were themselves parents upon the Earth plane or not, they all undergo an extensive course of training before they are adjudged fit to fill the post of teacher to the children and to conform with, and uphold, the rigidly high standards of the work. And, of course, they must all be temperamentally fitted to hold the position of teacher.

The work is not arduous, as you would judge it in the Earth world, but it demands a multiplicity of special attributes.

The mental and physical growth of the child in the spirit world is much more rapid than in the Earth world. You will recall what I told you about the absolute retentiveness of the memory here. That retentiveness begins as soon as the mind is capable of grasping anything at all, and that is very early. This seeming precocity is perfectly natural here because the young mind absorbs knowledge evenly. The temperament is carefully guided along purely spirit lines, so that the possession of knowledge in one so young never takes upon it the obnoxiousness of earthly precociousness. The children are trained in strictly spirit matters first, and then they are usually taught about the Earth world, if they have not already lived in it, or if their Earthly lives were very brief.

The Ruler of this realm acts, in a general sense, in loco parentis, and all the children indeed look upon him as a 'father.'

The children's studies have an extremely wide range. They are taught to read, but many other subjects of the Earthly curricula are entirely omitted as being superfluous in the world of spirit. It would be more exact to say that the children are given knowledge of a particular subject rather than taught it.

As they grow they are able to choose for themselves the type of work that appeals to them, and so by specializing in their studies the children can become equipped with the necessary qualifications. Some of them, for instance, elect to return to the Earth plane temporarily to work with us in the exercise of communication. They make highly efficient instruments and thoroughly enjoy their visits. Such visits have the advantage of adding widely to their experience. It increases their depth of understanding of the trials and tribulations—and the pleasures—of being incarnate.

There is always one question that arises in the minds of Earth people in connection with children who have passed on: 'Shall we be able to recognize our children when we ourselves arrive in the Spirit world?' The answer is, most emphatically, yes, beyond all shadow of doubt. 'But how, if they have grown up in the Spirit world and out of our sight, can that possibly be?' To answer that, it is necessary to know a little more about one's self.

You must know that when the physical body sleeps, the Spirit body temporarily withdraws from it, while still remaining connected to it by a magnetic cord. This cord is the veritable life-line between the Spirit body and the Earth body. The Spirit thus situated will either remain in the vicinity of the Earth body, or it will gravitate to that sphere which its Earthly life, so far, has entitled it to enter. The Spirit body will thus spend part of the lifetime of the Earthly body in spirit lands. And it is upon these visits that one meets relatives and friends who have passed on before, and it is similarly upon these visits that parents can meet their children, and thus watch their growth. In the majority of cases the parents are not allowed within the children's own sphere, but there are plenty of places where such meetings can take place. Remembering what I have said about the retentiveness of the subconscious mind, you will see that, in such cases, the problem of recognizing a child does not arise, because the parent has seen the child and

200

observed its growth throughout the whole of the intervening years, in just the same way as the parent would have done if the child had remained in the Earth world.

There must be, of course, a sufficient bond of attachment between the parent and child, or else this law will not come into operation. Where such does not exist the conclusion is obvious. That link of affection or kindly interest must also exist between all human relationships in the Spirit world, whether it be with husband and wife, parent and child, or between friends. Without that interest or affection it is problematical whether there would ever be any meeting at all, except fortuitously.

The children's realm is a township in itself, containing everything that great minds, inspired by The Greatest Mind, could possibly provide for their welfare, comfort, education and the pleasure and happiness of its youthful inhabitants. The Halls of Learning are as fully equipped as are those larger establishments in our own sphere. Indeed, in many respects, they are more so, since they have all the equipment for the diffusion of knowledge and learning to those who are possessed of neither in the slightest degree, and who must therefore start at the very beginning, as they would have done had they remained upon the Earth plane. This concerns those children who have passed into the Spirit world in their extreme infancy. Children who leave the Earth world in their early years will continue their studies from where they left off, eliminating from the latter all that are of no further use, and adding those that are spiritually essential. As soon as they reach a suitable age, the children can choose their future work, and study for it accordingly.

And we all have the same great goal—perfect and perpetual happiness."

In both books, *Life In The World Unseen* and *Here and Hereafter,* Robert gives wonderful accounts of the spectacular world of nature which greatly surpasses ours with all life forms being incorruptibly perfect. All trees, plants, fruit and flowers have a palpable internal life force that emits uplifting and revitalizing energies to all. The flowers, both those we find on Earth and so many more that we do not have, are displayed in radiant glowing profusion of colors, tones and heavenly perfumes that fill the air. Not only that but they also emit certain musical tones that are interactive with the respective colors.

Flowers

"Of the flowers themselves, when I was able to examine them more closely, I must say that I never saw either their like or their counterpart upon the Earth of many that were there in full bloom. Numbers were to be found, of course, of the old familiar blossoms but by far the greater number seemed to be something entirely new to my rather small knowledge of flowers. It was not merely the flowers themselves and their unbelievable range of superb colorings that caught my

attention, but the vital atmosphere of eternal life that they threw out, as it were, in every direction. And as one approached any particular group of flowers, or even a single bloom, there seemed to pour out great streams of energizing power which uplifted the Soul spiritually and gave it strength, while the heavenly perfumes they exhaled were such as no soul clothed in its mantle of flesh has ever experienced. All these flowers were living and breathing, and they were, so my friend informed me, incorruptible. There was another astonishing feature I noticed when I drew near to them, and that was the sound of music that enveloped them, making thirteen such soft harmonies as corresponded exactly and perfectly with the gorgeous colors of the flowers themselves.

...Flowers are essentially beautiful, evolved from the Supreme Creative Mind, given to us as a precious gift, showing us in their colorings, in their formations, and in their perfumes an infinitesimally small expression of that Great Mind. You too have this glory on the Earth plane.

We have the most glorious flowers here, some of them like old familiar cherished blooms of the Earth plane, others known only to the spirit world but all alike are superb and are a perpetual joy to all of us who are surrounded by them. They are Divine Creations, each single flower breathing the pure air of Spirit, upheld by their Creator and by all of us here in the love that we shower upon them.

It is not only the smaller growing flowers that we have here. There is no single flowering tree or shrub that the mind can recall that we do not possess, flourishing in superabundance and perfection, as well as those trees and shrubs that are to be seen nowhere else but in the Spirit world. They are always in bloom, they never fade or die, their perfumes are diffused into the air where they act like a spiritual tonic upon us all. They are at One with us, as we are with them.

When we are first introduced to the flowers and trees and all the luxuriance of spirit nature, we instantly perceive something that Earthly nature never seemed to possess, and that is an inherent intelligence within all growing things. Earthly flowers, although living, make no immediate personal response when one comes into close touch with them. But here it is vastly different. Spirit flowers are imperishable, and that should at once suggest more than mere life within them, and spirit flowers as well as all other forms of nature, are created by the Great Father of the Universe through his agents in the Realms of Spirit. They are part of the immense stream of life that flows directly from Him, and that flows through every species of botanic growth. That stream never ceases, never falters, and it is, moreover, continuously fed by the admiration and love which we, in this world of Spirit, gratefully shed upon such choice gifts of the Father. Is it then, to be wondered at, when we take the tiniest blossom within our hands, that we should feel such an influx of magnetic power, such a revivifying force, such an upliftment of one's very being, when we know, in truth, that those forces for our betterment

202

are coming directly from the Source of all good. No, there is no other meaning behind our spirit flowers than the expressed beauty of the Father of the Universe, and, surely, that is enough. He has attached no strange symbolism to His faultless Creations. Why should we?"

Like everything else in the perfect Spirit world of nature, water and the ocean and its inherent qualities take on a whole and expanded new meaning. So many times people who have visited these realms, whether it be from Near-Death Experiences or passing over, are greatly restricted by our Earthly limited minds awareness and comprehension to be able to express and do justice to the magnificent splendor that these realms represent.

Water

"We followed a path that led for part of the way beside a brook, whose clear water sparkled in the light of the heavenly Sun. As the water pursued its course it gave forth many musical notes that constantly changed and weaved themselves into a medley of the most dulcet sounds. We drew to the edge that I might look at it closer. It seemed to be almost like liquid crystal, and as the light caught it, it scintillated with all the colors of the rainbow. I let some of the water run over my hand expecting it, by its very look, to be icy cold. To my astonishment I found that it was delightfully warm. But still more it had an electrifying effect which extended from my hand right up the arm. It was a most exhilarating sensation and I wondered what it would be like to bathe fully within it. My friend said that I should feel myself being charged with energy, but there was not a sufficient depth of water here to immerse myself in it properly. I should have the opportunity, as soon as we came to a larger body of water, to indulge in a bathe. When I withdrew my hand from the brook I found that the water flowed off in flashing drops, leaving it quite dry!

We and our clothes were perfectly dry! And now another word about the water. It was as clear as crystal, and the light was reflected back in every ripple and tiny wave in almost dazzlingly bright colors. It was unbelievably soft to the touch and its buoyancy was of the same nature as the atmosphere, that is to say, it supported whatever was on it or in it. As it is impossible to fall here by accident, as one does on Earth, so it is impossible to sink in the water. All our movements are in direct response to our minds, and we cannot come to harm or suffer accident. It is, I am afraid, rather difficult to give a description of some of these things without going beyond the range of Earthly minds and experience. So much has to be witnessed first hand to gain any adequate idea of the wonders of these lands."

The Ocean And The Birds

This was Robert's tantalizing account of going to the ocean for the first time.

"We were soon walking along a beautiful stretch of open country with the grass like a green velvet carpet beneath our feet. There were no trees, but there were many fine clumps of healthy-looking shrubs, and, of course, plenty of flowers growing everywhere. At length we arrived at some rising ground and we felt that the sea must be beyond it. A short walk brought us to the edge of the grassland and then the most glorious panorama of ocean spread out before us.

The view was simply magnificent. Never had I expected to behold such sea. Its coloring was the most perfect reflection of the blue of the sky above, but in addition it reflected a myriad of rainbow tints in every little wavelet. The surface of the water was calm, but this calmness by no means implies that the water was lifeless. There is no such thing as lifeless or stagnant water here. From where we were, I could see islands of some considerable size in the distance. Island's that looked most attractive and must certainly be visited!

Beneath us was a fine stretch of beach upon which we could see people seated at the water's edge, but there was no suggestion of over-crowding! And floating upon this superb sea, some close at hand—others standing a little way out, were the most beautiful boats—though I think I am not doing them full justice by calling them mere boats. Ships would be more apposite. I wondered who could own these fine vessels and Edwin told us that we could own one ourselves if we so wished. Many of the owners lived upon them, having no other home but their boat. It made no difference. There they could live always, for here it is perpetual Summer.

A short walk down a pleasant winding path brought us to a sandy seashore. Edwin informed us that it was a tireless ocean and that at no place was it very deep by comparison with terrestrial seas. Storm and wind being impossible here, the water was always smooth and in common with all water in these realms, it was of a pleasantly warm temperature that could occasion no feelings of cold—or even chilliness—to bathers. It was, of course, perfectly buoyant, possessed no single harmful element or characteristic, but it was, on the contrary, life-sustaining. To bathe in its waters was to experience a perfect manifestation of spiritual force. The sand upon which we were walking had none of the unpleasant features associated with the seashore of the Earth plane. It was never tiring to walk on. Although it had every appearance of sand as we had always known it, yet to the tread it was firm in consistency although soft to the touch of the hand.

In fact, this peculiar quality rendered it more like well-kept lawn to walk on, so closely did the grains hold together. We took some handfuls of the sand and allowed it to run through our fingers. Great was our surprise to find that it lacked every trace of grittiness but seemed to the touch more akin to some smooth soft powder. Yet examined closely, it was undeniably solid. It was one of the strangest phenomena we had seen so far. Edwin said that that was because we had, in this particular instance, carried out a more minute examination of what we were beholding than we had done hitherto in other things. He added that if I chose to make a close scrutiny of all that we saw, whether it the ground we walked on, the substance of which our house were made, or the thousand and one other objects that make up the world of Spirit, we should be living in a state continual surprise and there would be revealed to us some small idea—but only a very small idea— of the magnitude of the Great Mind—the Greatest Mind in the Universe—that upholds this and every other world.

Indeed, the great scientists of the Earth plane find, when they come to live in the spirit world, that they have a completely new world upon which to commence a fresh course of investigations. They begin de novo as it were, but with all their great Earthly experience behind them. And what joy it brings them, in company with their scientific colleagues, to probe the mysteries of the spirit world, to collect their data, to compare their new knowledge with the old, to record for the benefit of others the results of their investigations and discoveries. And all through they have the unlimited resources of the spirit world upon which to draw. And joy is in their hearts.

Our little experiment with the sand led us to place our hands in the sea. Ruth fully expected it to taste of salt but it did not, much to her surprise. As far as I could observe, it had no taste at all! It was sea more by virtue of its great area and the characteristics of the adjacent land than anything else. In all other respects it resembled the water of the brooks and lakes. In general appearance the whole effect was totally unlike the Earthly ocean, due, among other things, to the fact that there was no Sun to give its light from one quarter only and to cause that change of aspect when the direction of the sunlight changes. The overspreading of light from the great central Source of Light in the spirit world, constant and unmoving, gives us perpetual day, but it must never be assumed that this constancy and immobility of light means a monotonous and unchanging land—or seascape. There are changes going on the whole time; changes of color such as man never dreamt of—until he comes to the Spirit world. The eyes of the spirit person can see so many beautiful things in the world of Spirit that the eyes of incarnate man cannot see—unless he be gifted with the psychic eye.

We wanted very much to visit one of the islands that we could see in the distance, but Ruth felt that it would be a nice experience to travel over the sea in one of the fine vessels that were close to the shore. But the difficulty arose—that is, it seemed as though it might arise—as to the boat! If, as I understood, these were 'privately' owned we should first have to become acquainted with one of the owners. Edwin, however, could see how Ruth was so longing to go upon the water that he soon explained the exact position—to her unbounded joy.

Edwin introduced them to a friend of his who owned one of these beautiful yachts who was only too pleased to take the trio across to one of the Islands.

205

The yacht was traveling through the sea with the most perfect, steady motion. There was no vibration, naturally, from any machinery, but the very movement through the water could be perceptibly felt, while the sounds from the gentle waves as the boat cut along made loveliest musical notes and harmonies as the many colors of disturbed water changed their tints and blends. We observed in our wake the water quickly settled into its former state, leaving no appearance of our having passed through it. Our host handled his craft skillfully and by increasing or diminishing its speed could create, by the different degree of movement of the water, the most striking alternations of color and musical sound. The most brilliant scintillations of the sea showing how alive it was. It responded to the boat's every movement as though they were in complete unison—as indeed they were

We had by now approached sufficiently near to the Island be able to view it quite well, and the boat turned in her course and followed the coastline. After continuing along in this fashion for a little while, we sailed into a small bay which formed a picturesque natural harbor.

The Island certainly came up to our expectations in its scenic beauty. There were not many dwellings upon it; those that were to be seen were more summerhouses than anything else. But the great feature of the place was the number of trees, none of them very tall, but all were of particularly vigorous growth. And in branches we could see scores of the most wonderful birds, whose plumage presented a riot of color.

Some of the birds were flying about, others—the larger variety—were walking majestically along the ground. But all of them were unafraid of us. They walked with us as we strolled along and when we held out our hands, some small bird would be sure to perch upon our fingers. They seemed to know us, to know that any harm coming to them was an utter impossibility. They did not require to make a constant search for food nor exercise a perpetual vigilance against what on Earth would be their natural enemies. They were, like ourselves, part of the eternal world of Spirit enjoying in their way, as we do in ours, their eternal life. Their very existence there was just another of those thousands of things that are given to us for our delight.

The birds which had the most gorgeous plumage resembled slightly the kind that live in the tropical parts of the Earth plane but the likes of these birds are never seen by the eye of man until he comes to the Spirit world. By the perfect adjustment of temperature they were able to live in comfort with those of less spectacular appearance. And all the while they were singing and twittering in a symphony of sound. It was never wearying, in spite of the quantity of sound that was going on, because in some extraordinary fashion the musical sounds blended with each other. Neither were they piercing in quality despite the fact that many of the small birds' songs were themselves high-pitched. But it was their trusting friendliness that was so delightful by comparison with the earthly birds, whose life there takes them into an almost separate world. Here we were part of the same free world, and the understanding between the birds and ourselves was reciprocal. When we spoke to them we felt that they knew just what we were saying and in some subtle way we seemed to know just what their thoughts were. To call to any particular bird meant that that bird understood, and it came to us.

The perfect blaze of color from all the birds we could see about us was almost too much for us to take in at one visit. They were beyond description, and I shall not even attempt it. We strolled on through delightful groves past the musical murmuring of the many brooks, through glades of velvet grass, as in an absolute fairyland of nature. We met people on the way, who called a greeting to us, or waved their hands. They were all happy among the birds. We were told that this part of the Island was exclusive to the birds and that no other form of animal life intruded upon them. Not that there was any fear or danger that they would come to harm, because that would be impossible, but because the birds were happier with their own kind."

Due to the evenly sustained warm and revitalizing sunshine and the utter permanence and incorruptibility of all substance in these Realms, nothing ever deteriorates, gets dusty, rusty, moldy or dirty. None of the customary Earthly signs of deterioration ever happens! How wonderful is that! Coupled with this there are no weeds, mosquitoes, harmful insects of any kind!

Perfect Weather and No Housework!

"We have only the glories of perpetual Summer. ...Now if you were to take the most perfect Summer's day upon Earth that you can recall to your mind, in so far as the weather itself were concerned, you would still be far, far below the splendour of the heavenly Summer of these Realms. And with us every day is Summertime.

Incidentally, we never become tired of it. I have not found one single, solitary individual in these regions who has at any time expressed the wish for a change of weather. When you come here and sample it for yourself, you will feel the same about it, I am certain. If not, then you will be the one interesting exception to the rule!

You can see how this will affect not only our lives but our homes as well. Our windows and doors can always remain wide open; there is a genial warmth penetrating into every nook and corner of our houses, just as the light diffuses its rays throughout. There is therefore no need to consider what means of heating we shall employ when ordering the disposition of our home.

And now an important matter arises. How do we arrange for the maintenance of our houses? By which I mean: who does the cleaning for us, and generally looks after things? That is, those of us who need such help.

This is another point which irritates some minds. The incarnate person, upon the mention of Spirit world houses, immediately thinks of them in terms of cleaning and upkeep, and the idea of houses in the Spirit world then becomes distasteful.

Here again arises a confusion between your world and ours. Recollect what I have said about our world being incorruptible, and you will see at once that the two words dust and dirt, which are such a nightmare to those of my friends on Earth who have the care of their own homes in their hands, simply cannot have any meaning in the Spirit world. Dust and dirt are merely disintegration in progress, and so, where you have no disintegration, as in the Spirit world, so you will have no dust and dirt.

Every house here in these realms is of a cleanliness where immaculate is the only term with which to describe them. Without the means to cause the dirt, you cannot have the dirt. Whereas on Earth the gradual but persistent process of decay will always show itself in dust and dirt. You cannot avoid it. The most you can do is to invent and provide mechanical means with which to clear it away. But it will return and continue to return. I am, I know, stating what is a painfully obvious fact to so many good people, but I must do so to emphasise one of the outstanding qualities of our homes in this Spirit world, namely, their superlative and everlasting cleanliness. In this respect, therefore, our homes will require no attention throughout the whole period of their existence, and that may be hundreds of years of your time. A house wholly unoccupied for such a protracted period would be, at the end of that time, as immaculate as on the first day of its erection. And that entirely without the least attention having been paid to it.

The fabric of the house comes under the same conditions, and these conditions are a Law. We have no winds in the Spirit world that will wear away the stones or bricks of which a house is built, nor do we have a smoke laden atmosphere which will eat into the surface of our buildings or cause them to crumble away into dust. We have no rains to cause rot and rust to set in, and so to require various replacements. All our possessions within doors, our furniture and our hangings, our personal belongings, such as our books, all alike are subject to the same splendid Law. They cannot deteriorate, receive damage, become soiled; the colours in our hangings and upholsteries cannot fade or become shabby. Things cannot get broken or cracked with age. We cannot loose our small possessions by mislaying them. The floor-coverings on which we walk can never become worn out with constant tread of feet. "

With there being nothing of a negative nature in these Spirit Realms to contend with, we can see that life is but one pleasurable experience after another. There is no work we have been conditioned to *begrudgingly* to pay the monthly bills. There are no bills or energy sources to have to pay for such as electricity, gas and petrol or even any food to pay for. Everything is provided free by Source by the sheer love for all of His/Her Creations.

Work Is Not Work As We Know It

"Here in spirit lands we have nothing to disturb us. On the contrary, we have everything that will bring us contentment. Our true natures thrive and expand upon such glories and splendours as the spirit world alone has to offer. We work, not for an earthly subsistence, but for the joy that comes with doing work that is both useful and congenial, and above all things, work that is of service to our fellow beings. The reward which the work brings with it is not a transient reward as is the case with so much mundane labour, but a reward that will lead us eventually to a higher state of living.

To us here in the spirit world, life is pleasure, always pleasure. We work hard, and sometimes long, but that work is pleasure to us. We have not the tiresome wearying toil that you have upon Earth. We are not solitary beings fighting for our existence amidst a world that can be, and so often is, somewhat indifferent to our struggles. Here in these realms wherein I live, there is not one solitary individual of whatever nationality under the sun who would not come immediately to the assistance of anyone of us upon the merest glimmering of our needing help. And such help it is! There is no false pride that precludes our accepting help from a fellow creature anxious to give it.

Millions of us though there be, yet there is not one sign, not one atom of discord to be seen throughout the immense extent of these realms. Unity and concord are two of the plainest characteristics to be observed and understood and appreciated to the full.

The joy of living is a phrase of which you cannot have even the barest understanding while you are yet upon the Earth plane.

All that is great in man survives and is taken with him into this very Spirit world where new avenues, far greater, finer, and broader, are for ever opening before him. There is no limit to what immense heights he can reach, whether he be scientist, or artist, or musician, or a follower of any other of the myriad worthy occupations that are to be found upon Earth."

It becomes obvious from all that Robert is describing that everything good we are accustomed to upon Earth takes on a grander, more comprehensive and exquisitely beautiful form in these Realms. None more so than the music in these Realms as we can almost feel and see the intricate blending of colour and sound

209

within this glorious *exposé* of Edwin taking Robert and Ruth to their first concert performance.

Music Unlike Anything Experienced On Earth

"We had observed that the Hall of Music stood in grounds far more extensive than those we had already seen, and the reason was soon made clear to us. At the rear of the Hall was the great centre of concert performances. It consisted of a vast Amphitheatre like a great bowl sunk beneath the level of the ground, but it was so large that its real depth was not readily apparent. The seats that were farthest away from the performers were exactly upon ground level. Immediately surrounding these seats were masses of the most beautiful flowers of every possible hue, with a grassy space beyond, while the whole area of this outdoor Temple of Music was encompassed by a magnificent plantation of tall and graceful trees. Although the seating arrangements were upon such an expansive scale, much more so than would be at all practicable upon Earth, yet there was no sense of being too far from the performers, even in the farthest seats. It will be recalled that our vision is not so restricted in spirit as upon Earth.

Edwin suggested to us that we might like to hear a concert of the Spirit world and then he made a strange proposal. It was that we should not take our places in the seats of the Theatre, but that we should take up a position at some distance. The reason, he said, would be manifest as soon as the music began. As a concert was due to start very shortly, we followed his mysterious suggestion and seated ourselves on the grass at some considerable distance from the actual Amphitheatre. I wondered whether we should be able to hear very much so far away, but our friend assured us that we should. And, indeed, we were joined by numbers of other people at that very moment, who doubtless had come for the same purpose as ourselves.

The whole place, which was empty when Edwin had first brought us in, now contained many people, some strolling about, and others, like us, seated contentedly on the grass. We were in a delightful spot, with the trees and flowers and pleasant people all about us, and never have I experienced such a feeling of real, genuine enjoyment as came upon me at this moment. I was in perfect health and perfect happiness, seated with two of the most delightful companions, Edwin and Ruth; unrestricted by time or weather, or even the bare thought of them; unhampered by every limitation that is common to our old incarnate life.

Edwin told us to walk over to the theatre and look down over the seats once again. We did so, and to our astonishment we found that the whole vast hall was packed with people, where there was not a soul to be seen but a short time before. The musicians were in their places awaiting the entrance of their conductor, and this great audience had arrived as if by magic, or so it seemed. As it was apparent that the concert was about to begin, we returned to Edwin at once. In answer to our question as to how the audience had arrived so suddenly and unperceived.... In the case of this concert, the organizers had merely to send out their thoughts to people at large who were particularly interested in such performances, and they forthwith assembled. As soon as Ruth and I had shown our interest and desires in these concerts, we should establish a link, and we should find these thoughts reaching us whenever they were emitted. We could, of course, see nothing of the performers from where we were situated, and so when a hush came upon all around us, we were thus sufficiently informed that the concert was to begin.

The orchestra was composed of some two hundred musicians, who were playing upon instruments that are well known to Earth and so I was able to appreciate what I heard. As soon as the music began I could hear a remarkable difference from what I had been accustomed to hear on the Earth plane. The actual sounds made by the various instruments were easily recognizable as of old, but the quality of tone was immeasurably purer, and the balance and blend were perfect. The work to be played was of some length, I was informed, and would be continued without any break. The opening movement was of a subdued nature as regards its volume of sound and we noticed that the instant the music commenced a bright light seemed to rise up from the direction of the orchestra until it floated in a flat surface level with the topmost seats, where it remained as an iridescent cover to the whole amphitheatre. As the music proceeded, this broad sheet of light grew in strength and density, forming, as it were, a firm foundation for what was to follow. So intent was I upon watching this extraordinary formation that I could scarcely tell what the music was about. I was conscious of its sound, but that was really all.

Presently, at equal spaces round the circumference of the theatre, four towers of light shot up into the sky in long tapering pinnacles of luminosity. They remained poised for a moment, and then slowly descended, becoming broader in girth as they did so, until they assumed the outward appearance of four circular towers, each surmounted with a dome perfectly proportioned. In the meanwhile, the central area of light had thickened still more and was beginning to rise slowly in the shape of an immense dome covering the whole Theatre. This continued to ascend steadily until it seemed to reach a very much greater height than the four towers, while the most delicate colours were diffused throughout the whole of the etheric structure. I could understand now why Edwin had suggested that we should sit outside the Theatre proper, and I could follow, also, why composers should feel impelled to alter their Earthly works after they have arrived in spirit. The musical sounds sent up by the orchestra were creating, up above their heads, this immense musical thought-form and the shape and perfection of this form rested entirely upon the purity of the musical sounds, the purity of the harmonies, and a freedom from any pronounced dissonance. The form of the music must be pure to produce a pure form.

211

By now the great musical thought-form had assumed what appeared to be its limit of height, and it remained stationary and steady. The music was still being played and in response to it the whole coloring of the dome changed, first to one shade, then to another, and many times to a delicate blend of a number of shades according to the variation in theme or movement of the music. It is difficult to give any adequate idea of the beauty of this wonderful musical structure. The amphitheatre being built below the surface of the ground, nothing was visible of audience, of performers, or of the building itself, and the dome of light and colour had all the appearance of resting on the same firm ground as were we ourselves.

This has taken but a brief while in the telling, but the musical thought-form occupied such time in formation as would be taken by a full length concert on the Earth plane. We had, during this period, watched the gradual building of the outward and visible effect of music. Unlike the Earth where music can only be heard, there we had both heard and seen it. And not only were we inspired by the sounds of the orchestral playing, but the beauty of the immense form it created had its spiritual influence upon all who beheld it or came within its sphere. We could feel this although we weren't seated within the Theatre. The audience within were basking in its splendor and enjoying still greater benefit from the effulgence of its elevating rays. On the next occasion we should take our places in the huge Auditorium.

The music at last came to a grand finale and so ended. The rainbow colors continued to interweave themselves. We wondered how long this musical structure would survive, and we were told that it would fade away in roughly the same time as would be taken by an Earthly rainbow, comparatively a few minutes. We had listened to a major work, but if a series of shorter pieces were played, the effect and lasting power would be the same, but the shapes would vary in form and size. Were the form of greater duration, a new form would conflict with the last, and the result to the eye would be the same as two different and unconnected pieces of music, when played together, would be to the ear.

The expert musician can plan his compositions by his knowledge of what forms the various harmonic and melodic sounds will produce. He can, in effect, build magnificent edifices upon his manuscript of music, knowing full well exactly what the result will be when the music is played or sung. By careful adjustment of his themes and his harmonies, the length of the work, and its various marks of expression, he can build a majestic form as grand as Gothic Cathedral. This is, in itself, a delightful part of the Music Art in spirit which is regarded as Musical Architecture. The student will not only study music acoustically, but he will learn to build it architecturally, and the latter is one of the most absorbing and fascinating studies.

In the Spirit world all music is color and all color is music. The one is never existent without the other. That is why the flowers give forth such pleasant tones when they are approached, as it will be remembered of my early experience with flowers. The water that sparkles and flashes colors is also creating musical sounds of purity and beauty."

Next, we briefly explore a subject that was at the core of why Robert gave these enlightening transcripts to his friend Anthony and subsequently to all of us who are still incarnate upon planet Earth. A subject that was Monsignor Robert's life whilst alive on Earth but which he soon learnt had very different connotations in the spirit world where *only the truth of Cosmic Law exists.*

What of Religion?

Robert was asked the following question by one of the readers of his books and he elaborates.

"How is it that a person who was a clergyman during his earthly life and who was a firm upholder of his Church's teachings and of what is orthodox in religious matters - how is it that such a person can, in communicating with the Earth, give every sign imaginable of having quickly thrown off his religious beliefs and his orthodoxy?

The same question could apply to a large number of people to a greater or lesser degree according to the views which they held upon Earth. Orthodoxy is not the only thing that can mentally and intellectually shackle a being on Earth.

Religious beliefs, both orthodox and unorthodox, can exert a most powerful hold upon the minds of human beings. The former, in general, are too widely known to need amplification, but of the latter, the unorthodox, there are many forms. A great many people hold that a firm belief in a book of ancient chronicles, (without even remotely understanding a tithe of its contents), is fully sufficient to assure them of a safe journey to 'the next world', and the certainty of a residence in some salubrious spot among the 'elect'.

Some people hold that a staunch belief in the merits of another will achieve the same results. Whatever form these beliefs take, they are most of them of the crudest description, and upon arrival in the spirit world, the ardent upholders of the childish creeds discover their true worth, which is precisely nothing. It is exactly according to the mental and intellectual make-up of an individual when he arrives in the spirit world as to how long it will take him to shake off the erroneous beliefs and mistaken ideas which he has accumulated during his life on Earth. The person with an 'open mind', provided that mind is not too 'open' and therefore too easily swayed in one direction or another without perceiving the truth, such a person will more quickly see what his new life involves in the matter of altered outlook. If he is ready to throw off the old life at once and take up the new life with equal clarity, then so much the better and happier will that person be.

To come more specifically to the terms of our friend's question, it depends upon what is meant by quickly as regards the time taken by an inhabitant of the spirit world to abandon orthodox religious views. Here we are measuring time in earthly terms. A few hours taken to achieve this end would doubtless seem the extreme of rapidity in which to relinquish beliefs that have been held for a lifetime. But with the right type of mind it can be done; indeed, it has been done on many occasions to which I can bear witness of personal experience.

The age of the new arrival must also be taken into consideration, whether he (or she) be young, middle-aged, or elderly. So, you see, there are a number of factors to be taken into account, either singly or in conjunction with each other. There is, for instance, another element which will weigh in the matter: how firmly were the beliefs held? Were they deep rooted, or merely superficial? People will sometimes make a demonstration of holding certain religious beliefs because they have been brought up in those beliefs from childhood. They may not have bothered to think very much for themselves, and so they have proceeded through their Earthly life in an easy fashion religiously, not really caring, but content to follow the rest of the family in their practices. So much for general terms. I can, however, speak from my own personal experience.

During my Earthly life I was a clergyman of the orthodox church, but I was not entirely ignorant of the presence around me of an invisible world over which, so it appeared to me, my church had no jurisdiction whatever. My own psychic faculties were not very powerful, but at least they were strong enough for me to disbelieve what my church most emphatically taught in this connection, namely, that such manifestations as I was permitted to see were all the work of 'the devil'. Now here I could perceive no evidence at all of diabolic intervention. What I did see was decidedly harmless in every way. I therefore frankly disbelieved what the church taught me and told me to teach others upon the subject. But I did not voice this disbelief. That was a secret which I carried with me into the spirit world. I should have done no good had I expressed what I thought openly.

And so, I kept these discoveries to myself. Naturally, I believed in a future state of life, and what I saw for myself, psychically, confirmed that belief. Secretly, I differed from the church in its attitude towards this."

Prolonged Mourning

In this book I have outlined the various stages of Grief. When you lose someone precious, grief is a naturally resulting process. It is wise, however, to address grief that has become pro-longed mourning that is perpetuated to the point where it has

214

moved into self-pity and a non-ability to see past this, resulting in subsequent depression. If this happens it is both hindering your loved one from progressing to his/her natural spirit place of abode and YOU are drawing back to YOURSELF those same negative energies you are giving out in even greater amounts. This HAS to happen as it Cosmic Law; whatever energy we give out we draw back to us in greater amounts, both positive and negative. It is the Law of Cause and Effect or the Law of The Circle. Here is the truth conveyed from one who has passed over and who witnessed this first-hand on countless occasions.

"The spirit world disapproves of mourning in every shape and form. Genuine, heartfelt sorrow is a human emotion that none of us is secure from, but too much mourning is spurious. Here, in these Spirit Realms, we can see just what is taking place in the minds of the mourners. Mourning as a rule is utterly selfish because people are not sorry for the soul who has passed on, except in so far as it is thought that he or she is now infinitely worse off 'dead'. The great majority of people are sorry for themselves at the physical separation, not happy and glad that their friend or loved one has gone to a greater, grander, more beautiful life. Of course, I am now speaking of those who are destined for the realms of light.

Even where the sorrow is perfectly genuine and inspired by true affection, every effort should be made to curb the over-indulgence of it. The Soul newly arrived in spirit lands will feel the determined drag of the thoughts of those who are left behind, unless those thoughts are constructive thoughts for the present and future well-being of the friend or loved one who has gone.

Extenuated thoughts of the wrong kind can draw the soul back like a magnet and prevent it from making a steady and natural transition into its proper sphere. It is no exaggeration to say that it would be immeasurably better, things being what they are upon Earth, if mourners on Earth were to pass into a complete state of physical insensibility for some days after the passing of a loved one into the Spirit world. There would then be no danger of the thoughts of others circumscribing the actions of the newly departed Soul.

The strong attachment to the physical body that exists in the minds of so many people would be largely broken down if those same people were to become fully acquainted with spirit truths such as I have relayed in my books.

A short prayer, efficiently directed, asking for help, will bring an instantaneous answer. That response will be invisible to you on Earth, but to us here it means a downpouring of light and power that we most need for the case in hand. Pray that the Soul, your loved one, may soon receive the light of understanding of the new situation in which he finds himself, (if he is entirely ignorant of spirit truths), and that he may be happy and contented in the life upon which he has just embarked.

We have found by experience that where prayers are offered such as I have suggested in bare outline to you, we are enabled to carry on our work in the easiest, most effective, and most straightforward fashion. (Robert and Ruth are helping souls newly departed to transition so he has seen first-hand these consequences playing out).

Now transitions have been taking place since the world began thousands of centuries ago, but mankind in general is content to remain in ignorance of what is to happen to him when he leaves the Earth for the spirit world. He either asserts that it is impossible to know, or else he prefers to abide in his ignorance. And yet if he had but the knowledge of even the simple facts such as I have detailed to you, what a wealth of difference it would make to his mind. It would drive out that dreadful fear of the unknown 'hereafter' which can be, and is, such a crushing nightmare to sensitive minds. (One of the reasons why I collated this book).

I am disposed to believe that not only is it fear of the unknown that distresses people, but also the thought that physical dissolution is a painful process. A study of the facts and truths of life in the Spirit world is the best antidote indeed, it is the only antidote for fears such as I have mentioned. Great faith may go a long way, but faith can never take the place of facts. And then instead of giving the departing Soul a harrowing, sorrowful send-off, with a knowledge of the truth the same Soul could be given all the help he needs in a powerful, bright and happy Godspeed.

In place of fears of a speculative 'hereafter' we try to show you something of the brilliant prospect that lies before you when that happy moment arrives for you to take up your true and undoubted heritage in the Spirit world.

It has been my very pleasant occupation to give you some details of this land, and I am very conscious of the many thoughts and feelings of kindness and goodwill that are constantly coming to me from my friends upon Earth after reading these book(s). Your thoughts always unfailingly reach me and each is answered though, alas, you may be unaware of it. It is because of the inability to hear my personal and direct reciprocation of your good thoughts that I here thank you for them with all my heart.

We have travelled some distance together in our discussions of life in the Spirit world, although we have touched but briefly upon so vast a theme.

And so, in taking a brief leave of our subject, I will take also a brief leave of you, and in doing so I would say to you:

'Benedicat te omnipotens Deus

May Almighty God Bless You '"

Anthony concludes.

"Interested readers may be wishful to know, perhaps, how Robert views the results of his achievement regarding the previous books and their penetration into many lands. He says with warm appreciation: 'I am delighted with the results that have far exceeded my expectation.'

A voluminous, world-wide correspondence has itself been a 'revelation', our readers being folk of all ages, from a youthful 20 to an equally youthful 80 years of age. Throughout all the letters, I have been almost overwhelmed by the writers' many expressions of appreciation and gratitude, of cordiality and warmth. 'Life in the World Unseen,' writes one minister of the Church, 'has given me much inspiration. Thank you most sincerely.' And the wife of a clergyman wrote to say: 'I have read your indescribably lovely book through twice already, and hope to read it many times more.' It is not surprising, therefore, Robert should have feelings of justifiable gratification."

Anthony Borgia also transitioned into the Spirit world, no doubt guided *home* by his friend Robert, in 1989. Now that would have been a grand reunion! The above extracts are only a small selection contained within, the books, *Life In The World Unseen* and *Here And Hereafter*. There is also another book in this series entitled, *More In The World Unseen.*

I would like to say to you Robert and Anthony–on behalf of all the readers of this book and the ones you jointly collaborated on–you have our heartfelt deepest gratitude and may the warmest of Blessings go out to you both. Your books have been a tremendous International success and if I can add in some small part to the International distribution of this much needed information about what we can ALL potentially experience when we too pass over, then I am well pleased.

I would also like to say a heart-felt thank you to Julie of Global Grey e-books. For 8 years now Julie has passionately developed her website which currently has over 3,000 e-books and/or publications that she has personally collated and often transcribed after the original Copyright of the older books has expired. You will find her great website at www.globalgreyebooks.com and should you partake, please consider a small donation. Julie is offering the public a great free service and certainly has costs to maintain relative to maintaining and expanding it. Well done Julie!

CHAPTER SIX

AFTER DEATH COMMUNICATION BY 'SIGNS'

The ADC Project was created in May 1988, to conduct the first in-depth research of After Death Communications. The founders, Bill and Judy Guggenheim, interviewed 2,000 people who live in all 50 American states and the 10 Canadian provinces. They collected more than 3,300 firsthand accounts from people who believe they have been contacted by a loved one who had died. Their website is www.after-death.com. Remembering that this was collated over thirty years ago. This will only represent a minute proportion of actual experiences. They are very real and happen regularly all over the world.

The following excerpts are all taken from *Hello From Heaven* by Bill & Judy Guggenheim. This is a wonderfully inspiring book devoted to personal stories from all the different types of ADCs (After Death Communication). Many thanks to Bill and Judy for their gracious consent to reprint these extracts.

Walter, a 58-year-old real estate broker in Arizona, had his transcendent moment after his wife, Arlene, died of cancer.

"It was a misty, rainy, totally overcast day. There was no sky visible anywhere. I spread Arlene's ashes around a tall Ponderosa pine tree up in the White Mountains and said a prayer. Then I walked to my car about forty feet away and said another prayer. As I stood up, a shaft of bright, golden light came through the clouds and shone around the base of the tree. It only lit up that particular spot

where Arlene's ashes were. The light did not illuminate anything else. It was an amazing experience – it was just incredible! I thanked the good Lord. I knew it was God letting me know that Arlene was with him again.

Several people reported seeing a beam of bright light suddenly shining on a particular object or place as Walter did. Some of these accounts describe a ray of golden light illuminating a casket during a funeral service or highlighting a memorial stone at a cemetery."

(That is exactly what transpired at my sister's funeral as described later in the 'Terminal Illness' chapter.)

Flowers can also play a significant role in symbolic ADCs as the next two accounts reflect.

Joanne is a secretary in Missouri. She was given a consoling sign after her 28-year-old son, Matthew, died by suicide.

"Right after Matthew's funeral, I removed a gorgeous Mum[43] from his coffin. Mums last a very long time, so I took it home and put it in some water and placed it on my kitchen windowsill.

A couple of weeks later, Mum was totally dead. I remember thinking, 'I can't bear to part with this.' And I chastised myself because I couldn't even throw away a flower. But I put the Mum in some freshwater anyway. The next day the Mum was totally alive again! I took that very definitely as a sign that Matthew was trying to tell me he was okay."

Flowers are very popular not only for their natural beauty but for their powerful emotional and spiritual healing properties as well. In this instance, the revitalized Chrysanthemum became a symbol of life after death for Joanne.

Peg is a day care worker in Pennsylvania. Her prayers were answered by her 17-year-old son Skip after he was killed in an automobile accident caused by a drunk driver.

"Skip always gave people roses. If anything special ever occurred, he gave a rose. He gave his girlfriend roses every Monday from the time he met her because he

---

[43] For those of us who don't live in the USA – a 'Mum' is a type of Chrysanthemum.

had met her on a Monday. If it was my birthday or if he wanted to get on the good side of me, he would bring me a rose. A month after he died, I was talking to him saying, 'Please Skip, give me a sign that you are okay.'

Later, my three sisters were with me when I stopped at the cemetery. I said, 'I wish Skip would just let us know he is okay.' One of my sisters said, 'In time, he will.' Afterwards, we went on to the church, and all during the service I was praying, I would get a sign. When we came out and got in the car, I saw there was a rose stuck under the windscreen wiper! It was a long-stemmed red rose. I knew immediately it was from Skip. I just knew it! My sisters all started crying as they too knew the rose was from my son.

I still have this rose, and it's still as red as the day it was put there for me!"

The power of heartfelt prayer is truly remarkable. When we sincerely pray, we actively demonstrate our openness, willingness, and readiness to receive ADCs and other gifts from the spiritual realm.

It is the extraordinary behavior of many kinds of animals that is so highly noticeable in this beautiful symbolic ADC account. Such signs are unmistakable to the experiencers because they often dramatically reflect the deceased loved one's long term affinity for a particular animal.

Phillip is a retired hotel pool and cabana manager who lives in Florida. He had these two outstanding symbolic experiences after his son Gregory died of Leukemia at age twenty-seven.

"When Gregory and his sister were very young, we took them on vacation to Key West, Florida. During this trip, Gregory was able to swim with a porpoise at a recreation area. That was the biggest thrill he ever had as a child. Through the years, Gregory loved the environment, loved the water, and of course, he loved porpoises. In fact, he loved everything in life. Before he died, he requested his ashes be placed in the Gulf Stream at sunrise so his ashes could travel all across the world.

After Gregory's death, a friend of ours picked my wife and I up very early in the morning in his boat. Our daughter came with us, and a friend of ours who would recite the kaddish, which is a Jewish prayer for the dead. We started out from Miami Beach, and it took about an hour and a half to get to the Gulf Stream. Exactly at sunrise, my friend said the kaddish, and my wife placed Gregory's ashes in the water. No sooner were the prayers finished than a school of at least 6 to 8 porpoises came alongside the boat. The porpoises stayed with us, swimming on both sides, as they escorted us practically all the way back to the beach. But that's not the end of the story.

A few years later, my wife and I went to a regional Compassionate Friends conference in Clearwater, Florida. At the end of the conference, everyone tied a message of love for their child to a helium-filled balloon. We all faced the Gulf of Mexico and released the helium balloons at 3.00. I asked Gregory if there was some way he could send us a message that he loves us, would he please do so. No sooner did we release our balloon than a single porpoise came swimming towards us to within 40 to 50 feet from the shore. It disappeared a moment, came back up again, then just glided away. These two experiences have given me delicious moments to think about and to keep inside my heart forever."[44]

---

[44] *Hello From Heaven*, Bill & Judy Guggenheim, Self published by the ADC Project, 1995 edition.

CHAPTER SEVEN

AFTER DEATH COMMUNICATION BY 'APPEARANCES'

Sue Ellen is a homemaker in Florida. Her father delivered a personal message when she was 24 years old.

"I was lying on the sofa. Suddenly, I saw my father very clearly! He was definitely there with me – I could see his smiling face. I heard him say, 'It's all right, honey. It's beautiful over here! I'm really happy, so don't you worry,' Then he laughed and added, 'Now I don't have to pay for all that furniture your mom and sister bought.' Of course, I didn't know what he meant. Almost simultaneously, the phone was ringing. I could hear my husband in the background, saying, 'Oh my Gosh!' He learned that my father had just died from a heart attack. My father was only 53 and had been in excellent health!

After that, we got a letter saying my mother and sister had gone out and bought a house full of furniture just before my father died! But my father's insurance paid for all of it! That was verification to me that my experience was real. I believe my father came to me because he wanted to be the first one to tell me he had died."

For Sue Ellen, her father's sense of timing was perfect, as so many ADCs. He arrived just in time to cushion the shock his daughter would have felt when she learned of his unexpected death. Her father also provided her with a subtle piece of information about the new furniture, perhaps anticipating that Sue Ellen would ask her family for more details. And when she did, they confirmed everything he had told her, thereby validating the reality of her experience.

Claire is a certified public Accountant in Oregon. She had this thought-provoking experience with her 56-year-old friend Hugh.

"Hugh and I had known and worked with each other for fifteen years. He was somebody who was very special to me in understanding and friendship. While I was waking up early on a Monday morning, Hugh came to me. He pinched me to get my attention! I saw him! He stood there by my bed, wearing a white shirt with the sleeves rolled up. His mood and expression were really sad, as though he'd lost it all. He said, 'I'm sorry, Claire. I didn't make it.' He added, 'Goodbye,' as if forever. Then he just vanished. I sat on the edge of the bed contemplating his message. I was wondering, 'What on earth?' Then my clock radio switched on with the early morning news. They announced that Hugh's seaplane had gone down in the Columbia River the day before. He didn't make it ashore and had drowned!"

Hugh had the foresight to visit Claire before she learned of his death from an impersonal source. His consideration for her feelings is reflected by his impeccable timing.

"One night I went to bed early and drifted off to sleep. All of a sudden, the whole room lit up, and grandma was standing there! She was standing upright. (She had cancer of the spine which had caused her to be bent over and in extreme pain.) She was under a trellis with beautiful roses around her. There was a mist at her feet and a very vivid blue sky and cushiony clouds behind her. Grandma said, 'Marilyn, tell your mom, that I'm at peace now. Tell her that she has to understand how I died. I'm with our loved ones here. Someday you will share this love and joy with us.' I said, 'Grandma, what are you doing there?' She said, 'I'm at peace, Marilyn. Just tell your mom. Ask her to understand my messages.' But I didn't know what she meant! I started crying, and Mom came running in and said, 'What's the matter?' I said, 'You have got to call Grandma!' She asked 'Why? It's a quarter after ten. She's already gone to bed!' I said, 'You gotta call her. Something's the matter!'

Mum called Grandma's house. The phone was answered by another grand-daughter Lucy, who was sobbing. Ten minutes before, Lucy had seen the lights on at Grandma's and stopped by. She found Grandma dead in the bedroom! The sad thing is that Grandma had committed suicide. She was in such pain from her cancer that she just couldn't take it anymore. She had laid out her clothes for her funeral – her dress, her shoes, everything. And she had left written messages asking everyone to forgive her.

Marilyn's Grandmother took her life because she couldn't bear the pain of spinal cancer. But, it seems she didn't suffer any negative consequences from committing suicide under these circumstances."

Understandably, most people with a terminal disease fear the physical pain that may accompany it. Receiving hospice care can be of great assistance to them because the personnel are trained experts in all aspects of pain management. If you or someone you know has a terminal illness, we urge you to contact a local hospice to learn about the outstanding physical, emotional, and spiritual support its programs provided to patients and their families.

"I opened my eyes, and my grandfather was standing beside me. He looked opaque, not like a solid person. He looked very healthy and had a glow about him like a shining golden light was coming from his body. He bent down toward my head, as though he was going to tell me a secret. He said, 'I will be a great-grandfather in the spring. I will have a great-grandson!' Grandpa was born in Hungary and had a very strong accent. I had an overwhelming feeling of comfort and warmth, and then he was gone. I got up immediately and went into the living room to tell my husband what had just happened. The next day I had a pregnancy test, and I was indeed pregnant! When our son, Tyler, was born the following May, I kept saying, 'Grandpa, you were right!'"

This is one of several ADC accounts we received in which a deceased loved one informed a woman she was pregnant. Some of these heavenly birth announcements also revealed the gender of the unborn child, and this information was later proven to be accurate.

This account is from Carolyn, a labor relations manager in Florida. She had this sentimental reunion with her father two months after he died suddenly of a heart attack at age 63.

"I was living in Colorado. I was out in my garden around 10:30 in the morning digging up some weeds in my salad patch where the green peppers were. I clearly heard my father saying telepathically, 'Hi Cricket!' Only two people in the world called me Cricket – one was my dad, and the other was my mom. I turned, and my dad was there, sitting on a log with his legs crossed, about three feet away. I could almost reach out and touch him, but I knew I shouldn't do that. He wasn't quite solid – his density was 'soft', like cotton candy. Dad just looked a million bucks! He had the most wonderful smile, and I could see the wrinkles around his eyes. He was wearing his old chinos, a light blue oxford shirt, and his white deck shoes. He looked a little younger, and all his health was there. He said, 'How are you doing sweetheart?' I said 'Daddy! I'm so happy to see you! I'm fine.' And he said,

'I just want you to know that I'm okay, and I'm watching over you.' Then he said, 'I'll see you, sweetheart.' And he was gone."

This experience was wonderful, because Daddy didn't have a chance to say good-bye to me before he died. It taught me that love is enduring and that my father's love for me continues. This was God's way of showing me that death doesn't stop love, and it doesn't take away relationships.

Faye is a court reporter in the Southeast. She was overcome with grief after her 16-year-old son, Chris, died from an undetected heart ailment.

"Chris' father took his own life right after Chris died, which was a double tragedy for all of us. I was beyond consoling.

My experience occurred shortly after his father's death. It was right before morning, and I was somewhere between awake and asleep. I guess you would call it twilight sleep. Chris sat on my bed! He was very solid and very real. I could feel his presence, and I could smell him. I could look into his eyes and see his smile. I could even see the little beauty mark under his eye and the little cleft in his chin. He looked peaceful, golden, and beautiful. He appeared at his exact age and in very good health. He said, 'Mom, I wanted to come and tell you that I'm fine. I love you. Don't worry about me.' He also said his Dad was alright, but he was going to have to work through his problems.

I just lay there for half an hour, basking in the simple bliss that you sometimes have when you're a child. All I could think was 'This is a gift! Chris really came!' And I was elated.

Faye's account is unusual, because it's one of only a few in our files in which the experiencer gained information about someone else who had died. The news she received regarding Chris' father implies that ending our life before its natural time to die may carry consequences that we will have to resolve following our death."

Gary is a purchasing assistant for a university in Washington. He had this heartening experience with his 3-month-old daughter, Lauren, who died of sudden infant death syndrome, and with his father, who had died of a heart attack in his early 40s.

"This internal vision in my mind occurred as I was driving about 5 days after Lauren's death. My eyes were open, and my eyes were focused on the road. All of a sudden, I had this image of my daughter sitting on my father's knee. He had one of his arms wrapped around her waist. Lauren was wearing a pink pinafore dress and was happy and smiling. My grandmother was standing next to them, and my uncle was behind my father. In the background were some of my other relatives who had passed on. It was a very calm place, and everybody was happy. I could tell from my father's expression that he was really proud of Lauren. The vision ended with my dad saying, 'She's okay.' I smiled, and it gradually faded out. I felt totally relieved as if a burden had been lifted from me. Lauren was happy and was going to be alright. I knew she was with my family, and I really felt at peace."

As Gary's and other ADC's in this book indicate, our deceased children are promptly met and lovingly cared for by a multitude of family members who welcome them with open arms and open hearts. With such nurturing and wise guidance, we can expect our children will continue to grow emotionally, mentally, and spiritually until we are united with them again.

Betsy is the manager of a retail store in the US Southeast. She was at the wheel of her car when she and her sons, Nathan, age 6, and Travis, age 4, were in an accident. Though Betsy was not seriously injured, her two boys were killed instantly.

"While I was in the hospital, I didn't want to live. Nothing made sense, and I just wanted to give up and die. I didn't want to live without my sons.

An angel came to me and took me firmly by the hand. I felt a love that I had never felt before. He took me to this beautiful meadow. It was the prettiest emerald green with the most vibrant blue sky. The colours are hard to describe because they are not like the colours we see here. There was a bright white and lavender light around this meadow, but it didn't hurt my eyes. It was a very loving, soothing atmosphere. As the angel and I were hovering above the meadow, I heard a lot of laughter. I heard my sons – Nathan and Travis! I looked down to see what they were doing. My vision was really, really good – I could zoom in on them with my eyes. Nathan and Travis were with a bunch of other boys and girls. They were vibrant and healthy, all happy and running and playing. There was so much beauty, so much love, that it filled the air. The angel told me, 'Your sons are fine, and you will see them again. Do not worry.' As I went to reach for Nathan and Travis, I was suddenly thrust back into my bed in the hospital. And that was the end of my experience. The angel knew I had to see that my boys were okay.

I have never known a greater love than this. "[45]

The least talked about, and possibly the least common of the ADC's is the complete manifestation of the deceased person. Elisabeth Kubler Ross experienced this unusual phenomenon with a former patient who came back to give her a vitally important message which was to shape her future work.

Elisabeth was walking to a lift with her boss, about to tell him she was quitting when a woman appeared before her. She described her as almost transparent and hovering in the air. She soon realized that she was the only one who could see her. The lady appeared to know her and came towards her. She called her Dr Ross and said she only needed a few minutes with her. Initially thinking she may have been losing her mind Elizabeth walked to her office where this lady opened the door for her, and it was then it dawned on Elisabeth who this was, Mrs. Schwartz! But ten months ago, she had died and was buried. She thought she had better sit down before she passed out. How could she be standing beside her?

Mrs. Schwartz explained that she had to come back for two reasons. The first reason was to thank her and the Reverend Gaines for all they did for her in the hospital. The second reason was to tell Elisabeth that she must not give up her work on death and dying. Not yet. Elisabeth wondered how she could possibly know that she was planning to quit. It had all got too hard. Mrs. Schwartz went on to say, *"Your work has just begun,"* she said. *"We will help you. "[46]*

Elisabeth could not believe this was happening to her and was about to ask for proof when Mrs. Schwartz seemed to have read her mind and she scribbled a note for the Reverend. Then she disappeared. The writing on the note was real and able to be passed on to the equally stunned Rev Gaines who had also worked with Mrs Schwartz in the hospital.

---

[45] *Hello From Heaven*, Bill & Judy Guggenheim, Self published by the ADC Project, 1995 edition
[46] Elisabeth Kubler Ross, *The Wheel of Life* (Bantam Books, London, UK, 1998) Pg 183

CHAPTER EIGHT

AFTER DEATH COMMUNICATION BY 'FRAGRANCES'

Dominic is a 38-year-old physician in Florida. He gained an important awareness while he and a classmate isolated themselves in a country cottage to study for their medical school exams.

"While my friend and I were studying, I experienced the extremely strong and distinctive smell of a medication that my mother used on Grandmother: camphor and alcohol. This home remedy was used as a cold compress that was applied to her forehead when she was feeling weak. There was definitely no camphor of alcohol in the cottage. Yet the odour was so strong that I told my friend that I believed that my grandmother had just died. He sort of brushed it off, but I noted the time when it happened, 10:10 a.m.

Shortly after that, I felt a very peaceful presence of my grandmother. I realized that something extraordinary was happening! The whole feeling was that she was saying, 'Goodbye. Don't worry. Everything is fine.' Grandmother had Alzheimer's disease. In the last months of her life, she was incoherent. But when I felt her presence, it was the person I had known before she became ill. She left me with a sense of relief and serenity and peace. When I went home, that day, mother was waiting for me. She said, 'Your grandmother has taken a turn for the worse.' I told her, 'Don't worry. I know what happened. She died at 10.10 this morning.' Then my mother confirmed that my grandmother had died at exactly that time.

When Dominic's grandmother visited him, he was given an invaluable lesson that is rarely taught in most Western medical schools. He learned that his grandmother is an eternal being who merely discarded her earthly body like an

228

old, worn-out garment. Imagine a world in which all medical caregivers have such knowledge."

This ADC also illustrates that when someone is afflicted with Alzheimer's or another debilitating disease, only the physical body is impaired, while the spiritual body is not affected. This explains how Dominic's grandmother could be healed and whole immediately after dying, despite the fact she had been severely incapacitated before she made her transition.

Vera is a hairdresser in Arizona. She was given a dramatic new appreciation for life from her father about 15 years after he died of cancer at age 40.

"I was in the hospital to have our first child. We were thrilled because we had wanted a baby and had waited so long to have one finally. Suddenly, I was in a lot of trouble! My contractions were strong, yet I stopped dilating, and nothing was happening. The doctor said they had to do an emergency caesarean.

On the way to the operating room, we stopped at the blood lab. I was alone in the corridor when suddenly I could smell the aroma of my father. He had been a furrier by occupation. His aroma was the combination of animal skin and tannic acid he had used to tan hides. It's a very distinct odour. There's no other smell like it. It's a very clean fragrance and was very much a part of my father. I could feel my daddy was there with me, and I relaxed. A peaceful feeling came over me, and I knew everything was going to be fine. My son was born easily – the whole thing proceeded like a piece of cake!"

Lorraine is employed by an optometrist in New York. Her daughter Tammy was 25 years old when she was killed in an automobile accident.

"When my daughter, Tammy, went to the Bahamas, she bought me a bracelet and a necklace. The night that she died she had the bracelet on and it was destroyed. For over two years since the accident, I had been trying to find a new bracelet to match my necklace. I would have paid anything for it!

It was night time, and we were coming out of one of the attractions at EPCOT centre at Walt Disney World. My other daughter, her friend, and my husband were with me. My daughter turned to me and said, 'Ma, do you smell that?' I said, 'Oh yeah!' We were smelling the Gloria Vanderbilt perfume that Tammy always wore. But as we looked around, there was nobody near us. Her girlfriend smelled it too and said, 'Why don't we go in here?' So we all went into the store, and I began browsing in the front. My daughter called, 'Mom, Mom, come back here! I went to the back of the store, where they were selling jewellery. And there was the bracelet – the exact match to my necklace from Tammy! It was unbelievable!"

It seems reasonable to assume that Tammy wanted to replace her mother's bracelet and found a clever way to provide guidance to her family. Her choice of time and place to contact them indicates she probably knew in advance that they could discover the priceless bracelet in the nearby gift shop.

Spontaneously smelling a fragrance that you associate with a deceased loved one may trigger a flood of warm, loving memories of that person. This can provide much comfort and support when you realize you are still in the thoughts and in the heart of the one who has died.[47]

---

[47] *Hello From Heaven*, Bill & Judy Guggenheim, Self published by the ADC Project, 1995 edition

CHAPTER NINE

AFTER DEATH COMMUNICATION BY 'VOICES'

Philip is a psychiatrist in Kentucky. He was caught off guard when he heard from his 15-year-old daughter Tina after she died in an automobile accident.

Tina had friends all over the city. We didn't realize how involved she had been with so many kids. She was quite a force for good in the community.

She had told one of her friends from Sunday School that if she should die, she would like everyone to have a party for her and not to mourn. Her friend reminded us of this statement.

"So the night of Tina's funeral, we had a very large gathering at our home with 200 to 300 kids, some with their parents. It was wall-to-wall people!

I was passing through the hallway downstairs when I heard Tina say, 'I love you, Daddy!' I wheeled around as this was an audible, external voice.

I am a board-certified psychiatrist, and I am not given to hearing things that are not there. Having lived my professional career as a pretty hard-headed scientific person, I really hadn't expected this.

However, this experience took a good bit of the sting out of the loss because you know you really haven't lost them.

Philip recognized Tina's voice despite the large number of people who were in his home at the time. What words could be more meaningful to any bereaved father than the ones his daughter chose, 'I love you, Daddy!'"

Sherrie, a 31-year-old corporate recruiter in Washington, was widowed when her husband Scott died from a cerebral aneurism at age 3.

"About three weeks later, on Christmas day, I was asleep in the living room of a friend's house. It was about 3:00 or 4:00 in the morning. A sound woke me up. It was Scott's voice, just as clear as ever! I recognized his voice and speech manner. It was an external communication that was totally outside of me.

He said, 'Don't ever be afraid. You will always have the people around you that you need.' He said that with such conviction that it seemed he knew more about things than I did. This statement made me feel like everything was going to be okay, even though Scott was gone.

That experience really changed things around for me. A big burden was lifted off me."

Scott's voice was so strong and so real that it literally awakened Sherrie from her sleep. And, he spoke with such authority that his message gave her the emotional support she needed to go on with her life.

Patricia is a customer service representative for a bank in New York. She was contacted by her husband, Herbert after he died of emphysema at age 59.

"When Herb passed away, I cried every day for a whole year, because I missed him so much and worried about him. He wasn't only my husband; he was also my very best friend.

A little after the first anniversary of his death, I was sleeping, and Herb's voice woke me up. He called 'Patsy, Patsy.' I heard him through my ears.

When I was fully awake, I heard him say, 'I'm all right. I'm okay. I'm fine.' I had a distinct feeling he was trying to tell me not to worry about him.

I felt Herb was right there, and by some grace, he was able to communicate. I heard his voice so clearly. There was no laboured breathing – just his normal, healthy voice, like before he got sick."

There are no words to describe the calmness that came over me. It was a blessing, and it felt so good.

Vicki is a 36-year-old office manager in Florida. She was consoled and renewed by her father after he died suddenly of a heart attack at age 66.

"I didn't get to see my father when he passed away, so I guess I took it harder than everyone else. I was given a two-week leave of absence from my job to recuperate.

After my first day back to work, I was driving home and the dam burst. I started crying and crying. I had to stop on the side of the road. I bowed my head in my arms on the steering wheel and cried uncontrollably.

About two minutes later, I felt a presence right there in my car. I felt encapsulated in a cloud of love and heard my father's voice as clear as a bell. He sounded elated and said, 'I am fine. I am happy! Just take care of your mother.' I heard him through my ears.

It was a miracle, a blessing! In that one instant, I was filled with so much love and joy that it completely took all my hurt away. I knew my father was totally at peace, and I was a different person from that point on."

Rhoda is a classical musician in Texas. She was nineteen years old when she had this transforming encounter with her grandfather, who had just died from a heart attack.

"Just 48 hours after his death, I was awakened. I peeked at the clock, and it was 2:10 a.m. I knew my grandfather was there! I felt he was standing at the foot of the bed. He started talking to me and said, 'I want you to know that everything is fine over here. Please tell everyone not to worry about me. I'm happy. I did everything I needed to do on earth, and I want you to tell that to everybody. And tell them that I love them.' It wasn't a voice I heard – it was like ideas and thoughts. It was truly telepathic, and I simply let it come. It was such a peaceful feeling – I felt flooded with peace all over. Grandpa was really saying goodbye. I feel he needed to do that as much as I needed to hear it. It was the most powerful message I could have ever had of life after death. It catapulted me into a deeper search for the meaning of life."

Rhoda's account shows that some people don't actually hear a voice, either externally or internally. Instead, they mentally receive thoughts that they are certain originate outside and independent of their own mind. This is known as thought transference.

Beth, a 56-year-old writer in Florida, had this informative ADC after her father, Norman, died of congestive heart failure.

"The night my father died, I was lying in bed, and lo and behold, I sensed his presence. He said, 'Hi, Honey!' I said 'Daddy! You're okay!' He said, 'Honey, there's nothing to it. Dying is as easy as falling off a log!' I was so overcome that I really didn't know what to say.

My father continued, 'I just stood up and there was Carl! He shook my hand and said, 'Hello, Norman. It's good to see you.' Carl and I used to play together when we were little kids, but I hadn't seen him in years. All these other people were there who I hadn't seen in ages, and Carl introduced me around.'

I was lying there crying with joy and said, 'Oh, that's wonderful!' Then my father said, 'I just wanted you to know. Don't worry about me.' I said, 'Thank you, Daddy.' It was all telepathic and that was the end of it. I fell asleep very, very happy. I wanted to share all this with my family, but I knew they would think I was crazy. So I just used it as support and let it warm me inside."[48]

Elisabeth Kubler Ross witnessed her dying father conversing with her deceased Grandfather shortly before he passed over. She was nursing her dying Father, who was in excruciating pain. He had been sleeping, and suddenly he woke abruptly asking Elisabeth to open the window so he could hear the church bells clearly. He then proceeded to converse with his own deceased father (Elisabeth's Grandfather) as if he was in the room, asking him for forgiveness for leaving him to die alone in a nursing home. He told his father that maybe all his suffering had been his punishment, and he promised to see him soon. The next morning he was dead.

Elisabeth felt sure that her Grandfather had taken him into Heaven to be *"embraced by the unconditional love of God."*[49] At this point in Elisabeth's life,

---

[48] *Hello From Heaven*, Bill & Judy Guggenheim, Self published by the ADC Project, 1995 edition
[49] Elisabeth Kubler Ross, *The Wheel of Life* (Bantam Books, London, UK, 1998) Pg 127

she had no knowledge of life after death, but she intuitively knew that her father was at peace at last.

One of the reasons for collating this book is to present as many as possible of these remarkable first-hand experiences from a diversity of people and situations to propose that it is time for humanity to gain a different perspective on 'death' and on interaction with other dimensions that are just as real as ours. A perspective that then negates the fear of death and dying and accepts that we live eternally, with sojourns on Earth and in the spiritual dimensions. Inter-dimensional communication happens regularly in many different ways. We are only temporarily separated from those we love. In Earth years it may seem a long time, but relative to our *eternal* life - it is but the blink of an eye. I look forward to the day when these facts of life are generally known and accepted.

So where do deaths from seeming *accidents* fit into the premise that, as a general rule, they are predestined? The more interesting question might be, *are there any accidents?*

CHAPTER TEN

WAS IT AN ACCIDENT?

How many of you reading this book have known of a beautiful child or adult that died prematurely by a freak 'accident,' illness or through seeming negligence of another?

On my journey, I have met various people who have lost loved ones in accidents. Two of those people were friends who lost their beloved sons while young.

An old friend of mine lost her only son when he was 19. He was a very loving, much adored young man who accidentally fell off a cliff to his death. Another friend lost her younger son when he was six while playing in our street on his bike. Another acquaintance lost a favorite Aunt in a head-on collision where a drunk driver hit them. At the time, this woman lost her faith in God as the lady who died was an amazing person that spent her life doing good for others.

What if every individual chooses before they are born how long they are going to live, the major life lessons they are coming in to experience, their parents, their siblings, and every other major factor of that particular lifetime? What if this is decided by the individual together with Higher Dimensional Beings and their own All-Knowing, All-Seeing I AM Presence, and their immediate family's I AM Presences to make the most of everyone's learning and growth in that life for particular reasons, (some karmic, some not), which is unbeknownst to them and their immediate families at the time of the accident. Remembering that our own I AM Presence knows and sees all our collective lifetimes and what we have chosen to overcome to fulfil our Divine Destiny.

I was delighted to find this piece written by author Dr Doreen Virtue which had been *given* to her in meditation regarding our life purpose.

236

"Before your birth, you and a spiritual council of guides created a life plan tailored to meet your material, spiritual, and karmic needs. This divine plan has three elements: a purpose, personal growth lessons, and relationships with other people to support the overall plan.

Your purpose is a task you are to do through your career, volunteer work, or a special project that uses your natural talents and interests to benefit humanity. Your plan's second element entails well-timed life events that teach you about love and how to shed self-defeating personality traits. The third element involves pre-birth arrangements you made with certain people who will serve as catalysts for your purpose and personal growth. These people may function as your family members, co-workers, friends, or acquaintances. Your interactions with these people simultaneously help them to fulfil their own plans.

You predestined your plan as a rough outline of what your life would look like, including your purpose, significant life lessons, and relationships with particular people. Because the plan is only a rough outline, you must choose the finer details of your plan as you go through life. You are free to ignore the plan completely, but the emotional and societal consequences of this choice can be devastating."
[50]

Look how similar this extract is that was given to Neale Donald Walsch on this subject.

"You may, however, select the persons, places, and events – the conditions and circumstances, the challenges and obstacles, the opportunities and options – with which to create your experience. You may select the colors for your palette, the tools for your chest, the machinery for your shop. What you create with these is your business. That is the business of life.

Your potential is unlimited in all that you've chosen to do. Do not assume that a soul that has incarnated in a body which you call limited has not reached its full potential, for you do not know what that soul was trying to do. You do not understand its agenda. You are unclear as to its intent.

Therefore, bless every person and condition, and give thanks. Thus you affirm the perfection of God's creation—and show your faith in it. For nothing happens by accident in God's world, and there is no such thing as coincidence. Nor is the world buffeted by random choice or something you call fate."[51]

---

[50] Virtue, *The Lightworkers Way*. (Hay House Inc., Australia. 2006). Pg 72.
[51] Walsch, *Conversations With God, Book One*. (Hachette Livre, Sydney, Australia. 2007). Pg 46.

I was involved in this heart-breaking experience when my boys were young. It was one of the first that made me reflect on what a seeming *accident* might actually be.

"It was a hot, sunny morning in Auckland, New Zealand, and Jason was bringing his Mummy a cup of tea in bed. Six-year-old Jason had woken up wanting to do some special things for his Mummy this morning. He wanted to show her how much he loved her. The weak tea was lukewarm with four teaspoons of sugar but his wise mother saw the pride in his eyes at having made it all by himself. She hugged him and drank it with a smile, telling him it was great and how clever he was to have made it all by himself.

An hour later, Jason appeared in the kitchen beaming from ear to ear.

'Mummy I picked all your favorite vegetables from our garden. Don't they look yummy?'

Jason had done something he had never done before and gone all the way down to the bottom of the garden and picked all the vegetables he could find that he knew Mummy liked. He had displayed them beautifully in a straw basket. Once again, very surprised, Mummy thanked him profusely, and he skipped off.

Another hour elapsed, and Jason appeared at the doorway. 'Mummy, can I go and play with my friends?' Mum said yes, and he rushed up and gave her the biggest hug and kiss ever. 'Goodness,' thinks Mum to herself. 'You'd think he was never going to see me again with that goodbye!'

Thirty minutes later, his Mum and I, in our separate homes in the same street, hear a sickening scream and with dread in our hearts rush down to the road not knowing whose child it was we had heard. All I could see were two little feet sticking out from under our elderly neighbor's car. Jason had just enough time to tell his Mum he loved her, and he passed away.

When his Mum was able to talk to me about that morning, she relayed the above to me and said it was as if sub-consciously Jason knew they were going to be parted. He acted as if he was never going to see her again. It makes complete sense to me. It was his chosen time to go for whatever reason, and at a Soul level, he knew."

A dear friend from my High School days lost her beloved only son Daniel in an apparent *accident* while he was on a surfing holiday on the rugged Great Barrier

238

Island in New Zealand with my son and their friends. Some of the last words he spoke to her were. *"You should come with me Mum. I'm going to paradise!"*

His Mum thought nothing of those words as he thought of Great Barrier Island as a beautiful place, but I believe at a Soul level, those words had a deeper meaning.

Early one morning, the group had walked up to the clifftop to watch the first rays of the golden sunrise creep over the horizon. They sat around talking for some time and then gradually made their way back in small groups at different stages. No one could understand how it even happened. One moment he was there – the next he wasn't. No one saw him fall or heard a scream. No one knew what had happened until after they had scoured the island and discovered his body on the rocks below.

The rest of the family had gone away themselves that weekend, and Diane was out walking early in the morning and twisted her ankle at the precise moment she believes Dan could have died. Apart from the pain of a twisted ankle, she had a sick feeling in the pit of her stomach, and she asked Tony to take them all home – NOW.

Diane recalls how on the drive home, she had looked out over the ocean and said to his little sister, *"Dan's out there somewhere."* At the time she remembers being shocked by his seven-year-old sister's strong response who adamantly retorted, *"Don't say that Mummy, I love him too much!"*

Little did they all know that he was indeed out there on a boat as his body was being ferried back to Auckland as they spoke.

Later, when they finally went to his flat, they found that Dan had neatly packed everything up ready to be moved with ease. This is not uncommon that the sub-conscious, prompted by the Soul of the person, pre-empts the time of their death and tidies everything up beforehand.

I spoke to Diane later, and she said that while she was pregnant with Dan, she had a dream that he was killed in an accident and that he sustained head injuries. So, before he was even born, Diane had a premonition that he could die prematurely. In fact, she had an underlying fervent desire to protect and watch over him. Diane recalls a sense of urgency with him from the moment he was born.

Dan was an extremely happy, fearless and adventurous child who always ran ahead of everyone else and Diane had the feeling that she was continually having to *"hold him back"* so he didn't injure himself, even in his teenage years. The family saying with regard to Dan was often *"He's gone on ahead."* So much so that when Tony asked Diane what to put in his funeral notice for the paper, she replied without hesitation, *"He's gone on ahead."*

Diane had never forgotten when Dan, at the age of seventeen, was chatting with her in their kitchen and completely out of the blue he stunned her by saying,

"I hope I know the moment I die. It must be phenomenal. I don't want to miss it!"

Dan had no fear of death; his Soul knew his mission this time around. And what a mission that was. It seemed that all those who knew him were deeply touched by this young man's desire to protect and look after them, of his ability to give selflessly, of his acceptance and non-judgment, his loyalty and his integrity.

One of his friends at the time was gay and having a difficult time at High School. He recalls many times when Dan had just *"appeared out of no-where like a Guardian Angel"* broke up whatever was going down quickly and easily and then vanished. This friend was so impacted by Dan's protective friendship and non-judgment that he calls Diane every year without fail to remember him.

After the funeral, Dan's friends would come and visit to support Diane and Tony for months afterwards. They came around and created a Photo Board of his life at school, balls, rugby trips, and of course surfing and camping at Great Barrier Island.

His closest friend, who was at Great Barrier when he died, later named his son after him. Dan's first love still rings Diane on his Birthdays to remember him, even though she is happily married with her own child now.

Everyone who knew Daniel loved this young man. He was special. He always helped those around him and gave unselfishly. It seemed so utterly senseless. However, if he originally chose to live until age 19 to help and teach specific people specific things until then, and if he, together with his immediate family and God chose this for their own karmic reasons unbeknownst to them in the *now*, then it does make some sense. Understandably that would be extremely hard to accept for the distraught family at the time.

No words anyone else can say to parents who have lost a child can erase the grief and pain they have been through. I pray that the knowledge that your young one pre-elected that particular time to transition back to his/her heavenly home and that they are still very much alive and awaiting the time that you will all be reunited, is of some solace. Earth time doesn't exist in the higher dimensions, where they now reside. To them, it will be but a blink of the eye before you are together again.

I also reiterate that at the point of *death* in accidents the person feels no pain at all – just a shift in consciousness where often they find themselves looking down detachedly at their body in a state of All-Enveloping, All-Encompassing love from their Divine Creator, (as is mentioned numerous times by the NDE'rs in this book).

240

Apparently, many children instinctively know when they are close to passing over, just as little Jason and Dan did. Elisabeth Kubler Ross experienced this with a young friend while seriously ill in hospital.

When Elisabeth was a young child, she had her first encounter with *death*. She had contracted pneumonia and pleurisy and was in our equivalent of the Intensive Care Unit. Lying next to her was a chronically ill little girl a couple of years older than herself.

Although they were too sick to speak, they communicated telepathically and comforted each other silently. One day Elisabeth looked across at her, and they had a silent, moving conversation as her fragile little friend told her not to be upset but that she was going to be *"leaving"* that night. She reassured Elisabeth that she would be fine as *"the angels were waiting for her."* She also told Elisabeth that she must keep fighting to make it and that she was going to get better.

She reassured Elisabeth that she was going to be fine as her real family was *"on the other side."* Neither child had any fear of the *"journey"* one of them was about to make to go to her heavenly home. It seemed perfectly natural to both of them.

The next morning when Elisabeth awoke, her little friend's bed was empty

Similarly, this next wise young patient of Elisabeth's knew exactly what was happening.

Jeffy's story is one Elisabeth Kubler Ross remembered telling countless times as it is so full of wonderful messages and shows this little boy's acceptance and inner knowing as to when he was going to die. He, like so many of Elisabeth's young terminal patients, would tell her exactly what was needed for him to find peace. Elisabeth's quest was to ensure as many doctors and parents as possible saw the importance of listening to their dying child's needs and actioning them, which included taking them home to die if that was what they wanted.

241

"Jeffy's central nervous system had been affected, and he was like 'a drunk little man.'52 He could barely stand up, and he had experienced losing all his hair many times after Chemotherapy.

Jeffy was nine years old, and he had battled with Leukemia most of his young life. At this time Elisabeth was aware he would probably only live only a few more weeks. She overheard Jeffy's new physician telling his parents that they were going to give him another round of Chemotherapy. Elisabeth asked both the doctor and the parents if they had asked Jeffy if he wanted another round. They hadn't, and all agreed to do so.

In Jeffy's childlike innocence, he replied, 'I don't understand you grown-ups. Why do you have to make us children so sick to get us well?' In a courageous and authoritative voice, he politely declined, 'No, thank you.' His parents were unconditionally loving people who respected his wishes. He then went on to ask if he could please be taken home that day and would Elisabeth come home with them. Elisabeth was extremely busy, but in her wisdom and from her past experience, she realized that when a child asks to go home with urgency in their voice, they should be listened to. Jeffy, noticing Elisabeth glancing at her watch told her she wasn't to worry that it was only going to take ten minutes.

They all agreed to take him home then and there and drove home together. Elisabeth innately knew Jeffy was going home to finish some unfinished business and was interested to see what it was.

They drove into the garage, and Jeffy got out and immediately asked his father to get his bike down off the wall where it had been hanging for the three years since his father had bought it for him. His dream, for a very long time, had been to be able to ride his new bike around the block all on his own. He hadn't been able to.

Humbly but firmly he asked his father to put the training wheels on. Tearfully his father obeyed. As Elisabeth said, a nine-year-old does not want to be riding a bike with training wheels on, but he knew it was his only option. Here was this beautiful, very sick little boy, who was barely able to stand, asking to be allowed to have his dream fulfilled—to ride around the block on his own on his new bike.Once again showing maturity beyond his years he told Elisabeth that she was there to hold her Mum back and his father was there to hold Elisabeth back from following him. How hard must that have been for all involved. Off he went.

After what seemed like forever, he came around the corner beaming from ear to ear as if he had just won Gold at the Olympics. He asked his father to take the training wheels off and to carry it up to his bedroom. He turned to Elisabeth 'very

---

52 Elisabeth Kubler Ross, *The Wheel of Life* (Bantam Books, London, UK, 1998) Pg 189

242

unsentimentally, very beautifully and very straightforwardly'53 and said she could go home now!

When his first-grader brother, Dougy, came home, Jeffy asked his Mum to send him up to his room with one condition attached—there were to be no grown-ups. This took place, and after a while Dougy came down and told his Mum he couldn't talk about what they had talked about. Jeffy had asked his brother to keep it a secret until after his birthday in two weeks."

Jeffy died the week before his birthday. After his birthday Dougy shared what had transpired in Jeffy's bedroom the day he had called him up there. The book continues.

"In his bedroom, Jeffy had told his brother that he wanted the pleasure of personally giving him his most beloved bicycle. But he could not wait another two weeks until Doug's birthday because by then he would be dead. Therefore he wanted to give it to him now.

But only on one condition: Dougy was never to use those damn training wheels."54

Young children so often have no fear of death as they see it as a natural returning home – which it undoubtedly is. That is such a beautiful story, one with a sad, but happy ending as the parents and doctors honored a dying, brave little boy's wishes. By doing so they had helped Jeffy complete everything that was on his mind and in his heart, thus enabling him to pass over in peace.

A fact that not too many reflect on, or are even aware of, is that our precious children, of all ages, are only *"loaned"* to us by our Mother/Father God. Our Mother/Father God who Creates vast Galaxies, breathes life into the tiny human fetus at the exact pre-arranged, Cosmically aligned time that the Soul enters the body and sustains that human body with all its intricacies and complexities of physiology and anatomy. Our limited conscious human mind could never conceive of how to do this let alone implement it! Our 'job' as parents is to unconditionally love them, guide and nurture them until they are adults, but we don't *"own"* them per se. They are God's own, just as each one of us are God's precious children.

---

[53] Elisabeth Kubler Ross, *The Wheel of Life* (Bantam Books, London, UK, 1998) Pg 191

[54] Elisabeth Kubler Ross, *The Wheel of Life* (Bantam Books, London, UK, 1998) Pg 192

Yes, the Mother's heart connection to her children is so strong and the pain is very real. Even more reason to call upon our Divine Mother, whose depth of unconditional love defies human understanding, to bathe you, immerse you in Her Love and dress those wounds so they can heal. Ask and you shall receive the Divine soothing balm to assist you in easing the pain of losing your precious young one.

To love them is to let them go so they can move on unrestricted in their Higher Spirit Realms where they are sublimely happy and radiantly healthy. This is equally important to enable you to also move on and find those blessings in each now moment that our benevolent Father/Mother God bestows on us daily. The miracle of life and the miracles within God's glorious Creations in nature that are all around us if we but take the time out of our busyness to notice.

My husband's father died prematurely at 58. In the last couple of days before his fatal heart attack almost all the family, (six children), had gone out of their way to visit him. That was very unusual on its own. Naturally, none had any idea of what was about to happen. He was fastidious about his diet eating little to no sugar, and on the day before he died, he was seen eating a plate piled high with desert, something he never ever did. When questioned, he jovially replied that, *"it didn't matter anymore."* Subconsciously his Soul knew he was shortly to pass over.

Then the unimaginable happened right here in Australia! The world listened incredulously to the news that our seemingly indestructible, irrepressible *Crocodile Hunter* Steve Irwin had been killed in a *freak accident* by a stingray!

Steve Irwin was one of those rare people who exuded unconditional love. Steve's pulsating passion for life, of living every day to its fullest, captivated both young and old right around the world. He had no fear. He became *one* with whatever species of animal he was with.

I remember watching one program in stunned amazement as Steve edged his way, on all fours, closer and closer to an enormous *wild* Mommy Orangutang in the jungle until finally, he sat right beside her. And what did she do? (They can be overly aggressive and protective when their young are around, which they were.) She put her huge, hairy arm around him and gave him a hug! *"Wow, this is a really special man to be able to do that,"* I thought to myself at the time.

Terri said Steve would sometimes get up in the middle of the night and say he had to go down to the zoo as one of the animals was in trouble! He would go down, no matter what time it was, find and help the animal whose distress signal he had picked up on, and go back to bed! Now that is being *"at one with the animals"* – *he was literally on their wavelength*!

Not until after his death did I realize how well known and how loved Steve was outside of Australia, especially in America.

Shortly after his death, I was watching Ray Martin's poignant interview with his wife Terri, with tears streaming down my face. Terri's openness, honesty, and her obviously still raw anguish over losing a part of herself, so touched me, as I am sure it did all who watched that emotional interview. Here was another special and extremely wise person, not afraid to bare her soul to the world to continue to spread Steve's message to love, respect and protect all animals—especially wildlife.

From the interview, I could see just how much of a devoted father and husband Steve was. Steve was *"a big kid"* who would spend as much quality time as he could in between his busy schedules with Bindi and Bob entering into their world as they played just as he would enter into the animals' world when he interacted with them.

Here was a man who lived Godly principles for the world to see. I believe he taught millions about unconditional love and how precious all of God's creatures are. His raw enthusiasm was infectious. His appreciation for the gift of life was so apparent.

Here he was, with a wife and two children he adored, seemingly senselessly snatched away in the prime of his life. I, for one, do not believe he died from an accident. I feel it was his chosen time to go – that is, *chosen by him*. If this were the case, then the spirits and souls of the whole family agreed to this before incarnating and on some unconscious level knew they would only have their precious Steve for a certain length of time!

Are they separated forever? No, they are not. He will still be watching over them and guiding them from another dimension until it is their time to return *home* to be forever reunited.

In this interview, Terri said she and Steve had spoken about what would happen if he died! Steve had an intuitive feeling that he would die young. Terri had an uncomfortable feeling whenever Steve went diving! Steve had hand-held scorpions, the world's most venomous snakes, and I once saw him stand on a deadly stonefish. And yet, how did he die? A stingray tail-spike pierced his heart in exactly the right spot, at exactly the right time to end his life! The chances of that happening must be something like a trillion to one!

Are Terri, Bindi and Bob carrying on his dream? You bet they are. Did they let his death stop them? No. Bindi and Bob also have their Father's passion, enthusiasm, and love for all animals. I believe, they are now comfortably wearing their father's mantle. It appears to me that to walk in their father's footsteps is their pre-chosen destiny. That they all worked this out before they entered this lifetime is the only thing that makes any sense to me.

If Steve and everyone else did die from accidents beyond their control and often at the hands of someone else's negligence, then our Divine Creator would seem completely unfair, and our world would be totally chaotic and out of control. For myself, I know without a shadow of any doubt that the 'I AM of All That Is,' our God of love, is very much in overall control and we are living out what we have chosen for our growth and learning, although, when you have personally lost someone dear to you, this is understandably hard to accept at the time of loss.

Dr Melvin Morse MD, clinical Pediatrician, in his scientific research presents research showing that over 25% of the time, parents were warned of their child's impending death by a specific premonition or vision. They often took the children to the doctor or wrote their fears in a journal, all before their child died.

All of the cases of children and young adults I have known who have passed away prematurely, often in *accidents*, were very special souls with much to give and teach those around them just by being who they were. Similarly, it explains how some people seemingly defy death and live against all odds. In their case it wasn't their time to go. This also takes away the unfair guilt and blame on the part of the parents, caregivers, and friends who otherwise could spend their life thinking they could have prevented that person's death by keeping them away from whatever situation it was that caused them to pass over. It is simply the various parties living out their chosen part for whatever reason.

On that note, I would like to address the traumatic situation of losing a baby through SIDS, (Sudden Infant Death Syndrome), or Crib/Cot Death as it is sometimes known.

SIDS has confounded the medical fraternity as no apparent medical reason for these premature deaths has ever been found. So, if there has been NO medical reason for all these deaths, (which is large number of cases worldwide with approximately 3,000 a year in the USA alone) then surely this suggests that the underlying cause and reason is a spiritual one rather than a physical one.

Dr Melvin Morse, with the aid of Carrie Sheehan, associated with the Southwest SIDS Alliance and herself a SIDS parent, studied a large group of SIDS parents. Carrie had discovered, through a detailed questionnaire they sent to SIDS parents, that many had had very strong premonitions, dreams or visions of their baby's death. These premonitions would often come just at the point of going to sleep. The point where the conscious mind has *"let go"* and the sub-conscious and spirit can communicate to that soul. Dr Morse explains.

"In the middle of this huge questionnaire was a single question: 'Did you sense something was going to happen to your baby?' An astonishing 21% answered yes. A large number of those said that their premonitions were so strong or their visions so vivid that they wrote about them in their diaries. Some even told their physicians or ministers before the baby died.

.... Many of those in the study felt that they had witnessed a physical event.[55]

The majority explained these 'dreams/visions' in the same way NDE people relate to their near-death experience. That it was not remotely similar to the normal dream state but that it was an ACTUAL experience that they could recall with vivid detail. As one SIDS Mom said, 'The difference between my vision and a dream was like the difference between television and actually being there.'[56]

These SIDS parents were being prepared and being shown what was *to be* and, in some cases, like the one below, they were shown that their child had returned to their eternal *home* with their heavenly Father.

This case study in Dr Morse's book, *Parting Visions*, shows how the mother's guilt and anguish over the loss of her baby were relieved by her vision which she was given at exactly the same time as her baby passed over. She explains.

"I was in my early twenties when Kathy died. I had no reason to expect anything was wrong. I fed her and burped her like I always did and then put her down to sleep in the crib.

I went to bed myself about an hour later. I was tired like most new mothers are, and I went to sleep. All of a sudden, it was like I was there. I could see a beautiful country that seemed to be made of light. The hills and grass and sky were spectacular. There were various shades of light that glowed in the most generous way.

---

[55] Morse & Perry, *Parting Visions-Uses and Meanings of Pre-Death, Psychic, and Spiritual Experiences.* (Harper Collins, N.Y. 1994). Pg 51.

[56] Morse & Perry, *Parting Visions-Uses and Meanings of Pre-Death, Psychic, and Spiritual Experiences* . (Harper Collins, N.Y. 1994). Pg 53.

I could see my daughter there in this field, a place that looked like a meadow. She wasn't lying there, but she wasn't walking either. Maybe she was floating.

I felt as though I had finally come home, as though this beyond place was where I should be. And then I woke up."[57]

Linda realized that something was wrong and ran to her daughter's crib, only to find that she had *gone*. Naturally she and her husband were traumatized, sold their house and never returned to that area. However, the vision had a comforting element. Linda continues.

"When things got tough, I thought of that dream. It helped me overcome the pain because I know that I saw where she was going."

My desire for including this portion is for any readers who have experienced this tragic situation, or if you have someone close who has, to realize that no blame should be apportioned here. That comfort can be drawn from the realization that, once again, we see that the spirit/souls of ALL concerned have pre-elected to endure this experience for reasons we cannot understand here in the physical realm. Our God of love would never inflict such circumstances upon anyone, anywhere. The only other possible explanation is that at some fundamental level it was pre-chosen by all parties concerned. The wonderful message here though is the fact that your wee one continues to live in a stunningly beautiful 'heavenly' realm where one day you can be reunited.

After reading Robert Benson's wonderfully illuminating and inspiring first-hand experience of visiting *The Children's Spheres* you can find comfort in knowing your little one is continuing to grow up in this beautiful place where his/her every need is being taken care of with love, tenderness and understanding.

For all those people who read this who are in this situation, I pray God will speak to your heart and soul and impart the truth to you that you may be comforted in knowing it was not your fault and that there was nothing you could have done that would have changed the ultimate outcome. If you wish, you and your loved ones can pray this prayer which will also help to draw these things to you.

God thank you for giving me the peace
Within my heart and soul that I so desire.
A peace that passes all understanding,
Knowing that.............. is alive and well with you and your
Angels,

---

[57] Morse & Perry, *Parting Visions-Uses and Meanings of Pre-Death, Psychic, and Spiritual Experiences*. (Harper Collins, N.Y. 1994). Pg 57.

In safety, radiant health and enveloped by your love.
I lift my burdens of .... (guilt) or .... to you,
Thank you that you are helping me to understand
At a soul level and helping me to Forgive myself and all people concerned.
Thank you for cleansing me and restoring me with your love.

PART TWO:

COPING
WITH LOSS

PRACTICAL APPLICATIONS, SUPPORT AND INSIGHTS FOR THOSE DEALING WITH GRIEF

One cannot write a book on understanding 'death, dying and coping with grief' without acknowledging the woman who, for three decades, pioneered the then unacceptable open and honest examination of 'death' and dying. A selfless, tireless Angel whose devotion to her calling of listening to the needs of the terminally ill and many times supplying those needs from a heart overflowing with unconditional love and compassion, was both inspirational and remarkable. A woman who met with much resistance at the time as she vowed to change the way orthodox medical practitioners treated the terminally ill. She was the epitome of living a Christ-filled life of unconditional love for all and the subsequent healing impact living that way had on all she touched.

Naturally, I am speaking of Elisabeth Kubler-Ross, who passed away on August 24, 2004. When I read Elisabeth's autobiography *The Wheel Of Life* I cried in almost every chapter. The struggle, the heartache, the terror, the loneliness, the pain, the deprivation, the intense judgment, the ridicule, the courage, the strength to live her dream, that she experienced—I realized that our pioneers that initiate lasting social reform and leave behind treasuries of wisdom and knowledge for following generations, survived only through their extreme faith, dedication, tenacity and perseverance, often against all odds. Their lives were so often wrought with pain and hardship.

Elisabeth's work left an enormous legacy for all medical practitioners, the terminally ill and their carers and to humanity in general. Elizabeth launched some of the very first research papers on Near-Death Experiences, the afterlife and publicly advocating the fact that we never 'die.' Her books are full of timeless, practical wisdom and poignantly illustrate the importance of living with love and compassion. Her message is one of hope, encouragement and the absolute healing power of unconditional love.

During her time as an Intern and Doctor in State hospitals, Elisabeth discovered that the dying were being treated as badly as her former Psychiatric patients. *"They were shunned and abused. Nobody was honest with them. A cancer patient might ask, 'Am I dying?' and the doctor would reply, 'Oh, don't be silly.'"*58

Elisabeth had learnt from her success with her psychiatric patients that healing was more than drugs and science. It was about **one human being reaching out**

---

58 Elisabeth Kubler Ross, *The Wheel of Life* (Bantam Books, London, UK, 1998) Pg 123

and touching another with tenderness and compassion. She discovered that what her dying patients wanted was *"honesty, closure and peace."*[59] Elisabeth describes what she found.

"During my consultations, I sat on beds, held hands and talked for hours. There was, I learned, not a single dying human being who did not yearn for love, touch or communication. Dying patients did not want a safe distance from their doctors. They craved honesty. Even the most suicidally depressed patients could often, though not always, be convinced that there was still meaning left in their lives. 'Tell me what you're going through,' I would say. 'It will help me to help other people.'"

"But tragically, the worst cases—those people in the last stages of illness, those who were in the process of dying—were given the worst treatment. They were put in the rooms farthest from the nursing stations. They were forced to lie under bright lights they could not shut off. They were denied visitors, except during prescribed hours. They were left alone to die as if death might be contagious." [60]

Elisabeth learned that many Doctors viewed death as a personal failure and as a result, avoided talking about it, especially to their patients. In fact, she found in her day that no-one wanted to talk about it: the doctors, the family, the carers or the friends.

Elisabeth did something that was considered to be revolutionary. She began conducting Death and Dying seminars. Weekly seminars where a terminally ill patient that was different each time and who had previously consented, was interviewed as the subject for that week. Her students were able to listen to Elisabeth interviewing the patient as to their needs. Likewise, the patient was able to express often repressed feelings and air their grievances about the way they had been treated and how they felt it could be improved. That was the absence of compassion and honesty about the fact that they were actually going to die rather than the actual medical treatment, which was fine. The auditorium was always full, and after the patient had left lively, animated discussions ensued. Soon, doctors, social workers and priests joined the weekly seminar. Elisabeth describes the awe-inspiring results,

"In these discussions, doctors, priests and social workers confronted hostility and defensiveness. Their fears were analyzed and overcome. By listening to dying

---

[59] Elisabeth Kubler Ross, *The Wheel of Life* (Bantam Books, London, UK, 1998) Pg 149

[60] Elisabeth Kubler Ross, *The Wheel of Life* (Bantam Books, London, UK, 1998) Pg 124

patients, all of us learned what we should have done differently in the past and what we could do better in the future."[61]

Through Elisabeth's courage, monumental life-long changes took place for all these people who attended her regular seminars. What a wonderful gift she gave them all.

The dying became Elisabeth's greatest teachers, and her life's work had begun. She went on to educate people that death should be openly and honestly discussed with all parties. That death is nothing to fear and that the actual time of transition can be a wonderful experience, one of sublime peace and reuniting with loved ones that have passed on. That death equals new life.

Another much debated topic is that of suicide. Once we realize that we never truly die, as such, that changes the whole perspective of suicide. It will be comforting for parents who have lost children to suicide to know that they are still alive and they can be reunited with them when it is their time to pass over.

Many religious factions teach that it is *wrong* and that God will punish those who do. I personally do not believe that a God of Love, which our Divine Father/Mother God undeniably is, would do that.

For anyone reading this book who has lost a loved one through suicide I trust this next passage is of some comfort in which Source is conversing with Neale Donald Walsch on the subject of suicide.

"Comfort may come from knowing that the person who has committed suicide is all right. They are okay. They are loved and God never forsakes them. They will simply not have achieved what they set out to do. That is important for anyone who is contemplating suicide to understand.

There is no such thing as 'punishment' in what you call the 'Afterlife.' It is those who are left behind who feel punished. They experience an incredible shock, from which some never fully recover. All of them feel an enormous loss. Many spend the rest of their lives blaming themselves. They wonder what they did wrong. They agonize over what they could have said that might have changed things.

What you die with is what you will continue to live with.

---

[61] Elisabeth Kubler Ross, *The Wheel of Life* (Bantam Books, London, UK, 1998) Pg 148

I want you to be very clear here. You will encounter yourself on the other side of death, and all the stuff you carried with you will still be there. Then you will do the most ironic thing. You will give yourself another physical life in which to deal with what you did not deal with in your most recent one.[62]

Suicide has become so prevalent in our world today. Especially amongst our young ones, many of whom are unable to cope with the pressures of today's society and don't know where to turn. These 'New Children' do not fit into the old paradigms, neither should they be expected to or forced to.

A good friend of mine is a medical practitioner, one of the top in his field; patients stay with him, they have children and then their children are also treated by him. In his clinic alone, which is not a large one, he is seeing an average of 2 suicides a MONTH! We have a large problem that no-one is talking about – our world needs to change.

One day I pray that there will be many places that educate children *from a young age* that they are ALL beautiful, powerful little God-Beings having a spiritual experience on Earth in these bodies – that they are here to treat others as they would like to be treated and to love each other rather than to judge each other. To be able to express their God-given creativity freely. To be taught the power and consequences of their thoughts and words. That they all have a Guardian Angel watching over them. That their God Presence is always there to give them the inner strength to overcome whatever they are facing as long as they ask for help. That they are always loved beyond measure by their Mother/Father God. Imagine the difference if children through to young adults were taught these fundamental Universal Truths as a part of their basic foundational education.

These precious ones are literally our 'hope' for the future. They are here to change the very foundations of society in all arenas. Many incarnating now are coming in with their relevant Soul memories intact, they know a lot more than we do and they have come in *as our* teachers to make the necessary changes upon our Beloved Planet! We, the adults, would be well advised to listen to what they have to say.

All people are precious in God's sight irrespective of anything they do or have done. This is an experiential planet of learning from our 'not so good' and 'good' experiences. There are no perfect people and our Father/Mother God does not expect us to be. Although we pass into another realm whole and healed from our previous physical ailments we can see from the Life Reviews that we are accountable to ourselves and our Creator for any *unfinished business* that we had originally elected to carry through to completion that didn't eventuate.

---

[62] Walsch, *Home With God*. (Hodder & Stoughton, London.2006). Pgs 61,63.

CHAPTER ELEVEN

LIVING WITH GRIEF

We, as vulnerable human beings, do not need to cope on our own in times of grief, trauma, and disaster. We were fashioned out of bones that break and hearts that break. We were designed by God to be able to depend on Him/Her and the myriads of Angels and Higher Dimensional helpers at such times for added strength and guidance.

For those of you who do not know God, I pray this book may quicken your spirit to seek Him/Her out and begin your journey with Him/Her and that it may be of some solace if you have lost a loved one. Let me assure you that our Divine Creator is a God of immeasurable love: endless, limitless, bottomless love, that endures for eternity. Every one of his precious creations that is you and I, are a priceless facet, an individualized part of our Divine Creator, that He/She cherishes. We need to ask for God's help. Our Divine Creator gave us all Free Will here on Earth, and Universal Law is such that we must ask for help in order for it to be given. We must choose to do this whenever we need that inner strength and Divinely guided insight.

Our God is indeed the ultimate creator of All That Is as He/She breathed life into our very core at conception and designed a unique masterpiece of anatomy that only a Divine Being could create. She/He knows every cell in your body, your strengths and your weaknesses and, above all, your vulnerabilities. Your own Guardian Angel and I AM Presence want to walk with you, to carry you when the pain overwhelms you, to encourage you and strengthen you with their immeasurable love, hour-by-hour, day-by-day, and year-by-year.

For those of you who don't know God and would like to, you can pray this prayer regularly, it will be faithfully answered. (Simply replace your name for our Divine Creator if necessary)

PRAYER

Dear God/Jesus/Source, thank you for helping me to know you.
Thank you for guiding me to a person, people, and/or place where they know you.
Where they will embrace me just as I am and love, support, and guide me.
Thank you for leading me to a church or group that truly practices your principles.
One that does not judge and condemn, but one which edifies and builds up.
I desire tender loving care and sensitive and understanding people around me who will listen.
Show me you love me.
Thank you for walking with me and being my strength and refuge from the storm that rages all around me and within me.
Wrap your arms around me and envelope me in your love.
Thank you, God, for protecting and covering me.

Grief is a process that cannot be hurried. Just as there is no one exactly the same as you, no one's experience of grief is the same as yours. It should never be compared and you should be given all the time you need to work your way through the various stages.

C. S. Lewis wrote, *"Stitches of love, support, happy memories and faith in God will pull the wound together to make it hurt less."*

Please do not try and go through the grieving process alone without your Divine Creator at your side. Invite Source/God into your life and ask for Divine strength and support.

THE PROCESS OF GRIEF

Grief is the response we experience as a result of a loss. For example, it can occur through loss of a loved one, miscarriage, loss of a limb, divorce, loss of a beloved pet, and many other of life's losses. Any painful life event can be the precursor of a range of painful human emotions which might include sadness, fear, anger, relief or a mixture of all of these emotions.

Grief from death-related loss strikes a severe blow because it so final. The person is gone forever out of this life. Expressing grief in whatever way is right for each person helps to reduce the intensity of the pain that initially feels like a raw, gaping wound, as long as the environment feels safe and supportive.

In this section, I refer to the book *Coping with Grief* by Mal and Dianne McKissock. They are professionals in the field of bereavement, whereas I most certainly am not. It is a book I highly recommend reading. Mal and Dianne are the founders and co-directors of a bereavement care centre and also have a service, especially for children. Their websites are www.bereavementcare.com.au and www.childhoodgrief.org.au.

Dianne says, *"Grief is a chaotic experience – forwards, backwards, all over the place. The process is determined by many things; the person who is grieving, the event, the person's relationship with the deceased, the nature of support, concurrent events and so on."* Dianne and Mal have categorized the process of grieving into five main stages – Shock, Numbness and Crying, Anger, Guilt and Despair.

SHOCK

"Denial is a natural defense mechanism. It is inconceivable that their loved one is dying or has died. Even more inconceivable if it is happening to themselves. While in denial and shock, they do not want to look at the reality of the situation.

In the beginning, most people feel shocked when they first learn of the death of someone they love, even when the event has been expected. It is hard to believe that person will now be physically absent, harder still to understand and accept the foreverness of death."

My Oxford Reference Dictionary describes shock as *"a sudden violent effect upon the mind or emotions."* If possible, ensure you have someone with you who is able to handle the practical details such as answering and making telephone calls, driving you around, and helping in the house and home where possible. You may feel confused, disorientated, and each moment may tend to blur into the next. Time may seem to stand still.

Many people, including children, find it beneficial in the long term to spend time with the person who has died to make the most of last opportunities to touch them, to say the things that are in their heart.

NUMBNESS AND CRYING

Mal and Dianne McKissock say.

"In conjunction with emotional responses to grief, there are a host of physical responses. One of these is designed by nature to decrease pain to a more manageable degree. When someone we love dies, our body produces a number of narcotic-like chemicals similar to heroin and morphine. They are powerful pain-killing chemicals and are produced to create the numbing effect most people

experience in the beginning. For those who cry, these chemicals are released through tears. That's why it is important to be allowed to cry if you are able to.

Then, gradually, as the weeks go by, the production of these chemicals decreases, and around four to six weeks after the death, they are significantly low. The resultant increase in distress is both an increased awareness of reality and the body's attempt, through increased crying for example, to produce more chemicals to assist further in survival. Some people never cry but access a similar numbing chemical effect through strenuous activity or from constructive expressions of anger.

With this in mind, it is easier to understand the role and importance of crying and other grief behaviour. Don't associate crying and getting upset with going downhill. In fact, they show you that you are going up-hill and it is a difficult haul – but you can make it. Be kind to yourself – let go, as much as you are able, your need to be in control.

Bereaved people are very vulnerable and susceptible to the criticisms and judgments of others. Many people believe that grief occurs in neat, sequential stages or phases, and tend to give the bereaved symbolic gold stars when they appear to have moved from one neat, predictable stage to another. However, while grief is a potentially healing or healthy process, it is chaotic, dynamic, and ever-changing. The bereaved need supporters who will let them be themselves rather than people for whom they have to change their behaviour in order to pass some mythical test."

You are the only one who can feel what you feel. You are the only one who can determine how to express what you feel. Others affected by the bereavement have their own feelings and their own way of expressing them, but if you feel like going to bed for a couple of days –do it!

If you feel you want to stay with a friend for a couple of days – do it! If you want to yell, scream, cry, and curse – do it discreetly (for a time only). If you want to withdraw and have time to yourself – do so (for a time only).

ANGER

Anger is a natural part of grief for some people. Not everyone experiences this emotion. As numbness subsided the reality sets in, anger may appear and can be a frightening and intense reaction.

As Mal McKissock says *"Unexpressed anger often builds up on the inside and may explode at an inappropriate time, or worse, cause physical problems."*

Find a safe means of expressing it. It may be a punching bag, beating an old pillow with an old tennis racket, or throwing old plates in the garage. For most people,

258

the need to express anger openly in this way is for a fairly short period of time, although, like most other grief emotions, can be re-stimulated when something or someone brings raw grief back into the foreground.

GUILT

Once again, I reiterate that the grieving person needs to be able to talk openly about their feelings.

This includes talking about the guilt they are feeling. As a caregiver, it is wisdom to listen compassionately and attentively without giving advice. At this point, advice is the last thing they want or need.

Mal McKissock says, *"The person experiencing guilt needs to be able to recount the story, tell it the way they wish it had been, apologize, repent, confess,—say sorry from the heart."*

Mal and Dianne's perspective on the relationship between despair and grieving is insightful and comforting. *"This occurs when the numbness wears off, when the reality of the foreverness of death penetrates, and all hope of seeing that loved person again is lost. The desire to see them may be intense, the longing to touch, hold, and speak to them feel overwhelming, and the thought of remaining this way forever seem unbearable. Despair may last for a long time, may come and go at intervals, but you won't feel this way forever. You will recover through support, acceptance, understanding, and many other caring things people can offer, as well as through your own internal resources, but the recovery may be slow."*

If you find your despair turning to depression that you can't seem to raise yourself above, then seek professional help. Find a bereavement counsellor or support group or turn to your pastor to assist you in finding suitable support people.

In the first year, it is suggested that the grieving person refrains from making any major decisions. Reach out to those around you who love you and with whom you feel comfortable and ask for help when you need it. Express your feelings openly and honestly. Don't hold back.

You are under extreme stress – look after your health. Where possible, take extra nutritional supplements, eat an easily digested, balanced diet. Of course, you'll need some comfort foods too. Have a massage. Meditate, exercise gently, spend time alone, and time with others as the need arises. Listen to yourself – trust your own instincts about self-care.

I encourage you to call on God/ your own I Am Presence/Guardian Angel for strength and the resilience to overcome the despair. You will always be given it-- if it is what you *truly* want.

259

It is unhealthy for both yourself and your departed loved one to hang onto them with excessive grief. This creates an energetic tie/hook that makes it much harder for your departed to move on to their newly chosen path. The energetic tie literally holds them back. This is common when people lose babies, children or young ones. Sometimes they create almost a shrine to that person or leave their bedroom exactly as it was. This also holds you back from moving on and can be a form of denial that it has happened. This can be quite natural in the early stages but not for any great length of time.

The only way to find any level of happiness for *anyone* is to live in the *now* moment appreciating what we do have rather than focusing on what we feel we do not. What we give our predominant focus to is what eventuates in our life. It is the Universal Law of the Circle that what we put out energetically through our thoughts, words, and deeds must come back to us and it shall gather even more of the same/like energy. A very good reason to watch what our predominant thoughts and words are; negative or positive. We are powerful Co-creators of either constructive happenings or destructive happenings in our own lives, and with God's help, we can turn our lives around armed with this awareness and by then putting it into practice.

You know you're on the home stretch when you have acknowledged your loved one's death, found ways of honoring and remembering them, and begin to re-organize your life in their physical absence—remembering that they would want you to move on and find a level of peace and happiness.

CHAPTER TWELVE

TERMINAL ILLNESS

For all the people who are living with or have lived with and cared for the terminally ill I pray you will draw your strength from your Divine Creator. If your loved one is still alive when you are reading this, then I would urge you, the caregiver, to seek lots of help for yourself as you bear the brunt of the pressure. Don't be afraid to ask for help and for time out. You need rest time yourself to replenish and revitalize yourself. If you do not have family or friends to help, ring the local community services or church and ask what is available.

It is so terribly hard to watch the one you love suffer in any way. I would be asking for help from God/Jesus/Angels that will definitely be around you, every day. Talk to him/her/them in your head just as you would your best friend. Talk, talk and talk some more, for you cannot be expected to bear this load on your own. They long to be there for you, but you must ask. As I've said before, we have Free Will on Earth, and that means God/Jesus/Angels cannot impose their will on us no matter how much they see we need help.

We must ask, and that then gives them permission to intercede and stand beside us. You may like to pray this prayer. In all my prayers, I would suggest you pray them until you feel the words becoming real for you. You may not feel that way at first.

PRAYER FOR THE CAREGIVER

*Heavenly Father/ Source/ Jesus, thank you for giving me the
strength and courage to face each day.
Thank you for helping me to be loving, compassionate, and
sensitive to ……… 's needs.*

Thank you for helping me to listen quietly and patiently
while ……… is needing to talk.
Thank you for helping me to know ……… will soon be resting in
your arms, free of pain and suffering.
Thank you for helping me to impart the importance of ………
making peace with his/her Creator.
Thank you for helping me to talk to ……… and give me the right
words to help ……… to lean on you and ask you into his/her life.
Thank you for helping me to show ……… how much easier it will
be for them if they focus on coming home to your loving arms, free
of pain, rather than focusing on the fear of the unknown.

Thank you for helping me to help ……… to understand you will
forgive anything and everything he/she has ever done, no matter
how bad it may seem, if only he/she will ask for your forgiveness.

Your grace is enormous, and you will ALWAYS forgive when the
person who is asking is repentant and sincere. Then ……… will
feel so much lighter, and you can truly minister to him/her in
his/her last days/weeks/months.

Thank you for helping me to explain how important it is for ………
to also forgive those he/she holds un-forgiveness towards and
lastly, for the strength and grace to forgive himself/herself for
everything that he/she has ever done.

Thank you for helping ……… and myself to realize there is no such
thing as judgment in the higher realms.

Thank you God/Source/Jesus.

He/she will then begin to find a new level of peace within. Maybe, if you think it is appropriate, read some of Robert Benson's chapter and the NDE and ADC accounts to your loved one from this book. I know if I was the one dying, I would love to read these highly reassuring, inspiring, and wonderfully loving testimonies of those who have experienced death. Maybe also, where appropriate, read to them the passages that refer to what we believe we will find once we have passed over is what we will initially find but more importantly that we can create a joyful experience of going straight to the bliss of heaven if that is what we choose.

Elisabeth Kubler Ross discovered through working with hundreds of terminally ill patients that had they been able to *"express their anger, to cry and grieve, to finish their unfinished business, to articulate their fears, to work through the above stages, they will reach the last stage of acceptance. They won't be happy, but they will no longer be depressed or angry. It's a period of quiet, meditative resignation, of peaceful expectancy."63*

If your loved one has been speaking of seeing people who have passed on or an angel or guide they have possibly entered into the Twilight Stage which precedes death and the person is able to see into other dimensions simultaneously. You can reassure them that this is okay and nothing to be feared.

PRAYER FOR THE TERMINALLY ILL

Father/Source, thank you for helping me to cope with the knowledge that soon
I am going back home to your loving embrace.
Thank you for helping me make peace with you.
Father/Mother God, I ask you into my broken life (if appropriate).
Thank you for helping me to let go all my fears and surrender them to you.
Thank you for forgiving me for all the things I have done. I am truly sorry.
Most importantly, thank you for helping me help me to forgive myself and put the past behind me.
Thank you for helping me to forgive those who have wronged me as you have said you will ALWAYS forgive me, but I must also forgive those who I have offences against.
Thank you for helping me to realize that when I have done this you can then touch me with your peace that surpasses all understanding and I can truly rest knowing I am coming home to your tender love.

Thank you God/Source.

One of my reasons for writing a book such as this is to assist people who are terminally ill to transition without unnecessary fears. To see from these wonderful alluring and illuminating near-death extracts and from Robert Benson's description of how glorious it is to live there, that where you can go is a wonderful place that, dare I be so bold as to say, you could actually look forward to: A place where you become free of all that you may be suffering from in the now in your physicality. A place where you will be caressed and wrapped in a cocoon of warm, deep unconditional love. A place of tremendous beauty and unlimited opportunities to become all that you aspire to become. A new, fresh beginning free from all judgment and condemnation. A place where you can look forward to

---

[63] Elisabeth Kubler Ross, *The Wheel of Life* (Bantam Books, London, UK, 1998) Pg 167

263

reuniting with deceased loved ones and pets. The list goes on and on. I'm certainly looking forward to it when my time comes! Naturally, there is tremendous sadness and grief at leaving loved ones behind. Know that you will be reunited as there is no time in the higher dimensions

On that note I have a personal dream that this book will find its way into as many hospices around the globe as possible – to shed light, give hope, reassurance and peace for those fearful about and burdened with their impending death. The thought of so many dying full of fear and alone unnecessarily is abhorrent to me. However, I am only one person who resides in one country-Australia. If you believe this book, with its amazing collective of insights and inspiration, could help ease the emotional pain of the terminally ill and assist in making their transition one of ease and grace instead of fear and struggle, as I do, then I would ask that *anyone who feels to* donate a book (or books) to their local hospice, please do so. I have no expectations with this request, just a heartfelt desire to get this message out to as many as possible. One spreading the word to another, and another and so on can become a powerful *human word-of-mouth chain* and accomplish much. If you do this in any way, big or small, please email me at christiners1@gmail.com, so I can send a personal thank you card in sincere appreciation.

Here is a quote from Neale Donald Walsch's book, *Home with God*, regarding the loving support that is available to us all to help us adjust to the transition of passing from one dimension to another. It is comforting to know that before we transition, (die), we can create a wonderful experience when our time eventually comes, eliminating all fear of death.

"In the moments after your 'death,' you will all find yourself in the Presence of the most loving Angels and guides and gentle spirits, including the spirit or essence of everyone who has ever been important to you in your life . . .

Those you have loved the most will be closest to you. They will surround you . . .

The Presence of these loved ones and angels will be of enormous help to you, assisting you in becoming 'orientated' and understanding exactly what is happening to you, and what your 'options' are . . .

It IS exciting. In fact, your 'death' can be one of the most exciting moments of your life. It all depends on what you believe. As in life, in death, what you believe is what you will experience."[64]

Cancer is rampant these days. In Australia alone, it affects one in three people. We see children dying of such illnesses as leukemia and brain tumors. Once again,

---

[64] Walsch, *Home With God*. (Hodder & Stoughton, London. 2006). Pgs 102,103.

these precious little ones are seemingly snatched away when they are just beginning to experience life.

I would re-iterate to the parents who have lost a child to terminal illness. These little ones are so special. They have some kind of precious quality or qualities that endear them to so many. They have that special intangible something. Often a perception way beyond their years and the ability to be grateful for what they do have rather than dwelling on what is wrong with them. I believe that these children would have chosen, together with God/Source before they were born, to return to their heavenly Father at an early age for whatever reason. You will find these children often teach those around them to love unconditionally, to be accepting, to find joy in the simple things, to appreciate each precious moment of life and to appreciate what we do have. How often do you see a child that has suffered some terrible disease or affliction, who has had operation after operation, with this extraordinary countenance that still laughs and loves and enjoys life? At these times, these beautiful Souls become our teachers.

Isn't it comforting to know your precious little one is alive, in radiant health and still growing up in the Heavenly Children's Spheres in a far more beautiful, loving, and harmonious environment than Earth is at present? Focusing on these facts may make it easier to cope with your child's passing. Robert Benson's first-hand account of the beautiful children's spheres and some of the children's NDEs listed in this book will reiterate these concepts.

We were never designed by God to go through life's traumas on our own. Just as we naturally reach out to our earthly parents to help us through the hard times, so too should we reach out to our Father/Mother God-Parents for support and understanding. Not only does God/Christ/Source give us constant support and understanding but even more importantly immense love, grace and forgiveness.

Forgiveness plays such a vital part in the healing process. I pray you can forgive yourself and any others you may hold responsible for your loved one's passing. The best way you can do this is with God's help. You may like to pray this prayer.

PRAYER

Father/Mother God, Thank you for helping me to cope with the
loss of ....
Thank you for your strength and support to get through this and
face another day.
Thank you that you are helping me to forgive myself and any others that I, in any
way, hold responsible for this loss. Together
we can do this.
Thank you that each and every day you are helping me let go of

any resentment or bitterness towards others knowing that
holding on to these feelings will only make it harder for me to
recover.
Thank you for helping me let go of any guilt or shame I have
towards the passing of ....
Father/Mother God, I know in you I can eventually find a peace
that passes all understanding.
I give you the burden that is too much for me right now. Thank
you for helping ease my pain.
I will trust in you, my Heavenly Father/Mother God. Thank you.

My sister Sylvia died of liver cancer and a brain tumor. She was a much-loved Christian lady who raised four boys and was very active in her local community. She was a conservative Anglican.

Upon hearing the news, she only had a short time to live, she understandably became very angry and un-accepting. She searched desperately for any possible remedies but found none.

She began to spend more time in prayer. One memorable day, she emerged with a serene smile and announced that the Holy Spirit had spoken to her very clearly that it was *"her time to go home."* From that moment, she developed a quiet acceptance of her destiny, and an inner serenity and tranquility that of course, those around her did not share.

She spent much time in prayer with God, and she would often speak in tongues during this time. Amazingly, she did not believe in speaking in *tongues* prior to her illness. (For those who don't know what Tongues is, it is described as the language of the spirit.) This seemed to give her even more peace, and at times she absolutely radiated God's love.

She had asked God that he would spare her from feeling too much pain. Even at her worst, she did not experience much pain, which was a miracle in itself, if you had seen her broken body near the end.

At her funeral, her local parish church was full to overflowing. Two other high-ranking ministers from another larger church also officiated, which was unusual. They all spoke of just how deeply this remarkable woman knew her God and how she had strengthened their faith and taught them so much. It was a dull, cloudy day but a golden ray of light suffused the hushed church and shone on the coffin. It stayed for about ten minutes and disappeared as mysteriously as it had come.

My other sister June and I knew it had been a sign from our sister who had passed on to be with her heavenly Father.

266

I realize not all patients will be like my sister, but I fervently believe that this God-given peace and serenity amidst pain and turmoil is there for anyone to partake of who hands everything over to their Father/Mother God and who surrenders, thus putting their complete trust and faith in their Divine Creator.

ONE OF GOD'S EARTHLY 'ANGELS' - KEN PRATHER

Don't you just love Divine synchronicity? It is always timed to perfection. The night before I had to have my manuscript complete, (for the first edition) and off to my publisher I received a seemingly random, (I don't believe in coincidence), email from Dr P.M.H. Atwater regarding this utterly inspiring man who, after his NDE, (which left him severely injured physically,) has founded two wonderful charitable organizations: Reaching For Joy; and A Day Away. I felt his story had to be included in this book. His work with the terminally ill knows no bounds. Ken is the epitome of how a Near-death experience can enlighten, strengthen and enable someone to become a living, breathing blessing to all he comes in contact with.

Ken Prather is described by Dr Atwater as a *"living, breathing miracle . . . .this special Angel manages to serve as a hospice caregiver, a joy-giving counsellor, and a huggie-bear source for children and their families to find happiness in the midst of poverty and pain . . .. Some claim that he is severely handicapped; I say he is a great spirit who has found a way to bring the pearls of wisdom he learned from his near-death experience back to earth . . . .for the benefit of all."*

Ken describes what took place.

"In 1998 I received a brutal beating by five men with baseball bats, it was due to this beating that I spent 32 days on life support, three months in the hospital and three years in a nursing home. It was during this time on life support that I experienced my second Near Death Experience of my life. It was truly my path of destiny, and on this path, the birth of 'Reaching For Joy' (inspired by my daughters business, Joy's House) not only became a vision and a gift from the Other Side, but mostly a reality on the Earthly plane.

It was during my three-year stay in the nursing home, where I was continuing my Spiritual Pilgrimage, along with my physical rehabilitation, that 'Reaching For Joy' was born. The elderly, the disabled, and the lost souls, all with the feeling that they had no self-worth or self-pride. As one man once told me, I have nothing to contribute to society anymore. How wrong he was. I explained to him that he had his life to share with others, and even just to listen, was sharing. Life's experiences and lessons are truly a gift that should be shared.

We then started group discussions which I named, Reaching For Joy, because that's exactly what we would be doing, reaching out to others. The group even grew so much that other nursing homes adopted my program. We even started taking residents from one nursing home to another, so they could interact with each other. It was also in the nursing home that the bond between myself (Reaching For Joy) and a Hospice organization was formed. I started counselling the terminally ill, right in the nursing home where I was a resident. I was also given an office in the nursing home, to use for Bereavement counselling with families left behind after the loss of a loved one. It was also during my stay in the nursing home, that I started volunteer classes at the local Zoo, to become a Docent - educator of animals. Reaching for Joy was starting to grow and mature, even in the nursing home. We were growing together.

Then one day I told everybody, I was making a trip to Colorado. I was Wheelchair-bound, and the doctors told me I would never walk again, but deep down in my soul, I knew different because I had been given a message on the Other Side, that on my return to the Earthly plane, that I was to follow my visions. That to find the answers, I would only have to look within. So, in a vision, I saw a mountain and a lake. So, Colorado, here I come. I spent two wonderful weeks in Colorado with my best friend and his family. I found my mountain and my lake and with it came answers from within to share the wisdom and knowledge of the Other Side.

It was made very clear to me to take everything that was negative in my life and teach and share it with others. Then I would be shown it was now positive, and it was always positive because it was my path of destiny. To be able to help and teach from your negative experiences in life on this Earthly plane is the greatest teachings of all.

On my return from Colorado, I had a very special surprise for everyone at the nursing home. It was in the afternoon, the nurses and doctors were milling up and down the hall, when I looked at them from my Wheelchair and said, "Hey guys, I brought a gift back from Colorado for everybody." It was at that point, I got out of the Wheelchair and walked. One nurse almost fainted and said, He's been given a gift. WOW! If they only knew who had given me that gift.

Reaching For Joy is not only about people helping others, but showing by helping others, you are mostly helping yourself, grow and mature, and realizing that this is our purpose on this Earthly plane, to share with others. I have been out of the nursing home for two years and Reaching For Joy has become Internationally known, and with the help of our local Zoo and other volunteers, Reaching For Joy is now taking Zoo critters up to our local Children's Hospital to visit with very sick children and their parents who are with them. We even upon request, make visits into the ICU rooms. This program is very rewarding to everybody involved.

It's the sole purpose of this website, not to judge anyone by their beliefs, religion, or faith. But to, in turn, let and show everyone that they have an individual Spirit that dwells within, and how to nurture and mature their Spirituality. I am also listing a profile of *Reaching For Joy*, and a list of the counselling services that I share with others.

Let it be known that *Reaching For Joy* is a volunteer program, with volunteers working within the program. I am also a writer of poetry and inspirational short stories and will have a message board where you can post poetry and stories in a tribute to your loved ones who have crossed to the Other Side. There are only two limitations on this website, and that is NO PROFANITY, and RESPECT the beliefs of others."[65]

Ken had just sent this communiqué to Dr Atwater and she had felt compelled to share it, as do I, as it is truly humbling and shows how much some people go through and how Ken has been making an awesome difference in his part of the world as a result of his near-death experience. In Ken's words, *"My major focus centers around making one-day wishes of respite come true for children who have a chronic or terminal illness."* He had recently just completed an animal presentation to over 120 children with cancer. Wow! What a man.

Ken continues.

"I just wanted to take the time to share a milestone and another blessing that 'A DAY AWAY' has been given. A DAY AWAY is in its 17th year and had just taken its 500th sick child and their family on a day away. It was truly a moment of NOW to remember. The little boy (seven years old) had cancer and was under hospice care, but his wish was to go to the zoo and see his favourite animal, the penguins. Just two weeks ago last Friday his wish came true, and he and his family had a very touching trip to the zoo. I received a phone call from his family stating that he had passed away. When I went to the viewing a couple of days later, I was embraced by his mother with tearing eyes. It was while I was hugging his mother that I could see the stuffed penguin I (we) had bought for him at the zoo—in the casket with him.

These are the precious moments (gifts) that YOUR donations are making come true for the children of A DAY AWAY. Next weekend A DAY AWAY and two of my volunteers will be taking a family who is driving over 100 miles to go on a day away. Both daughters 6 and 9 have cancer. Right at this moment, I have more than 30 children and their families on the waiting list to go on a day away. A DAY AWAY is now in its seventeenth year, and I couldn't have done this without you, the private and individual donors of A DAY AWAY or as I prefer to call them (you) 'the day away angels.'

Two more options have been added for the children to choose from. One is an amusement park with a petting zoo, and the other is a wolf rescue refuge. I had

---

[65] Ken's website is www.reachingforjoy.org

one young girl who was waiting for her father from California to join her on a day away, but then two weeks before he was to arrive in Fort Wayne he found out that he had Stage Four liver cancer.

So, A DAY AWAY paid for the little girl's airfare to go visit with her father. Of course, a nurse went along with the little girl.

Life has been a very humbling experience for myself. Your donations to A DAY AWAY has truly touched my soul, along with the souls of 500 children and their families. It looks to be a very busy summer, and any donations at all would be very much appreciated. There is no donation too big or too small. But the greatest gift of all has been your love and caring for the children of A DAY AWAY, and that is PRICELESS!"[66]

While in a nursing home recuperating after his NDE, Ken shared the message of hope and comfort his near-death experience had given him. What he has subsequently taught epitomizes the simplicity and power of these experiences – that it is in the giving of ourselves that we receive. **It is in acknowledging that everyone has something of value to share with another just by virtue of who they are and what they have experienced in their life. Our riches should not be judged by our material possessions but by what life has taught and given us. Compassion, wisdom and gratitude for life are acquired through our so-called negative experiences where we learn what not to do again.** Ken shows people that some of the greatest gifts we have been given are those that we would term our harshest and worst experiences as when we share the lessons that have been learned through those experiences people can identify with them and gain insight into just what the human spirit can endure and overcome. Our experiences are our *gold* that when shared, can help strengthen others on their journey through life.

Society, in general, suggests we should hide our mistakes and hardships, feel guilty and ashamed, but they are the clay that the Master Potter uses to mold us into discovering our own inner beauty and Divine Essence which we can then turn into our own unique and special masterpiece. A masterpiece which was never meant to be perfect as none are, but polished by the grace of God, love and respect of self and love and respect for others.

---

[66] Ken is also a powerful speaker having completed a nationwide speaking tour in the United States over three years. If you are a part of an organization that would like Ken to come to your part of the world with his special message of love and hope he can be reached on his email at ken.prather@yahoo.com If you wish to make a donation to A Day Away please email Ken on this email address.

Ken is the ultimate example of giving away one of our most priceless commodities – time. Time seems to be speeding up, and we seem to have less and less of it so to truly give of our time, to sit down with another, give them our undivided attention, and truly listen from our heart to theirs, is one the greatest gifts we can give.

Ken has become a living example of selfless love, giving, sharing and appreciation for the precious gift of life. His faith and obedience to his original mission that was given to him in his NDE resulted in a Divine blessing of miraculous healing for all around him to see. What a gift he is to those lucky enough to be touched by him.

I discovered this message from Ken on his website, which is so full of simple, honest truth and wisdom that I have also included it.

"Today was truly a blessing I should say. I received the most wonderful gift a soul could receive. I woke up, I looked in the mirror, and I saw my BEST FRIEND. To gaze upon the beauty of our Creators creation is truly a gift from above, but to do it with another soul is truly the essence of sharing.

Knowledge can be absorbed and devoured in many ways, but the wisdom and experience of life's lessons can be the greatest teacher of all. Remember, we are all the teachers of a gift, but most important of all is the gift from THE TEACHER

All beings travel a path of destiny in life, some just travel a longer path with many detours, but at the end of the journey, all paths shall lead home. Take care, and I shall see you at the end of the path.

The Essence of one's Soul is the nurturing of compassion towards others. Sprinkle with care, tend it with love, and from the seedlings of compassion, a loving Soul will bloom.

To listen is to learn, to learn is to gain knowledge, to gain knowledge is to have an open mind, and to have an open mind is to listen.

Now is the absence of the past, and the void of the future. Be true to the Now, embrace it, cherish it, and SHARE it. For NOW, shall be here FOREVER.

Compassion can be the greatest gift for a lost Soul, not theirs, but yours.

May you walk in the Light of the Creator forever, for you are a beacon of hope. His spirit will be with you forever, and how do I know? Because the Soul of Creation dwells within my soul and tells me so.

This new day is beautiful, a mystery, a challenge, an education, and a journey. I'm in unchartered waters, as I have never been here before. I'm one day older!

Light is the Essence of the Soul, to show the Soul the path of its own self destiny.

When imagination becomes a reality, its the birth of a vision, and visions are the success from within.

To gain strength in Spirit, and bring Peace to my Soul. To cry, then to laugh. To fail, then to succeed. To deny, then accept. To fall, then stand tall. To learn, then to teach. For this is my GIFT, THIS IS MY LIFE.

The greatest gift that humankind can give all is the gift of GIVING."

Thank you, Ken, you are indeed a precious gem, sparkling with love and compassion for all to see.

CHAPTER THIRTEEN

GRIEF FROM DIVORCE

For those of you who have never experienced Divorce, you may find my including this chapter in a book about 'death' strange. However, as one who has been through the process not once, but twice, I can affirm that it can feel like someone, who you gave a part of yourself to, has died. You will all know of friends and/or family who have divorced, and I hope these facts will aid in making people feel more compassionate towards those working their way through a divorce.

Most people are very sympathetic and supportive of the person who has just lost a loved one. However, society, in general, doesn't seem to be so supportive of the person coping with divorce. For those of you who are suffering or have suffered the anguish and enormous repercussions of divorce, I empathize with you

I know it well, as, in my first marriage, I walked out the coward's way with a lengthy letter of explanation and no prior warning. My only excuse now is that I was very young!

Guess what? In my second marriage, my husband left me with a lengthy letter of explanation and no prior warning! Talk about the epitome of what you give out you get back!!

The average time to stabilize from a divorce is five years. With divorce being so prevalent these days, we have a lot of wounded people out there who, more often than not, try to heal on their own with little support. That sounds easy, but it is not. The very best form of healing is a support group where you can see that everyone experiences all the devastating facets of divorce just like you.

When a divorce takes place, and one party has left the marriage, often suddenly, the other person is left with a gaping wound. The person who they had given their heart and soul to has gone. They had formed a deep bond and soul tie with that person, and often it seems like a large part of themselves just walked out the door. They feel crushed, broken, vulnerable, and usually, their self-esteem takes a spiraling dive. They have little or no energy, and the physical body needs a lot of help to cope. Ask for advice from your nearest health store, Naturopath or Doctor if necessary.

Often their own immediate family is not supportive, and overnight they have lost their in-laws and their extended families. I found that particularly devastating, as I loved the interaction with what was a large, happy extended family.

They will also move through the process of grief, potentially adding depression and loneliness to the list. It is so easy to get yourself stuck in the depression cycle where the light at the end of that long, dark, gloomy tunnel seems dimmer and dimmer until, if left unaided, the light disappears and hope fades. If this has happened to you, then it is time to join a support group or seek help from someone experienced in grief counselling.

Loneliness is paramount, especially in co-dependent relationships where one party lived for the other or lived their lives through the other person. In either case, it is very beneficial to go out and join hobby groups or local clubs of something you are interested in and meet new people. The worse you feel, the more insular you become which, of course, only compounds the feelings of loneliness. If at all possible, surround yourself with positive, uplifting people and avoid negative people while you are feeling low.

Shock is often the first feeling to set in. You feel numb and, initially, disbelieving that it is not a bad dream that will somehow pass. You hope the next day they will be back. In this state, you cannot function normally. It is even harder when there are children involved.

With the realization that this is real and permanent, the floodgates open, and grief can set in. You may not be able to function normally, think straight, or have a handle on time. It is wise to call in family and friends to help with arrangements for children, etc. It is wise to take more care when driving, as your reactions are usually slower.

It is about now that one or both parties can potentially start getting very angry and blame each other. A lot of heated words may be exchanged, and it is important not to have these discussions in front of the children no matter what ages they are. Sometimes it is helpful to engage a neutral party to mediate if you can't come to mutual agreements on your own.

After a while you can say your goodbyes and begin to move on. It is often easier for one party than another, which can also be painful.

Some more time elapses, and you can start the rebuilding of your new life. You know when you have reached this stage when the focus comes off the loss of the partner onto building a new life. Another reason for joining a group or enlisting support of one kind or another as it can happen faster than if you try to go it alone.

At the resolution stage, you are both moving on with your new lives. Maybe not happily for some, but you have worked through the necessary problems and found ongoing solutions.

My advice from my experience would be don't expect too much of yourself too soon, be gentle on yourself. Don't get into *"If only I hadn't done this or that."* That is what we call living in the past which only perpetuates how you feel and that keeps you in the past unable to find the strength to move on. Equally important for your own health, (as what you send out comes back to you in greater measure), endeavor not to get into the 'blaming game,' it does always take two in such matters and none of us are perfect. When you turn to Christ/God/Guardian Angel for the strength you need to overcome the grief and all the associated feelings that go along with it, it becomes easier. Pray for acceptance of the situation so you can physically and mentally begin to move on.

As with all feelings of grief, we need the strength of God/Christ to help us heal and overcome divorce even more so when it is one of those nasty ones with custody battles as you also have children who are bruised and battered from the experience.

Where children are involved the parents also have their children's feelings and emotions to contend with at the same time as their own. Please explain, no matter what age, that it is NOT their fault and that it has happened because Mummy and Daddy can't live together any longer. They don't need to know all the details unless they are older, and they insist. Even then use your discretion. Endeavour to explain why you are parting simply, without apportioning blame on the other party. Why? Because your children need both their Mummy and Daddy (where possible, I realize it is not always possible), and should not be made to feel they need to take sides.

Unfortunately, most children think it is their fault somehow. That they have not been good enough, etc., so making special quality time to be with your children, even if you are finding it all too much, will help all your collective healing. Their needs are great too, and often they will not tell you, as they know you are already terribly upset and stressed, and they feel that they might make it worse. Talking regularly with them and asking them how they are feeling also assists them to heal. If it is all too much for you, then it is wise to ask for help with the children from a relative or close friend your children know, like and trust.

There are many areas to be aware of where the children are concerned. It is wise not to use the children as go-betweens, as your messengers, or spies. Children do not want to have to choose between Daddy or Mummy, as both are equally important to the child's stability, under normal circumstances that is. The children will still need structure and routines so too many changes only add to their insecurities. To blame or criticize the other parent in front of the children can lead to further confusion and insecurities. If you promise something to them, ensure you keep that promise as they need to be able to rely on your word as their little world appears to them to have suddenly come crashing down just like yours may appear to have to you. If the going is getting too rough for you and the children seek help or find a support group. It is never too late to get help and turn to someone you trust.

Another area which usually adds to your stress at this time is finance. Often the main provider has gone. An emergency budget needs to be drawn up with what you have at your disposal. If you have no idea how to do this, ask for help from a family member, friend or community centre.

Often the family home and goods need to be divided. This can create enormous stress for all concerned. Once again, ask for help and seek legal advice/legal aid as to your rights.

For family and friends of the divorced couple, please try to remain as neutral as you can to both parties. (Obviously, I am not referring to cases where there has been abuse, etc.). I was horrendously judged by so many when I left my husband. No one except the two people concerned knows what took place behind closed doors, day in and day out. We don't have the right to an opinion as we don't have all the facts. It Is wise not to get emotionally involved in the inevitable *"he did this, and she did that"* conversations.

When family and friends do take sides that results in feelings of alienation and that person can feel even more alone and ostracized with no one to turn to. The old friends they had as a couple usually feel awkward around you and don't quite know what to do and say. Remember, we all have faults, and that is the very time that that friend particularly needs some grace and neutral friendship.

Each partner will benefit greatly from finding one friend they trust implicitly who can act as a sounding board. Someone they can just pour out all that has happened and get it off their chest, so to speak. Women have no trouble doing this, but often, the men find it harder. It is so important and speeds up the healing process. Otherwise, it remains locked inside as unexpressed emotion which can build like a dam, and when that person does blow, it can result in violence. The person

276

listening should do just that: LISTEN and not give advice unless the friend has specifically asked for it. Often, just by speaking it all out, the person finds their own solutions, sees it all with greater clarity, and it speeds up their healing. I trust this has been of some practical help from one who knows. Please continue to seek support and strength from Christ/God.

CHAPTER FOURTEEN

CONCLUSIONS

This book is designed to be thought-provoking, inspiring, and a pathway to expanded consciousness and Universal Truth for all races, ages and creeds. It has been designed to dispel any and all fears of 'death' and dying and also to give comfort and hope along the road to ultimate peace when you have lost a loved one. The inspiring and informative collective material also acts as stepping-stones along that pathway to peace in discovering there is so much more to life than what is seen. As it says in the Bible,

Therefore, we do not lose heart,

Though outwardly we are wasting away,

yet inwardly we are being renewed day by day.

For our light and momentary troubles are achieving for us

an eternal glory that far outweighs them all.

So, we fix our eyes not on what is seen, but on what is unseen,

For what is seen is temporary, But what is unseen is eternal.

2 Corinthians 4:16-18

We are never alone. There is limitless help from the unseen world to guide, strengthen, and help us along our own personal path with love of the unconditional kind. To assist us to discover our own precious facet of the One Divine Diamond. Our own All-seeing, All-knowing 'I AM' Presence, represented as The Dove.

Constantly we receive help from the myriads of Heavenly Helpers that our Divine Oversoul enlists to sustain our lives. If people only knew of, and could thus appreciate and give gratitude to, our Magnificent *"Builders of Form"* – not only of the Angelic Kingdoms, but also the Devic and Elemental Kingdoms - without whom NO LIFE WOULD EXIST anywhere! I am learning myself about these Divine Selfless Servers of Humanity and one day, when fully informed, I would love to write about them.

For anyone interested in learning more on this subject the best book I know of to do this is, *The Elemental Grace Alliance -The God Awakening* which can be found at www.elementalgracealliance.com both in e-book and hard copy format. Truly a Sacred Cosmic book of truth.

I speak to my angels every day and enlist their help in routine matters, even parking spaces in busy areas! This always works if done ahead and with a knowing it shall be done. The Spirit Dimensions where the Higher Dimensional Beings reside, are just as real as ours. In actual fact, they are more REAL, in a multitude of ways, as they contain only love-based energy with no distortions, no duality, no veils of illusionary perceptions to misguide or misinform us through the lower egoic mind of man.

Divine synchronicities and apparent coincidences are carefully orchestrated by our Divine Oversoul, our 'I Am' Presence, to ensure we are in the 'right' place at the 'right' time, often to meet specific people, according to our Divine Blueprint or Soul Contract for this lifetime, pre-agreed to by ourselves. Mind you, we do also attract additional occurrences to ourselves, be they positive or negative, as a direct result of our thoughts, words and actions through the fundamentals of The Law of Attraction.

Human life forms, as *seen* through our physical senses, are only a miniscule part of Mother/Father God's vast creations. We are *not* the only, and *certainly* not the most evolved beings in God's Multiverses. Why would the *original* Divine Creator of 'All That Is,' Primal Source Energy, in All His/Her Magnificence, who is a Creative Energy Force so vast that has no beginning or end, is All-seeing, All-knowing, be restricted to creating life only on our planet and give us only one life on that one planet, as some believe? What a *"gigantic waste of space,"* (no pun intended), that would be.

Take a look at these facts – the utter magnitude of which is incomprehensible to most mortal brains--definitely mine--however they illustrate just how mind-blowingly gigantic Prime Source's powers of creation truly are. Remembering that the Multiverses described below are **only** those our current telescopes have detected. Taken from NASA's website. Current telescopes have so far detected around:

"Two hundred billion Galaxies in the Universe, some of these Galaxies may hold up to one hundred billion Stars. For the Galaxies of middle age, as many as one quarter of the Stars may possess Solar Systems.

. . . . . the Sun is one of around 200 billion Stars just in the Milky Way Galaxy alone.

. . . . and current research suggests that there must be a further 90% of Galaxies in the observable Universe that are too faint and too far away to be seen with present-day telescopes!"

Those facts make planet Earth look extremely small in the grander scale of things, but none-the-less very important to our benevolent, gracious Father/Mother God. Highly evolved beings live in peace and harmony with complete respect for all life forms. This is one of Humanity's purposes on planet Earth. To aspire to, and live in, Brotherhood and Sisterhood, devoid of judgment, knowing no-one is lesser or greater than another. To treat *all* our 'Brothers' and 'Sisters' as we would like to be treated thus demonstrating little acts of kindness and compassion towards one another.

We can see from the Near-Death Experiences that when we *die*, or pass over, we re-remember and experience the fact that we are all a part of the giant whole and our perspective of life completely changes. The NDE's illustrate the fact that what 'we' do to one we do to the whole as we are ALL interconnected Individualizations of Father/Mother God.

As Peter Benson explains, as our awareness of spiritual truths expands so too do our experiences. This is another reason why Peter's first-hand experiences of living in these Realms, together with the experiences of our NDE'ers in this book, are so beautiful for the terminally ill to read. It expands their consciousness and can prepare them to experience **what they choose to create** rather than feeling that it is out of their control. All that we can take with us is our Consciousness so let's expand that to its maximum **before** we *die*.

Source discusses this with Neale Donald Walsch in his book *Conversations With God – Book Three*.

"This is what the Soul realizes at the moment of what you call 'death.' It is simply a change in perspective. You see more, so you understand more . . . . . . Then there will be new mysteries for you to ponder. As you move around the Cosmic Wheel, there will be larger and larger realities – bigger and bigger truths.

Yet if you can remember this truth – your perspective creates your thoughts, and your thoughts create everything – and if you can remember it before you leave the body, not after, your whole life will change."

And the way to control your thoughts is to change your perspective.

"Precisely. Assume a different perspective and you will have different thoughts about everything. In this way you will have learned to control your thought, and, in the creation of your experience, controlled thought is everything. Some people call this constant prayer."[67]

What a remarkable gift people like Dr. P.M.H. Atwater, Dannion Brinkley and all other NDE'ers have given us. People who have clinically died themselves, who have chosen to return to broken bodies to one degree or another, and who then have publicly recounted what their experiences were like. Dr Atwater herself having *died* three times and is therefore able to give us insightful descriptions of what death is and what happens when we die. Add to this Robert Benson's accounts of dying and what life is like to actually be living in these stunning Spirit Realms and we can see how all this knowledge and wisdom can assist us to transition happily and create for ourselves something to be looked forward to rather than to be feared.

Once we have read accounts such as Robert's and the NDEs in this book, how can we possibly believe there is no life after death? What detailed insights our Divine Creator has given us! Millions of people worldwide of all ages, races and creeds have experienced, in glorious detail, what it is like to *transition* into these spiritual dimensions and what heavenly beauty, peace and an All-Encompassing love is like. We need not fear death. In Lao Tzu's wise words.

If you realize that all things change, there is nothing you
will try to hold on to.
If you are not afraid of dying, there is nothing you cannot
achieve.

Lao Tzu

We have been given glorious, spellbinding accounts of life in these spiritual dimensions and that what awaits us, and our loved ones that have passed over, is, more often than not, joyous freedom, infinite knowledge, unimaginable beauty, bountiful health, and a love that is so immense and All-Consuming our brain can only comprehend but a fraction of it. A true *Heaven* where fear does not exist and all co-habit as an inter-connected part of the whole; *one* with the One God in peace, harmony, vibrant health, compassion, understanding and unconditional love. Utopia!

---

[67] Walsch, *Conversations With God, Book 3.* (Hodder & Stoughton, London. 1999). Pg 67.

This experience of becoming *one* with the All That Is, was 'given' to Yogananda by his Master Sri Yukteswar. It sums up the bliss of Omnipresent love and bears a striking resemblance to some near-death experiences. This Divine experience can only be given to a disciple in the physical who has strengthened his mind and enlarged his consciousness through regular meditation. Yogananda was a Self-Realized Indian Master who could Bi-locate--leaving his physical body in one location *and walking around in his chosen new location physically for all to witness.* Something he did frequently by the way.

Yogananda's poetic words bathe the Soul as he describes his wondrous experience.

"My body became immovably rooted; breath was drawn out of my lungs as if by some huge magnet. Soul and mind instantly lost their physical bondage and streamed out like a fluid piercing light from my every pore. The flesh was as though dead; yet in my intense awareness I knew that never before had I been fully alive. My sense of identity was no longer narrowly confined to a body but embraced the circumambient atoms. People on distant streets seemed to be moving gently over my own remote periphery. The roots of plants and trees appeared through a dim transparency of the soil; I discerned the inward flow of their sap.

The whole vicinity lay bare before me. My ordinary frontal vision was now changed to a vast spherical sight, simultaneously all-perceptive.

All objects within my panoramic gaze trembled and vibrated like quick motion pictures. My body, Master's, the pillared courtyard, the furniture and floor, the trees and sunshine, occasionally became violently agitated, until all melted into a luminescent sea; even as sugar crystals, thrown into a glass of water, dissolve after being shaken. The unifying light alternated with materializations of form, the metamorphoses revealing the law of cause and effect in creation.

An oceanic joy broke upon calm endless shores of my Soul. The Spirit of God, I realized, is exhaustless Bliss; His body is countless tissues of light. A swelling glory within me began to envelop towns, continents, the Earth, Solar and Stellar systems, tenuous nebulae, and floating Universes. The entire Cosmos, gently luminous, like a city seen afar at night, glimmered within the infinitude of my Being. The dazzling light beyond the sharply etched global outlines faded slightly at the farthest edges; there I saw a mellow radiance, ever undiminished. It was indescribably subtle; the planetary pictures were formed on a grosser light.

The divine dispersion of rays poured from an Eternal Source, blazing into Galaxies, transfigured with ineffable auras. Again and again I saw the Creative beams condense into Constellations, then resolve into sheets of transparent flame.

By the rhythmic reversion, sextillion Worlds passed into diaphanous luster, then fire became firmament.

I cognized the center of the empyrean as a point of intuitive perception in my heart. Irradiating splendor issued from my nucleus to every part of the universal structure. Blissful amrita, nectar of Immortality, pulsated through me with a quicksilver-like fluidity. The Creative voice of God I heard resounding as Aum, the vibration of the Cosmic Motor."[68]

I don't know about you, but to me, that passage was sublimely, ethereally delicious!

After reading all these inspiring and illuminating Near-Death Experiences one can see that the predominant, underlying message from our Divine Mother/Father God for humanity is a very simple one, revolving around one four letter word - LOVE. Not the fickle, conditional love as it is often portrayed here on planet Earth, but love of the pure, unconditional kind.

Jesus was the epitome of unconditional love in action and this was the foundational tenet of Jesus' messages to humanity 2,000 years ago. Love one another, treat all people the way you would like to be treated, judge not least you be judged, express little acts of kindness and compassion.

Rev George Rodonaia summed it up with this simplistic, profound wisdom when he said.

"Anyone who has had such an experience of God, who has felt such a profound sense of connection with reality, knows that there is only one truly significant work to do in life, and that is to love; to love nature, to love people, to love animals, to love Creation itself - just because it is. To serve God's Creation with a warm and loving hand of generosity and compassion – that is the only meaningful existence."

As the NDE'ers discovered, there are consequences for ALL our words, thoughts, and deeds that we haven't repented of, and that what is of the utmost importance here on planet Earth, is not how big and beautiful our house is, how many academic qualifications we have or which church we belong to, but *how we live our lives every moment of every day.* We are here on planet Earth as Spiritual Beings in a physical body expressing ourselves in a multiplicity of ways. Learning and developing from our life's experiences, and it is what we do with those experiences and how we treat our fellow man that most definitely determines what

---

[68] Yogananda, *Autobiography of a Yogi*. (Self realization Fellowship, CA. 2007) Pgs 126, 127.

spoke on the Cosmic Wheel we step onto when we pass over – remembering too, we are never judged.

NDE's show us common similarities that are experienced irrespective of age, race, creed or time and reveal reassuring information about the complexities of creation. They offer such a rich tapestry of interwoven spiritual insights and revelation.

They undeniably experienced that we are **all** interconnected, **all** Created by and of the same Source of Light. They experienced the beauty of the Oneness of life, devoid of separation.

Renowned filmmaker Mikki Willis of *Elevate Films* had this same potent *God Realization* and experience as a volunteer at Ground Zero assisting rescue services to look for survivors after the September 11th, 2001 bombings of the Twin Towers.

Disaster often brings with it unification and can potentially strengthen faith as people are forced to help one another and turn to God for solace. Source utilizes the outcomes of what could be termed 'evil' to break down, then to rebuild and recreate. The amount of collective compassion sent to all concerned in New York from around the World would have, on its own, been a powerful positive energetic force that our Divine Father/Mother God, could and I'm sure did, utilize behind the scenes to assist those in New York grieving and in shock. God is the ultimate Master Alchemist who can transmute a painful, devastating situation into one that can produce positive new growth and realizations. Here is an incredibly powerful illustration of just that, a life-changing event that happened to Mikki Willis, standing in the midst of the dust, rubble and chaos of *Ground Zero* on September 11th, that elucidates just what God can accomplish amidst anguish and turmoil. Mikki Willis relays his potent story.

"The fire chief stood up on top of one of the crushed fire trucks and did a role call. There were probably 400 names that he called off and at least half of them were not present. When the reality set in with all the fire fighters around that they were not present because they were not alive-they were in the building. They started to literally crumble like dominoes all around us, they fell to their knees, sat on curbs and these big hardened men were just in tears.

Earthmovers came in to clear the way for all the rescue vehicles – Wall Street was lined with extremely expensive automobiles so the only way to move them was to push them over one at a time-all the way down the road- just flipping cars out the way. I watched these material items go from being a car I was drooling over to just being trashed and we watched and stood there – twelve guys saying, 'Oh, my God, how can they do that?' But then it became really clear to me that they were

284

so irrelevant to the task of finding people alive that all the material world was just garbage at that point."[69]

What a powerful illustration of that point. Later Mikki continues.

"They put up a new work light. I looked around at all these people and everything instantly appeared different to me. I stood there, tears in my eyes, it felt like the world was in slow motion, I was watching people go by, and all I could see was just spirits crossing, and spirits working, and chain gangs of spirits, and it was so clear to me that everything was interconnected and it was all one big body of God.

Everybody had dropped their egos, they had dropped their identities, they had dropped their rank and they were working together for the greater good of all.

And I was so lit up with possibility for humankind of what it could be like when we are all working together in this way and I could really get beyond the concept of what 'Oneness' was.

Knowing that the entire world was experiencing what it was experiencing- all the separation and fear and chaos that was going on in the world. Here I was standing there experiencing the greatest bliss and beauty of my life and I remember just wishing that people could see through my eyes at this moment."

Thank you Mikki. Mikki continues to make amazing, ground-breaking films. He encouraged the film making world, then in Hollywood, to create positive uplifting material rather than those many films/movies that are fear-based. He and his team are masters of researching the facts, the hidden truths, behind important issues that *the masses are being told* and together with his film crew, creating enlightening films around such. He is a highly respected, principled, Man of God - making a difference in his part of the world.

It can sometimes be difficult to comprehend our true relationship with God and who we are in God. This piece that was given to Neale Donald Walsch by Source defines our relationship so beautifully. Personally, I love this analogy.

"Always remember, you are not the flower, nor are you even the fruit. You are the tree. And your roots are deep, embedded in Me. I am the soil from which you have sprung, and both your blossoms and your fruit will return to Me, creating more rich soil. Thus, life begets life, and cannot know death, ever."[70]

---

[69] Twyman, *The Moses Code*.(Hay House Inc., DVD 2008). Guest Speaker Mikki Willis

[70] Walsch, *Conversations With God, Book 3.* (Hodder & Stoughton, London, 1999). Pg 144, 145.

Our Father/Mother God—the Divine Creator of All That Is, is a Massed, Endless, Limitless Energy of the most glorious brilliance of pure *White Fire Electronic Light* and pure Unconditional Love. Like a vast, flawless diamond this Massed Energy continually splits and divides itself into every facet and expression of life in countless Cosmoses. A brilliance of Light Energy that by whom and through whom ALL Creation has been formed. We are *all* Individualized Facets of that original Divine brilliant Diamond gathering experiences of life in a human body.

Every man, woman and child are a precious facet of this pristine Light, an Individualized, unique expression of our Prime Creator. Minute only in comparison to the Whole, but Mighty in our capacity to give of this same love and Mighty in our capacity to Co-Create whatever we desire. Our objective being to acknowledge and discover our own special Divine Light within our own 'I AM' Presence and let it shine. To join with others' Lights to become brighter and brighter, igniting, fanning and expanding the flame of one another.

This is the message we see in so many of our NDE's. *We have come from One Source, One Light* and by spreading our own Light, our own Divine Essence, through loving unconditionally, we can help others to see their precious light and one little light becomes two lights, which becomes four, until millions of lights are illuminating the darkness and fear can be replaced by Love, complacency by compassion, judgment by forgiveness, deception by truth and war by peace. Thus, changing the mass consciousness and Co-Creating the quality of life our Beloved Father/Mother God wants for *all* His/Her children on Earth. This is beginning to eventuate as more and more Light is pouring onto our Beloved Earth, even though it may not look that way at times.

Life is to be lived, knowing that we are accountable for all our thoughts, words, deeds and actions. To live with the knowledge that we are Eternal Spiritual Beings and as such we never die. We are here on Planet Earth to serve each other rather than to be served. To share our lessons, to share our wisdom and to learn from one another. *Death merely serves to remind us that we are about to experience new life*. A sublimely *heavenly* existence devoid of judgment, pain and fear. A higher dimension of life that will wrap us in a warm cocoon of exquisite unconditional love, caress us, and say,

Welcome Home, Beloved Child of God.

CPSIA information can be obtained
at www.ICGtesting.com
Printed in the USA
BVHW051550090321
602118BV00003B/86